THE CRAFT OF POETRY

THE CRAFT
OF POETRY
Interviews from
The New York Quarterly

WILLIAM PACKARD, EDITOR

DOUBLEDAY & COMPANY, INC., GARDEN CITY, NEW YORK   1974

PHOTOGRAPH CREDITS

Photographs of W. H. Auden, John Ashbery, James Dickey, Muriel Rukeyser
and Richard Wilbur by John Briggs; photographs of Paul Blackburn and Robert Creeley by Elsa Dorfman; photographs of Anne Sexton and Denise Levertov
by Rollie McKenna; and photographs of Stanley Kunitz, Jerome Rothenberg,
Allen Ginsberg, Galway Kinnell, Jackson MacLow, Howard Moss, Erica Jong
and Diane Wakoski by Layle Silbert.

Library of Congress Cataloging in Publication Data

Packard, William, comp.
  The craft of poetry.
  1. Poets, American—20th century—Interviews.
2. Poetics.   I. New York quarterly.   II. Title.
PS135.P3   811'.5'409
ISBN 0-385-03468-7 Trade
ISBN 0-385-03496-2 Paperback
Library of Congress Catalog Card Number 74–2831
Copyright © 1970, 1971, 1972, 1973, 1974 by *The New York Quarterly,*
solely owned by The New York Quarterly Poetry Review Foundation, Inc.

To Lucille Medwick

INTERVIEWS

INTRODUCTION

We live in the age of the interview. Moderators interview celebrities on TV talk shows, newsmen interview Presidents at press conferences, and young people interview each other to see if they want to sleep together. Everywhere one turns, everyone is busy interviewing everyone else. There has never been such a passion to verbalize the world around us: there are panel discussions, encounter groups, workshops, seminars, symposiums, committee meetings and public hearings. All this talk talk talk talk talk must come from some very deep insecurity at the source of things. And, of course, there is the danger that charisma may take the place of character, and chatter may take the place of matter.

So it is no wonder if the practicing poet, caught up in an unreal world of words, may seek to keep his own counsel. For he alone knows that whatever is deeply intuitive cannot really be revealed except in rhythms and images. He may even feel that talking itself is a distraction from true communication. As Thoreau wrote in *Walden:* "Speech is for the convenience of the hard of hearing." And so the poet may choose to retreat from a Babel of tongues, and obey The Sermon on the Mount, when it says very simply:

> *But let your communication be, Yea, yea;*
> *Nay, nay; for whatsoever is more than these*
> *cometh of evil.*

Even so: there will always be a good deal of legitimate curiosity about poetry, and the poet will always be asked certain questions by readers who are eager to learn more about the art. It seems inevitable, then, that the poet should submit himself to be interviewed, along with everyone else in our universe.

Very well, then, but what kind of interview? There are interviews, and there are interviews.

James Joyce in *Ulysses* said that Shakespeare is the happy hunting ground for all minds that have lost their balance, and we can well imagine the sort of interviews which Shakespeare would be subjected to, if he were to return among us today. Because there are certain classic approaches to the interview form, and we think we can guess how these approaches might manifest themselves in relation to Master William Shakespeare.

First, there would be the professorial interview. This approach would try to clear up a lot of pesky questions about subtexts and footnotes in the various works. For example:

> *What is the correct spelling of your name? Why did you spell it differently on different documents? Or are you really Francis Bacon? In that case, did you hide a biliteral cipher in any of your plays? If so, what is the secret key to reading it?*

> *You have Hamlet say: "O that this too too solid flesh would melt." Instead of "solid flesh," what do you think of the variant quarto reading "sullied flesh"? Or what about the German critic Himmelbummer who suggested "soiled fish"? How about the 1807 edition reading of "salad flash"? Would you believe "smelly flush"?*

> *Who was the third murderer in Macbeth? Why did you drop Donalbain from the plot? And whatever happens to Fleance? And why did you never dispose of the three weird sisters? Were you saving these characters for another play? Is this a lost manuscript?*

Here we can imagine Shakespeare might smile, shrug and give a few mechanical answers. These questions would not be of any great concern to him, any more than they would be to most of his readers.

Then, there would be the opinionated interview. This line of questioning would focus attention on the subject's political, religious and socioeconomic attitudes. For example:

> *Shakespeare, do you believe in God? Or would you characterize yourself as a skeptic? A freethinker maybe? An agnostic? An atheist? Did you belong to the Church of England? If not, why not?*

> *What were your feelings about Queen Elizabeth? King James? What did you feel about the Essex uprising? What about his*

beheading? Were you sympathetic with the notion of civil disobedience, when it is warranted?

Are you in favor of constitutional monarchy? What do you feel about the concept of republican democracy? Christian socialism? Marxist communism? Freudian psychoanalysis?

Here we can imagine Shakespeare telling the interviewer that, for heaven's sakes, he had gone to some considerable pains during his lifetime to try and stay away from the various political and social arenas of his day, so he could remain relatively anonymous and try to practice his art with as much autonomy as possible. Wasn't that enough?

And then, there would be the gossipy interview. This line of questioning would dwell on Shakespeare's personality and his extrapoetic activities. For example:

What was Anne Hathaway like in bed? Did you recite poetry to her when the lights were out? And what did she do with herself back there in Stratford while you were off working in London?

Who was the Dark Lady of the Sonnets? Who was the young man? Did you ever have any homosexual experiences? If not, why not? If so, did you enjoy them?

What did you and Ben Jonson talk about in the Mermaid Tavern? What did you drink? Could you both hold your malt? Who picked up the tab?

Here, we can imagine Shakespeare might simply scowl and tell the interviewer to go to hell.

Finally, there would be the craft interview. This line of questioning would try to discuss the circumstances of an artist's work and not the work itself. And it would try to restrict its questions to those which might occur to a practicing writer. For example:

Your rate of writing comes to about two plays a year, and that means that in some years you wrote plays like Hamlet *and* The Merry Wives of Windsor *both in the same year. Did you ever feel any special problem in switching over from one type of play to another? Did you prefer doing one type of play, so far as the actual writing was concerned? Did your work habits vary, from comedy to tragedy to history?*

Was Ben Jonson right when he said you never blotted out a single word? Was there no revision? How much work did you do in your head before you began setting it all down?

Keats tried to imagine the physical situation of your writing. Did you always sit at a desk, or could you sometimes compose lying down or walking late at night through the streets of London?

Here, we can imagine Shakespeare giving matter-of-fact answers to the questions, because they are, after all, the sort of specific things which would concern him as a practicing poet.

And these are, in fact, the sort of questions we try to pursue in our NYQ Craft Interviews. With a profound respect for the innate privacy of a poet's own intuition, we try to approach the matter with as much tact and practicality as possible.

Granted, the poets we choose to interview will sometimes try to inundate us with their own opinions, professorial tidbits, footnotes, socioeconomic theories or plain gossip about themselves. But not as a rule. Usually they are grateful that we are that interested in their true identities as craftsmen poets.

Following are guidelines we have been using for NYQ Craft Interviews since the very first issue:

In approaching a craft interview, of course there is no substitute for a solid grounding in the work of the poet being interviewed, a familiarity with his own poems and his stated views on poetry, etc. The interview itself will reflect this familiarity if there are specific citations of sections of the work of the poet, which can serve as a basis for discussion between interviewer and poet. Ideally this discussion should be more in the form of an intercourse than a "question and answer" approach which sometimes feels more like a game of ping-pong. The questions below, then, are meant more as general suggestions of areas that might be covered with specific reference to the poet's own work, rather than as prescribed "questions" which must be asked at each and every interview:

1. *Would you describe the physical conditions of writing your poetry? Are you always at a desk? Do you do first drafts on typewriter or with pencil or with pen? On what kind of paper? As poems progress, what do you do with worksheets that you no longer need?*

2. *When you are away from your desk or writing area, do you carry a notebook with you? What do you do with thoughts*

or impulses that come to you when you are unable to record
them easily?

3. What would you say about revision? Is it a creative act
with you? Have you written anything that did not need
extensive revision? Do you have any special procedure for
revising a poem?

4. What do you feel is the value of the poetry workshop for a
young poet? Did you take any when you were beginning to
write poetry? What do you feel about student criticism of
each other's work?

5. Do you ever experience a dry period in writing, and if so
what do you do about it?

6. Do you ever play games with the craft of poetry, prosody,
for the fun of it, or for what it might lead to? Anagrams,
palindromes, etc.?

7. What do you feel about the need for isolation in the life of a
writer? How does it affect personal relationships?
Professional activities such as teaching?

8. Have you ever received lines of poetry which you were
unable to incorporate into a poem? What would you do
with them, as a rule?

9. If a poet is about to fall asleep and suddenly thinks of an
interesting poem or some interesting lines for a poem, what
should he do?

10. What reference books do you feel are useful for a young
poet to have on his desk, for consultation?

11. Do you feel we live in a particularly permissive age so far
as education and discipline in craft are concerned, and if
so, what effect is this having on the present stage of poetry
being written today?

12. What poet do you feel would be a good model for a young
writer to begin learning about poetry?

The following is a list of the poets and the individuals who
interviewed them:

Poet	Interviewers
1. W. H. Auden	Mary Jane Fortunato
	Linda Krenis
	William Packard
	Manuchehr Sassoonian

THE CRAFT OF POETRY

CRAFT INTERVIEW WITH W. H. AUDEN

NYQ: *What poets influenced the craft and form of your early work?*

AUDEN: I have always been a formalist. Now that I look back on it, I suppose the first poet I admired was Thomas Hardy. Then I went on to Edward Thomas. I read Frost before many others knew him.

NYQ: *What poets influence your work now?*

WHA: I'm reading a lot of medieval stuff. Like everybody, one has one's pets. Mine are Thomas Campian and William Barnes—both are minor poets but I adore them. Obviously, one doesn't need to mention the greats. I tend not to read much contemporary work. I am now on a Horace jag.

NYQ: *What musicians or composers do you admire?*

WHA: I was brought up on Bach. Later, I developed a love for Wagner and Schumann. You go through composers as people you will love in the same way you do poets. But one can't be influenced as a poet by a composer because they are two different arts.

NYQ: *Have you ever played a musical instrument?*

WHA: I play the piano very badly, not for other people to hear.

NYQ: *Have you ever been in a workshop situation, and what are your feelings about workshops?*

WHA: No, I've never been in a workshop. This is something quite peculiar to America. At Oxford, naturally one knew other people who wrote, and we used to read to each other. When I was there it was quite a small place —only four thousand including the girls. In a big city I suppose you have to plan these things up.

NYQ: *How much teaching have you done? Do you think teaching helps or hinders one's own creative work?*

WHA: I have taught all ages, from seven to seventy. I spent three years at Swarthmore. To earn my living, I started teaching boys from seven to fourteen, which is the age I prefer to teach because you can do something then, can give them standards and a sense of their own capabilities. When they are older, twenty or so, they have to do it for themselves. By that age, one should be able to say, "This book will interest you." Obviously one needs help with Chaucer or Milton, but I am always surprised when students want to have courses in modern literature. In England we read these for ourselves—the whole fun was in discovering for oneself. I have always refused to teach modern literature. It does affect my writing. Contemporary literature comes too near what one does.

NYQ: *What about poetry readings?*

WHA: I like doing it if one gets into it, it is something quite different. The thing you have to be careful about is not to try and think of a style of writing that is too declamatory. There are five hundred people out there in the audience, but they are thinking of you as speaking to one person.

NYQ: *Do you find, after you've written criticism, that your own poems may break some of the rules you've set down?*

WHA: No, I stick by whatever my principles are. I make it a rule only to review books that I basically like. In negative reviews, there is a certain malice. Reviewing books one doesn't like especially may be witty, but it isn't very useful. If one is right about a book, time will take care of it. If one is wrong, one will look a fool later. Bad art is bad in a particular way that is characteristic of the times.

NYQ: *Which critics do you find most useful for their craft principles?*

WHA: There are certain critics I owe a great deal to—Auerbach, Spitzer, C. S. Lewis, Valéry. They are good critics. And then, of course, Chesterton. Nobody reads him, now. I'm doing a selection of his nonfiction prose.

NYQ: *Do you feel in your own work there is a major area of strength? The visual, the aural or the conceptual?*

WHA: I don't know whether these areas are separable. All I know is the way I work, and I imagine others do the same. I have two things working—some kind of theme, and certain formal problems, metrical structure, diction. The language looks for the subject, and the subject finds the language.

NYQ: *Do you ever play games with craft, write poems in specific forms more for the joy of writing than for the content?*

WHA: Anyone interested in form has to do this, in a way. Everybody knows if you play a game you have to have rules. I would find it ghastly dull not to have some kind of formal thing. The fun of games is always present, but you have to have something to say as well.

NYQ: *Do you revise much?*

WHA: I do an enormous amount of revising. I think of that quote from Valéry, "A poem is never finished, only abandoned." Some people feel revisions have ideological significance. I revise if I feel the language is prolix or obscure. Your first idea is not always your best.

NYQ: *Do you ever revise published poetry?*

WHA: Constantly. In my *Collected Poems,* a lot of the poems have been radically revised.

NYQ: *In "September 1, 1939," you revised one line ("We must love one another or die") and then omitted the entire stanza in which this line occurs.*

WHA: I have scrapped the whole poem. I took out that section, then I decided the whole thing had to go. I will put it this way: I don't think a writer can decide how good or bad something he writes is. What he can tell, though, is whether the poem is authentic, really written in his own hand. I decided this poem is unauthentic as far as I am concerned. It may have certain merits but I should not have written it.

NYQ: *By rejecting entire poems outright, you must be arriving at a definition of your own style.*

WHA: You can see in the *Collected Short Poems* what I have removed. It is different from revising poems. When one revises, one is not revising emotions, but reworking the language. But the poems I decided were unauthentic went out. There was something false about them. The others which I have revised a great deal had more a question of language.

NYQ: *In "September 1, 1939" there is the line,*

           Find what occurred at Linz

         —which raises the question of specific reference, whether the reader should be expected to know that Linz was where Hitler spent his childhood years.

WHA: There is a terrible problem with proper names. Poets in older times had half the work done for them. Proper names were in poetry. Everyone knew them. Where I have used them, editors have glossed them. In one extreme case in a poem written, I suppose, in 1934, I referred to Garbo, and I was sure that everyone knew who she was. But an editor glossed the name, dropped a footnote. I thought everyone knew it, you see. I never was tempted to add a gloss to anything I've done. If a person does know it, the gloss looks rather superior: "You poor thing, you wouldn't know it."

NYQ: *A poet like Marianne Moore footnotes her work scrupulously.*

WHA: It is a sort of joke with her. I don't know when she does it, it really helps you to understand the poem. She is scrupulously honest. She will quote an idea from someone, then gloss it; it is a matter of literary honesty.

NYQ: *Can you work with music in the room?*

WHA: No. I must have silence. I work in my study upstairs.
I cannot work when people I know are about, but I can
work in a cafeteria, if there's no music and no one I
know and it's quiet. The people there might be cows or
trees.

NYQ: *Do you like to show unpublished work to friends?*

WHA: Yes, to people whose judgment I value, who can see
something is uncertain. They have to be poets because
other people's comments wouldn't be useful. They
wouldn't be able to put their finger on what was wrong.

NYQ: *Do you ever write with a specific person or type of
person in mind?*

WHA: One writes an occasional poem for a specific audience.
One can only say one writes a poem for people who read
it. One hopes for someone who will like it.

NYQ: *Do you ever need periods of isolation to work on your
poems?*

WHA: Some of the day one must be alone. I am a lot of the
time by myself. I don't go out much. But I don't seek
this.

NYQ: *What about extended periods, periods of withdrawal
from other activities?*

WHA: No. The need for isolation isn't a problem.

NYQ: *Do you feel that translating affects the technique and
content of your poems?*

WHA: I happen to enjoy doing it. Theoretically, it is
impossible. One has to try. But apart from the fun of
doing it, I do feel that translating is good to do. You
always find out something about your own language.
For example, you get into the habit of asking what does
it mean? It causes us to notice the decline in the
preciseness of language. I was six when I started Latin,
and nine when I started Greek.

NYQ: *What do you do with single lines that you haven't been
able to use in a poem?*

WHA: I jot down lines which I intend to use at some time or other. They are more apt to be words than lines.

NYQ: *Do you keep a journal?*

WHA: No, I don't keep a diary. That's more for novelists. All one puts down are things about the weather, or what happened in the garden, or when the first snow peas arrived. The lives of writers are not very interesting. The relationship between life and art is so obvious that nothing need be said and so complicated that nothing can be said. When Catullus wrote a love poem to whatever-her-name-was, no doubt you can see what is going on, but you can't find out why he wrote that particular poem. Investigations about the poem itself are necessary to tell me why that poem is any good. What I object to is simply keyhole peeping which is then called scholarship. About two years ago, there was a biography of Lytton Strachey. Some of the letters in this work were his private business. Why should anyone see them?

NYQ: *In your work, have you established a pattern of writing, a time and a place which are most conducive to productivity?*

WHA: I like to work in the mornings, also between tea and cocktails. I never work after dinner. Obviously, it's difficult to work if you are moving around. Most of my work I do in the summer, in Austria. There is no phone and it is nice.

NYQ: *Does a foreign environment influence the kind of poems you write?*

WHA: How can I tell? You are away from your native language. I share the house with a friend and we talk English. I happen to be fond of German as a language.

NYQ: *Living now in New York, do you find yourself getting images specifically related to the city?*

WHA: Yes, one picks up images. That obviously one does.

NYQ: *What sort of work are you engaged in now, and what are you planning for the future?*

WHA: My own view is that you never talk about what you are doing—what you have done, but not what you are up to. I'm very superstitious.

NYQ: *What books of craft would you recommend that poets keep on their shelves?*

WHA: Saintsbury's *A History of English Prosody*. All thirteen volumes of the Oxford English Dictionary. I have two sets, one in Austria and one here.

NYQ: *What advice do you have for young poets?*

WHA: You have to see their work, really. I have no advice in general for these people except to read fairly widely. It is necessary for a young writer to find his own models, the kind of language that may go through any period. On the whole, I am not in favor of one's reading very much criticism. When one is starting out it is not good.

NYQ: *Can you tell us something of the origin of* The Rake's Progress?

WHA: I can tell you about that quite clearly. I got a message from Stravinsky that he wanted to write an opera on the subject of *The Rake's Progress*. I went to see him and wanted to find out about it. He was looking at the Hogarth engravings, one of them a figure of a blind fiddler playing on one string, another of them in a brothel. The difficulty is that if you take Hogarth's engravings, what he gives you is the picture of low life in eighteenth-century London, and the only central figure is the Rake, and he has no story. We had to work to invent a story, and keep certain things intact, and everything else had to be changed. There was a problem in doing a character of a young man who always yields to temptation, who is a passive character, who still has speeches. So we gave him a sort of Mephisto, who would suggest things. Then we made him into a manic depressive so that he had a kind of emotional range.

NYQ: *What are your feelings about the level of technical competence today?*

WHA: There is a reaction against competence. And there is a lack of interest in the past which seems to be growing. But what one wonders at, at present, is that with all these young people, one cannot be distinguished from another.

NYQ: *There seems to be a reaction today against form. Now, your work had a tremendous influence on the technical competence of the forties and fifties—*

WHA: Did it? I wouldn't know about that. But there is a reaction now against form, and I wonder if there is any virtue in the reaction. We shall see. It may be I am getting old and can't get used to new things.

NYQ: *The two elegies that you wrote, on Freud and Yeats, seem to be more general as elegies than, say, elegies like "Lycidas" or "Adonais."*

WHA: Those elegies of mine are not poems of grief. Freud I never met, and Yeats I only met casually and didn't particularly like him. Sometimes a man stands for certain things, which is quite different from what one feels in personal grief.

NYQ: *To what extent do you feel a poet ought to be engaged, in social or philosophical or political issues?*

WHA: One must be engaged. All I see is that poetry can do nothing about it. I do not think that writing poems will change anything. I think Dr. Johnson was right when he said the aim of writing is to enable readers a little better to enjoy life or a little better to endure it. Would it really have been any different if all those great artists had never lived—Dante, Shakespeare, Mozart, Goethe, Beethoven? Simply talking in terms of social, political or historical things, I don't think I would say it would. There are exceptional places—in a country like Russia, where they have never had a free press. Sometimes a writer can say something within a political framework, and you don't hear it from anyone else.

NYQ: *Would you tell us something about the "shorts" you have given us to publish in* The New York Quarterly?

WHA: They are accentual elegiac couplets. It is a recent interest of mine, I have never done it before.

NYQ: *In closing, we'd like you to comment on the fact that we're not planning to run any book reviews in our new magazine. Perhaps an occasional review of a technical prosody book, but no reviews of poetry books as such.*

WHA: I find that interesting because my only complaint when I am reviewed is the critic's lack of knowledge. The one thing I am vain about is my knowledge of meters. I do think a reviewer should know his job. I look to see how a poem is made before I think what it says. Then I begin to read it.

SELECTED BIBLIOGRAPHY

The Collected Longer Poems of W. H. Auden, New York, Random House, Inc., 1969.

The Collected Shorter Poems of W. H. Auden, New York, Random House, Inc., 1967.

The Dyer's Hand, New York, Random House, Inc., 1962.

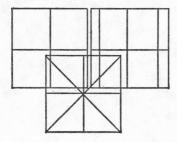

CRAFT INTERVIEW
WITH PAUL BLACKBURN

NYQ:

What poets have influenced your work?

PAUL
BLACKBURN:

W. H. Auden was an early influence. My mother
sent me a copy of his *Collected Poems* when I was
in the Army. When I was nineteen, I could write
a pretty good Auden poem, and I feel that I
picked up a formal sense of musical structure from
him. In college I began to read Ezra Pound. His
Personae, not to mention the *Cantos,* was an
incredible revelation to me as to what you could
do in terms of making music with different line
lengths, and how rhythm could be so rich and
varied. I think I learned a lot of my ear from
reading Pound. At the same time I was studying
Pound, I was picking up influences from my
contemporaries—Robert Creeley, Charles Olson and
Cid Corman. I was learning to strip my style of as
much as I could and get down to very simple
statements while still keeping it reasonably musical.
I think a lot of the William Carlos Williams
influence came to me, not through Williams so
much, as through Williams' influence on Creeley.
In a review of my first book, the critic blamed both
Creeley and me on Williams. I thought, "Oh, wow!
I've got to read Williams!" So I got ahold of
Paterson, and what was then his *Collected Poems.*
I wanted to find out where my influences were

coming from. I wanted to find out who my father was.

NYQ: *Those contemporaries you mentioned—Creeley,*
        Olson, Corman—didn't you all form the Black
        Mountain School of poetry?

PB: Black Mountain doesn't do at all as a label,
        because presumably it should apply to the people
        who either studied or taught at Black Mountain
        College, and it doesn't. Robert Duncan taught at
        the college and contributed to *The Black Mountain*
        Review, but he really can't be considered to be
        Black Mountain. He's much more musical than
        many of the Black Mountain people. And he
        doesn't necessarily work from speech rhythms—
        he's more formal. Mostly what this Black Mountain
        thing is all about is what we were all working at
        —speech rhythm, composition by field, or
        something from that set of ideas. By 1951, Olson
        had tied a lot of it together in that "Projective
        Verse" essay. So we even had a set of principles
        to keep in our heads. But this is not to say that we
        were developing similar styles. Does Creeley write
        like Olson, does Olson write like Denise Levertov?
        In the end, every poet is an individual, and if you
        can group them it's because they drink together
        once in a while.

NYQ: *You said that you "learned a lot of your ear from*
        reading Pound." Your ear must play a great part in
        the writing of your poetry.

PB: Certainly the ear is a prime judge of what I've
        accomplished or have not accomplished. I wouldn't
        even know whether a poem was finished or not
        unless my ear told me. I think music must be in
        the poem somewhere. Poetry is traditionally a
        musical structure. Now that forms are as open as
        they are, each poem has to find its own form. It
        has to do with the technique of juxtaposition and
        reading from the breath line and normal speech
        raised to its highest point. But that's abstracting
        a principle. When you're writing, these things are
        at the back of it. It's almost as though your

technique is in your wrists and you're sitting at a
typewriter instead of at a piano. As far as I'm
concerned, people who don't hear the poems are
missing a good deal, and a poet who doesn't hear
his own poems is missing everything. He's got to
hear his own voice saying it. It's got to come off
the page in a way that concrete poetry cannot.

NYQ: *What do you feel about concrete poetry?*

PB: Concrete poems are not written to be read aloud,
they're written as objects. In other words, they have
to stay on the page. It has to do with the
arrangement of sounds and words, of their
interpolations or their extrapolations, how they
mix or cross. I mean, it's there on the page,
whatever the joke is. And basically it is a game.
It can be a particularly beautiful game or a fairly
dull one, depending on who's playing it.

NYQ: *Do you play that kind of game?*

PB: No, I've never been able to stand crossword
puzzles, anagrams, that kind of thing.

NYQ: *What purpose do punctuation and indentation
serve in your poetry?*

PB: Punctuation serves much the way that spacing does
—that is, to indicate the length of a pause. For
example, if there is a space between the last letter
of a word and the period, the pause is longer than it
would be if the period were right beside the last
letter. If there is a period, the pause is longer than
it would be if there were no punctuation and you
moved over to the left margin to pick up the next
line. There is a longer pause between the end of
the line and the left margin than there is between
the end of the line and the succeeding line picking
up in the middle or three-quarters of the way
through the line. And certainly even less of a pause
(because this is the way the eye runs) if it moves to
the end of the line and simply drops off and
continues on the next line. So you're using the
common way of reading to control the speed of the
words as read.

NYQ: *What importance does form have in your work?*

PB: Strict form is by no means a necessity. Quite the
        opposite, each poem must find its own music, its
        own form. It's much harder to do that than to
        write quatrains all the time.

NYQ: *How do you respond to criticism?*

PB: It depends on who's doing the criticizing. If it's
        someone like Cid Corman, I'll listen, I'll consider
        it seriously, even if I think he's dead wrong. But
        there aren't many editors or critics who are in his
        category. He's a solid man. You wouldn't dare send
        him anything but your best work.

NYQ: *Have you published any criticism?*

PB: I've written two articles for *Kulchur*. One was an
        analysis of the whole Black Mountain thing, the
        other was about Robert Kelly. I consider Kelly to
        be a great poet. As a matter of fact, I considered
        him to be a great poet before he was thirty, and
        there aren't many people who are willing to make
        that kind of statement about a man who is under
        thirty. But I'm an amateur, I'm no professional
        critic. Anyway, I hate writing prose—I've never
        taken any pleasure in writing it.

NYQ: *Do you feel that poetry workshops are useful?*

PB: It depends on the student and what he's ready for.
        Certainly, to be in a group of people working
        together is often a very valuable experience for a
        young person. Not only what he may get in the
        way of advice from his instructor, but also the
        reactions of his contemporaries. However, it can be
        completely useless if a writer not only feels cut off,
        but wants to feel cut off, and insists on cutting
        himself off. He'll have a miserable time in the
        workshop because part of the learning process does
        depend not only upon his easy relationship to his
        instructor (and presumably the instructor has
        something to say that will be of use), but also
        upon his not building his defenses so great that he
        can't move past where he is. If he's already got his
        head set and he doesn't want to break it—if he

wants to stand there and prove how good he is to everybody then he's liable to get nowhere in the workshop. With such people it's sometimes useful just to blow their minds, to open them up and see what happens. So that's one value of a workshop —the opening up. Another value is giving the person a built-in audience. A young writer doesn't get a set of intelligent mirrors very often. Friends are something else. They may be helpful if they are themselves writers. Otherwise, they're liable to act as a dear reassurance which, God knows, is a necessity sometimes. But a workshop situation gives, at best, a fair cross section of a potential audience, lets you know if you're coming across—and how, and why.

NYQ: *Where do you write?*

PB: Anywhere, anytime, when it hits me I write. I don't ask any questions. It can be dead silence, the kid (his six-month-old son, Carlos) can be screaming, I can be sitting on the subway during rush hour. You write when you have to write, when it comes to you. Some people need a formal circumstance around them in order to write. I don't. Neither do I schedule myself when I'm writing poetry. However, I do schedule my translating. Translation requires a steadier concentration. But getting back to the question, what happens when you're being dictated to and you don't know where the dictation is coming from? All you know is you have to sit down and write it and you may not know what the damn thing means when you're done. And somehow, later on, you find out where the piece belongs—either in a long poem or as a separate piece.

NYQ: *Tell us something about your translations.*

PB: I don't become the author when I'm translating his prose or poetry, but I'm certainly getting my talents into his hang-ups. Another person's preoccupations are occupying me. They literally own me for that time. You see, it's not just a matter of reading the language and understanding it and putting it into English. It's understanding

something that makes the man do it, where he's
going. And it's not an entirely objective process. It
must be partially subjective, there has to be some
kind of projection. How do you know which word
to choose when a word may have four or five
possible meanings in English? It's not just
understanding the text. In a way you live it each
time, I mean, *you're there*. Otherwise, you're not
holding the poem.

NYQ: *How do you feel about writing in a travel
           situation?*

PB: I think travel is an ideal situation in which to
           write. In a way there's a kind of spiritual and
           sensory vacuum present. Take the subway, for
           instance. People blank out, you see the dullest faces
           there. What are they thinking, what are they
           doing? They're going from here to there and
           nothing's happening to them. They'd be lucky to
           have their pockets picked, at least that would be
           something. So you see, the demands on you as to
           movement or thought or even personal contact are
           minimal. And I have an idea that a lot of things
           come to the surface in such a situation that might
           not otherwise get there. The only thing left to come
           into this vacuum is whatever is in your head at
           that particular moment. And although the subway
           is moving, you're stationary; you're always looking
           at the same thing. Then there's the sound,
           trolleycars, trains, wheels on the tracks, will set
           rhythms going in your head, a kind of ground
           rhythm against which your own ear works, can
           turn you on, turn your voice into that emptiness.
           Buses also, especially on wet pavement. I always
           feel very sensual on buses, never so on planes,
           there's too much formality, all those chicks serving
           you drinks and food. I'd rather read or sleep or
           stare out the window at cloud formations. One is
           really stationary in a plane, you're being boxed or
           shipped, and the sound is a constant roar—no
           rhythm to it, and muted besides. Ginsberg wrote
           his *Wichita Vortex Sutra* on a plane, though, so
           we can't eliminate the possibility of that working

for some people. Allen has a panvision of the world anyway. John Keys has a couple of poems from an aircraft point of view. ". . . the clouds like a parking lot/sort of hump hump hump, if you see what I mean." It would be different on a boat because you could get up and walk around, vomit on the deck or something. At least there's a kind of personal movement on a boat which cannot be found on most other types of conveyances. It's not the boat that makes the waves, but where we are right now, as they say, the motion of the ocean. To come back to the city, though, the subway is an incredible place for girl watching. You find one face or a good pair of legs—you can look at them for hours. You think, "Oh god, I hope she doesn't get off at 34th Street."

NYQ: *What do you do when you have a dry period, when you can't write?*

PB: I don't get upset about it. As a matter of fact, I'm happy when I'm not writing. When I'm writing, I've got to work. Not that writing isn't a joy—it is at times, but there are great periods when I simply don't write anything or very little. In a very real way I use translations to fill in that time, because I do enjoy translating, getting into other people's heads.

SELECTED BIBLIOGRAPHY

The Cities, New York, Grove Press, Inc., 1967.

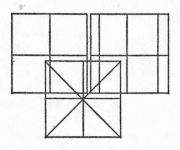

CRAFT INTERVIEW
WITH ANNE SEXTON

ANNE
SEXTON:

I have a terrible memory—it's all a mystery to me, it all just happens.

NYQ:

Do you revise much?

AS:

Yes, I've revised as much as three hundred times on one lyric poem. The title of that poem was "The Truth the Dead Know." I showed it to Robert Lowell after I'd rewritten it fifty times. He said the ending wasn't right. I don't remember—I ended it with the dead saying something. He said the dead don't speak. The more I thought about it the more I agreed with him, and that's when I turned them into stone.

NYQ:

How long did you work on that poem?

AS:

I don't remember how many months it took—maybe two. The poem "Flee on Your Donkey"—I rewrote that for four years. I hung onto it and revised it every six months. Everyone said it was a useless poem; even my best friend said, "It embarrasses me," and Cal Lowell said it was better to be a short story. I fussed with it and I played with it and I worked with it.

NYQ:

What physical conditions do you find best for revision?

AS:

I think that would depend on the physical conditions of the first writing. My play was written to music by Villa Lobos, and I put it on tape so I could play it all the while I was writing. When the kids were young, I would turn on a symphony to make a constant noise to drown them out so I could work. I wrote the poem "Vision Apart" to *Swan Lake*. I often write in silence, too. I can't just have the radio on. Any talking distracts me. I like quiet. Once I tried to write a poem a day. I wrote for eighteen days. The kids would walk by my room and say, "Shhh, Mommy's writing a poem!"

NYQ: *What do you think is valuable about poetry workshops?*

AS: They were very valuable to me. It's where I started. All you need is one friend to tell you to write a poem a day. It's not the criticism—it's the stimulation, the countered interest. It's a time to grow. My first workshop was with John Holmes in Boston, with George Starbuck and Maxine Kumin. If I'd gone to a real poetry workshop I'd have been scared. As it was, this was a friendly group. You'd always have enough ego to bring two poems. We all met once a month. We missed it very much when it ended.

NYQ: *Then you went on to study with Robert Lowell. Was it the beginning of your confessional poetry?*

AS: At that time Lowell had not revealed what he was doing. He was very stern. He went line by line. Sometimes he would spend five minutes on a first line. It was line dissection. What was inspiring was that he would take a poem by a great poet and relate it to the workshop poem.

NYQ: *That must have been stimulation in an advanced sense.*

AS: It was. Lowell introduced me to Lawrence, and to his own poetry. I came there at just the right time. I had *To Bedlam and Part Way Back* almost finished, and he helped me to hold it down.

NYQ: *Why did you choose to write poetry?*

AS: I haven't got the slightest idea. When I was eighteen or nineteen I wrote for half a year. One time I tried painting, but I wasn't good. When I was twenty-eight, I saw I. A. Richards on television. He was talking about the form of the sonnet, its images, and I thought, I can do that. I would like to be a photographer if the camera could work the way fingers work. I like to capture an instant. A picture is a one-second thing—it's a fragile moment in time. I try to do it with words.

NYQ: *Do you ever play craft games with your poetry?*

AS: I always call it tricks, not craft. Craft is a trick you make
      up to let you write the poem. The only game I ever
      played was with the word "star." I did everything I
      could with the arrangement of s-t-a-r. Conrad Aiken
      once saw a palindrome on the side of a barn: Rats Live
      On No Evil Star (and I want that to be on my
      gravestone, because I see myself as a rat, but I live on no
      evil star). Rats and star: I wrote a list of all the words I
      could make out of those letters. Then I sat down with
      the words and made up a poem. The game I do play is
      I say to myself, This poem is too hard to write. It is
      impossible for me, I can't do it. Then I start fooling
      around with some stanzas, running a syllable count. I
      use syllabics and rhyme. I get a good beginning to the
      poem. Then I say to myself, But I can't do the poem,
      it's too hard. I use this as a kind of superego. Then I
      proceed to do the poem. I make up the game, and then
      I don't follow it too carefully. Games don't get me
      involved. It's always the content that gets me involved.
      I make up the game to go along with the content. I start
      every poem with a powerful emotion. I write in the
      morning. I use yellow paper, sometimes lined school
      paper. I write at the typewriter and make extensive
      corrections. I sit at a desk, my feet up on a bookcase. I
      have cigarettes, naturally, burned down to one long
      gray ash. How do I write? Expand, expand, cut, cut,
      expand, expand, cut, cut. Do not trust spontaneous first
      drafts. You can always write more fully. The beautiful
      feeling after writing a poem is on the whole better
      even than after sex, and that's saying a lot.

NYQ: *How would you define confessional poetry?*

AS: How would *you* define confessional poetry?

NYQ: *We'd probably say it was autobiographical—associated
      with a certain purgation, and sometimes classified as
      therapy.*

AS: Was Thomas Wolfe confessional or not? Any poem is
      therapy. The art of writing is therapy. You don't solve
      problems in writing. They're still there. I've heard
      psychiatrists say, "See, you've forgiven your father. There

it is in your poem." But I haven't forgiven my father. I just wrote that I did.

NYQ: *Do you feel a tension between the narrative impulse and the lyric impulse?*

AS: I'm too rhythmic. You fight what you've got. I can't bear to be too rhythmical if I'm going to be confessional. I'm very fond of rhymes. I don't feel that off rhymes have the slam-it-home feeling of an on rhyme. Once in a while I use an off rhyme. I like double rhyme. Driving once into Boston, I suddenly thought that "cancer" rhymes with "answer." And so I wrote some lines. They are macabre, and yet it's an honest way of saying it. It makes it more real.

NYQ: *What do you do with lines that you can't use?*

AS: I put them all on paper, and then I put them in my rejection drawer. It's usually a set of lines, not just one.

NYQ: *Does anything keep you away from poetry?*

AS: Talking. Talking keeps you away from poetry. Not teaching, teaching keeps you close. I think I teach by instinct. I'm getting more vulgar in my old age. Now, what do I mean by "vulgar"? Not tasteless. Of the people. Common, is that it? Vernacular. A little less effete. Writing in the vulgate, but that sounds effete. We are being influenced now by South American poets, Spanish poets, French poets. We are much more image-driven as a result. Neruda is the great image-maker. The greatest colorist. Rilke is marvelous, but Neruda springs me loose, also Roethke. Images are the heart of poetry. And this is not tricks. Images come from the unconscious. Imagination and the unconscious are one and the same. You're not a poet without imagery.

NYQ: *To get images out of yourself you have to have a good relationship with yourself.*

AS: Yes—no, look at Hart Crane. He didn't have a very good relationship with himself, but look at his images. That's why I say you have to start with Neruda. Literal translation is best. When I am translated I want just the images, never mind the syllables and the rhymes. I'm proud of them, of my images.

NYQ: *Since, for you, images are the most vital part of poetry, what painters do you feel closest to?*

AS: I suppose Van Gogh, although that's sentimental to say —all the impressionists. Who was that wonderful man who painted all the jungle scenes? Rousseau.

NYQ: *How do you feel about concrete poetry?*

AS: What is concrete poetry?

NYQ: *Poems that are reduced to basic elements, as letters, letters as pictorial symbols.*

AS: A poem is spoken. A poem has to be spoken. I like it on the page, I like to see the stops of the lines.

NYQ: *How do you feel about public readings?*

AS: I care very much about my audiences. They are very dear to me, but I hate giving readings. I feel I've revealed so much of myself anyway, in the language. People always say, "You do it all so gracefully," and so forth. I can just see myself retreating, wearing a big hat and hiding behind dark glasses.

SELECTED BIBLIOGRAPHY

To Bedlam and Part Way Back, New York, Houghton Mifflin Company, 1960.

All My Pretty Ones, New York, Houghton Mifflin Company, 1962.

Live or Die, New York, Houghton Mifflin Company, 1966.

Love Poems, New York, Houghton Mifflin Company, 1969.

Transformations, New York, Houghton Mifflin Company, 1972.

Book of Folly, New York, Houghton Mifflin Company, 1973.

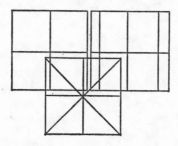

CRAFT INTERVIEW
WITH STANLEY KUNITZ

NYQ: *A few years ago, many of our poets were also serious critics. Today there doesn't seem to be the same interest in critical theory that there was when Mr. Ransom, Mr. Winters, Mr. Brooks and Mr. Warren—*

STANLEY KUNITZ: Oh well, it's part of the revolt against the establishment, which is also a revolt against conventions and standards, including critical standards.

NYQ: *And it seems also as if some poets are their own aestheticians, such as Mr. Olson. Now, does this take part of a poet's energy, part of what used to be given to him?*

SK: Yes, but on the other hand it means that the possibilities are more open; that nobody is required to write in the prevailing style or in the voice of the master. The danger, of course, is in thinking that anything goes in the new dispensation.

NYQ: *Perhaps there will be a swing back, perhaps there will be new criticism after this period is over.*

SK: I suspect there will be. These are energetic and confusing times. There will have to be an evaluation of the work of a whole generation. In fact, it is already happening—look at the spate of freshly minted anthologies. I note, by the way, that reputations are being shuffled faster than ever.

NYQ: *This must be one of the freest periods of your whole career, in terms of what can be done.*

SK: Freer than ever—but tied to the same old carcass! Incidentally, I can't think of it as a career. To me it's a life.

NYQ: *Mr. Auden has complained about the abuses of this period, that there seems to be a lack of interest in history on the part of some young poets, a lack of interest in meter, in craft, in prosody. He was very concerned, distressed.*

SK: Who will be left to admire his great craft? When I first began to teach, in the late forties, it seemed quite obvious that instruction in prosody was part of a workshop discipline. Today the young are mostly indifferent to such matters, not only indifferent but even strongly antipathetic. They praise novelty, spontaneity and ease, and they resist the very concept of form, which they relate to mechanism and chains. Few understand that, for a poet, even breathing comes under the heading of prosody.

NYQ: *You once said that the originality of any poetry consists to a large degree in the poet's finding his own key images, those that go back to his roots and traumas. Can a poet talk about these images?*

SK: Not unless he's very sick or very foolish. Some poets are both. One oughtn't try to explain everything away, even if one could. It's enough to reconcile oneself to the existence of an image from which one never gets very far. No matter how one turns or where one travels in the mind, there inescapably it is, sending out vibrations—and you know it's waiting, waiting to be seized again.

NYQ: *Several years ago you said that certain themes—those of the quest, the night journey, and death and rebirth—preoccupied you.*

SK: I must have been reading Jung then. Those are archetypes built into the structure of the mind.

NYQ: *In discussing "Father and Son" in the Ostroff book*

(The Contemporary Poet as Artist and Critic), *you referred to your sister and to the big house on the hill, and you said, "They belong to that part of my life which I keep trying to rework into legend." What does that mean?*

SK: What the alchemists meant when they spoke of converting dross into gold.

NYQ: *The voice in the poem you call simply "Poem" is intensely personal, and at the same time the events described have a sense of universal myth behind them.*

SK: When I wrote that poem I was young and ignorant. But even then, as now, I wanted to get below the floor of consciousness, to wipe off the smudge of the day. The poems I like best, I suppose, are the ones that are steeped in "the taste of self"—Hopkins' phrase. Such poems are hard fought for.

NYQ: *What do you feel about improvisations, about randomness as a prime creative principle?*

SK: My advice to myself is, Trust in your luck, but don't trust in it absolutely. I recall that after a couple of excruciating experiences as an amateur mycologist, John Cage saw that though the principle of chance operations was good enough for his music, it could not be extended to his mushroom hunting without killing him. Was he aware of the irony implicit in that revelation? Maybe he didn't pursue his insight far enough.

NYQ: *So far,* The New York Quarterly *is more or less dependent on the quality of the poems that are submitted to us. What do you feel about the level of the poems that are appearing in the* Quarterly, *and what should we do to improve the quality? We're always looking for that one poem that will be "below the floor of consciousness," as you have said.*

SK: Standards were easier to maintain in an aristocratic society. Emerson said somewhere that democracy descends to meet. All the modern arts are being threatened by the cult of the amateur. And being nourished, too. You have to know the difference between naiveté and simplicity, novelty and

originality, rhetoric and passion. The most insidious
enemy of the good is not so much the bad as it is the
second best. I mean particularly, in this context, the
inferior productions of first-rate reputations. Anyone
can see that we have plenty of talent around—what
civilization had more? The trouble is that our gifts are
not being used well. On the face of it, our literature
reflects a mediocre or silly age, sometimes an angry one.
When are we going to wake up to the fact that it's
tragic?

NYQ: *Have you had any experience with editing, with
magazines?*

SK: The only magazine I ever edited, after the Classical
High School *Argus* (Worcester, Massachusetts), was a
library periodical. But last year I became editor of the
Yale Series of Younger Poets, succeeding the late
Dudley Fitts. That means reading some five hundred
book-length manuscripts a year. Nobody believes me,
but I actually make an effort to read every one of
them, though not necessarily every page. It's a
responsibility I refuse to unload on others, because—
who knows?—the most miraculous, most original work
of all might get weeded out in the first round, as
sometimes happens in competitions of this kind. At
least half the submissions can be put aside at once as
hopelessly inept or maudlin—usually both. It isn't
asking much of a manuscript that it prove reasonably
competent and tolerably readable, but I've learned that
no more than a hundred out of the five hundred can
be expected to pass that test. Eventually it becomes
clear that there are only three or four manuscripts,
maybe, in the lot from which any sort of fire breaks
each time you turn to them. As far as I am concerned,
these finalists are all winners, and I wish the rules of
the game didn't require me to make an arbitrary
choice. I have always hated the business of ranking
poets. What was it Blake said? "I cannot think that
Real Poets have any competition. None are greatest in
the Kingdom of Heaven."

NYQ: *You have said that you used to play technical games
and do craft exercises. Have any of your poems come
out of one of those games?*

SK: Not that I can recall. But, of course, there is a game element in all poetry. In the very act of writing a poem one is playing with language, playing with the capacities of the mind to hold together its most disparate elements. The object of the game is to fuse as many of one's contradictions and possibilities as one can.

NYQ: *Before we began to record our interview, you said that most of your poems have begun with something that was "given" to you, a very strong opening voice. Doesn't, then, the challenge of realizing the poem require a great understanding of craft in extending the impulse through to the end? So many poems by mediocre poets seem to start beautifully and then are not brought off.*

SK: Practically all my poems start with something given to me, that is, a line or a phrase, or a set of lines, that take me by surprise. When that happens, the challenge is to accept the blessing and go along with it. Only in the process of writing the poem do you discover why the gift was bestowed on you and where it will lead you. Craft is there to sustain and fortify the original impulse, and to preserve the momentum, now by letting go, now by pulling back. Sometimes you find in the end you have to throw out the very lines that gave the poem its start, because they have become embodied in the whole act of the poem and are no longer necessary. Sometimes they require modification, because they may not have come to you perfect. For example, in "End of Summer," the opening lines, as they announced themselves to me, were *"The* agitation of the air,/ *The* perturbation of the light." At a certain point in the revision my ear told me that the four definite articles thickened the lines unpleasantly. I changed them to *"An* agitation of the air,/ *A* perturbation of the light"—much more open, airy, fluid.

NYQ: *Now surely this process of rewriting and trying to fulfill the intention of the given lines must require a full understanding of verse and prosody. This is the whole reason for craft.*

SK: As I indicated earlier, prosody isn't just metrics. It's closer to biology than to mechanics. It involves everything that has to do with the making of a poem, the way it moves, the way it sounds, the way it lives from word to word, the way it breathes.

NYQ: *It is interesting to hear that the beginnings of your poems often consist of "inspired" material, because so much attention has been paid to the way you have ended your poems—particularly those that turn at the end in a line or two in a way that seems both to come out of the poem and to be something new. Do you ever begin the writing of a poem with the ending?*

SK: Occasionally I am astonished to find, through all the devious windings of a poem, that my destination is something I've written six months or a year or two years before, and that is what the poem's been seeking out. The mind's stuff is wonderfully patient.

NYQ: *This process of retention, of being able to carry these lines for years and years, requires a tremendous memory. Is there ever any confusion with lines that have been written by other poets? Do you ever find yourself not sure if you wrote a line?*

SK: In the beginning, sometimes, I would say to myself, I wonder—is this line really mine? And I discovered quite soon that if I questioned it, the only thing to do was to forget it, because the mind has its own conscience, which has to be trusted. A little doubt is all you need to know.

NYQ: *You keep a notebook of quotations that mean something to you. Has an entry from that notebook ever inspired a poem of yours? Or, do you ever incorporate other people's words into the body of a poem?*

SK: The mind is a prolix gut. That's a phrase I suspect I stole from Woodrow Wilson, of all people, though I can't be sure. All poets are thieves—or magpies, if you want me to be euphemistic. The imagination keeps looking for information to digest, and digestion is a process of reconstitution. I don't really care much for paste-and-scissors jobs.

NYQ: *Do you consciously try to control the speed of lines in your poems? In "Benediction," the line "God drive them whistling out" has speed and force, and in the same poem the line "No shy, soft, tigrish fear" is suspended and slow.*

SK: The variable pulse of a poem shows that it is alive. Too regular a beat is soporific. I like to hear a poem arguing with itself. Even before it is ready to change into language a poem may begin to assert its buried life in the mind with wordless surges of rhythm and counterrhythm. Gradually the rhythms attach themselves to objects and feelings. At this relatively advanced stage the movement of a poem is from the known to the unknown, even to the unknowable. Once you have left familiar things behind, you swim through levels of darkness toward some kind of light, uncertain where you will surface.

NYQ: *It's improbable, isn't it, that this kind of experience would ever be given in sum to a poet, without the long struggle, without the long process of—*

SK: I wish it were easier. How I envy prolific poets!

NYQ: *To go back to your underwater metaphor for the creative process, what is the sensation at the point of surfacing?*

SK: Joy. As though a burden had been removed. One is freer than before.

NYQ: *Then a false ending to a poem would be an attempt to create this result without actually achieving it.*

SK: If you fake it, your rhetoric betrays you.

NYQ: *Have you always written in the way you have just described?*

SK: I think so. Even the earliest poems. "For the Word Is Flesh," for example.

NYQ: *How young were you when you began to write poetry?*

SK: Even in grade school I was rhyming—doggerel, mainly. But I enjoyed that. And I was reading all the bad poets, along with some good ones, and loving them equally.

Words always fascinated me, regardless of whether I knew what they meant. In fourth grade, I recall, I began a composition on the Father of Our Country with the sentence: "George Washington was a tall, petite, handsome man."

NYQ: *Which of the poets you read as a young person had the most influence on the development of your own writing? Did reading Tennyson affect the development of your ear?*

SK: During my high school years I admired Keats and Tennyson for their music. One day my English teacher read Herrick in class. Later, a neighbor gave me Wordsworth's collected poems. Those were red-letter days. At Harvard I discovered the metaphysicals and Hopkins, and they shook me up. Afterwards, in the thirties, the later Yeats became important to me, and I began my long friendship with Roethke.

NYQ: *Would you say something about your feelings concerning faith and religion? This process you describe of struggling with the given lines of a poem might almost be an Old Testament wrestling with the Dark Angel in order to find God through intuition rather than through outside revelation.*

SK: I suppose I am a religious person without a religion. Maybe because I have no faith, I need it more than others. And the wrestling is damn good exercise.

NYQ: *Do you often change words in poems after they have been printed? There are two versions of "Deciduous Branch" in print—the first says "Passion" where the later one has "Summer."*

SK: "Summer" made the metaphor harder and cleaner. I can't usually bear to read my early poems, but once in a while I am tempted to see whether I can make some small improvements in the ones I want to keep. I haven't the slightest interest in rewriting them *in toto,* even if I could, nor do I propose to make major changes.

NYQ: *This brings up the matter of a poet's going back and revising, or even disclaiming, early poems which the public has already come to know. How can he blot them out? Should a poet keep trying to bring his work up to date, or should he let the record stand?*

SK: A poet tends to be a perfectionist. I see no reason why he should be disqualified from trying to improve his own work, published or unpublished. As long as he's alive, it's his property. After his death, posterity will have the privilege of determining which versions of his poems, if any, it chooses to remember.

NYQ: *What prompted you to edit those massive collections of literary biographies, Twentieth Century Authors, European Authors, and the rest?*

SK: Simply that I had to earn a living. After college I went to work for a publisher in New York and soon discovered that I wasn't geared for an office existence. So I fled to a farm in Connecticut, where I produced a crop of herbs, flowers and reference books. And, perennially, poems.

NYQ: *Now you seem to be spending a good part of your time on Cape Cod, in Provincetown.*

SK: I'm truly happier there. I have a great world of friends in New York, but the city depletes me. I need to grow things and to breathe clean air. Then, I have my involvement with the Fine Arts Work Center in Provincetown. A few of us have banded together, with the help of some foundation money, including a grant from the National Endowment for the Arts, to invite a selected group of young writers and artists each year to join a productive winter community up there by the sea. We give what help we can. Alan Dugan and I are the ones most concerned with the poets. And we bring in all sorts of brilliant people from the outside for weekly seminars.

NYQ: *That sounds like an exciting program. How does one find out more about it?*

SK: By writing to the Fine Arts Work Center, Box 565, Provincetown, Massachusetts 02657.

NYQ: *Poetry seems to be the orphan child of the arts—it is always difficult to find public support for projects involving poetry. Do you see any sign of improvement? Will a person who wants to become a poet always have to look forward to a lifetime of struggling and working at vocations he doesn't really enjoy in order to support his art?*

SK: Hasn't that usually been true? I'm not sure that a poet should expect to be rewarded for his voluntary choice of a vocation. If he has any sense at all, he should realize that he's going to have a hard time surviving, particularly in a society whose main drives are exactly opposite to his. If he chooses, against the odds, to be a poet, he ought to be tough enough, cunning enough, to take advantage of the system in order to survive. And if he doesn't, it's sad, but the world is full of the most terrible kinds of sadness.

NYQ: *What do you think of the way in which poetry and literature have been presented to elementary school children through our present educational system?*

SK: Almost anybody would have to agree that the American system of education has been a dismal failure. Certainly one of the areas in which it has most significantly failed is in teaching students how to cope with poetry. The failure begins at the grade school level. But there are some promising signs—first of all, a general recognition of the failure. The new young educators, clearly, know the essential truth about the injury done to the imagination of the child, and there are many signs of revolt against the educational system, just as there is a revolt against the political system.

NYQ: *Many high school and college students feel that poetry has no importance for them, in their lives.*

SK: So many of the young today doubt that classroom instruction in general and the reading of poetry in particular is what they need most. I can understand their negativism. They fail to see that the work of the imagination is precisely what has to be achieved if we are going to save our civilization from disaster. And that a poem, regardless of its theme, can embody for us a principle of the free mind engaged in a free action.

NYQ: *Wasn't "The Mound Builders" written out of a political situation?*

SK: Many of my poems are, but in an oblique way. By its nature poetry is hostile to opinions, and the opinions of a poet on public affairs are, in any case, of no special interest. The poems that attract me most, out of the contemporary dilemma, are the peripheral ones that are yet obviously the product of a mind engaged with history. "The Mound Builders," I can recall, came out of the resumption of nuclear testing by President Kennedy in 1962, when I was traveling through the South, and looking at the archeological traces of a civilization that flourished in this country between 900 and 1100 A.D., the greatest civilization of the Eastern seaboard, and maybe the greatest civilization north of Mexico of which nothing now remains except a few shards. There in Georgia the inscription reads "Macon is the seventh layer of civilization on this spot." Macon, one of the seats of racist injustice in this country. So all these element entered into the making of the poem, including the fact that I was traveling, and reading my work, and talking to college students in the South. But most readers would say, not without justification, "It's a poem about mound builders."

NYQ: *Are you writing dramatic monologues now?*

SK: My new book has several poems that are basically dramatic in their structure. They're not quite dramatic monologues—I don't know really what to call them—but in each case there is a dramatic action incorporated in the poem, sometimes appearing and sometimes disappearing. The very last poem I wrote for the book is called "Around Pastor Bonhoeffer." Bonhoeffer, you know, was the Lutheran pastor in Germany who, after a great struggle with his conscience, joined the plot to kill Hitler. The plot failed, and he was exterminated. The conflict between his Christian principle of nonviolence and the political necessity for action seems to me a parable for our times. I myself am a nonviolent man with radical feelings about the way things are.

NYQ: *When will that book be published?*

SK: Next March.

NYQ: *And it's called* The Testing-Tree?

SK: With a hyphen.

SELECTED BIBLIOGRAPHY

Selected Poems 1928–1958, Boston, Little, Brown and Company, 1958.

The Testing-Tree, Boston, Little, Brown and Company, 1971.

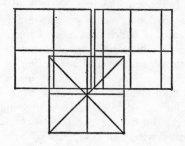

CRAFT INTERVIEW WITH JEROME ROTHENBERG

JEROME
ROTHENBERG:

I'll say one thing about interviews: I don't know if it'll be the case here, but there is a slight tendency to begin lying in the process of it. I think it's one of the problems of becoming self-conscious about writing in a public sense—when you're aware that somebody is listening in on you. A lie is sometimes more interesting than the truth and that's what poetry is about, to maintain interest and concentration.

I was writing poetry in some sense back to fairly early childhood. It was something that I could do, to play with language in that sense, and that I persisted in. To some point in my early twenties, when it became a serious matter or began to work itself out in ways that were different from what they had been. But I was calling myself a poet, say, from my middle teens, although I don't think I completely understood, nor do I think I completely understand now, what all of that's about. My first publication came, I think, when I was twenty-six or twenty-seven. It wasn't a period of early publications then, as it is today. There wasn't the great and marvelous overproduction of little magazines. It was more a question of waiting on line toward some possibility. I think being a poet was, in some sense, at that point more of a "professional" thing than it is today, which I think in many ways is wrong. That fake professionalism goes against the basic function of poetry.

NYQ: *You mean, that's the way it used to be.*

JR: The way it used to be, yes. In the case of poetry, it shouldn't be a question of submitting your manuscript to publishers who have no interest in poetry except for filling out a "list." Or of standing in line for submission, which is a literally demeaning concept, if you think about it. I suppose the best and historically earliest situation for the poet is in relation to some rather small and limited community for whom he is *the* poet, rather than the large and nameless, faceless society that poets and people in general face under contemporary circumstances. Poetry, it seems clear to me, grew out of a tribal and communal situation. Even into the ages of literacy and the political state—where we lost track of its beginnings—there was always a memory of poetry, of tribal poetry, from the first civilizations on. Poetry in a certain sense is a noncivilized thing. It is "primitive" in that it is one of the first high developments in cultures that haven't developed a political state. I don't think it ever really, in any significant sense, goes beyond that development. It always remembers its roots back in that primitive culture. It is a way of being in the world, and so the poet time and again in the history of civilizations comes into conflict with established authority, the proponents of another way. Those like Plato, for example, who idealize the political state and elevate it to a supreme position, see the necessity of eliminating the poets from that state because they tend to be, by their history, by their impulse, nonpolitical.

NYQ: *The poets were too independent?*

JR: Too independent and representing a different state of things: communal and anarchic, the customary or inspired order of poetry and vision—not the fixed

order of law. In a way their re-emergence as an
active force today is not unconnected, in its
reconsideration of tribal possibilities, with the
emergence of experiments in communal living. All
of which is closely connected with a kind of—if I
have the right term—poetic state of mind, primitive
state of mind.

NYQ: *You began working with Indian tribes, and more
recently you began developing a concept of the
identity of the Polish Jew. Was there any
autobiography in this new concept, and how does it
relate to the work you did with Indian tribes?*

JR: To concentrate on that kind of myth, to try to
approach the poem through those terms, to try to
construct a world out of that; that is pretty recent
for me, the last three years, but I've never been
particularly interested in myself as a subject for
poetry—autobiography. It doesn't interest me to go
through the process of the autobiographical poem.
I've never gone through that process, and I think
simply that there are other things in the world that
are more interesting than my personal,
psychological development. I don't think there is
anything astonishing about that. I find such things
as the history of a people, for example, more
interesting than most personal histories. I find
certain individuals interesting in terms of what
they do, but I just don't see—not being modest or
anything—I just don't see my own life as much of
a subject for poetry. There are things, of course,
that I am interested in pursuing, including mental
things, but I don't think poetry *is* autobiography.
Poetry is many things. Poetry may be
autobiographical, but to say that a poet must be
restricted to things out of his personal experience,
things from his psyche in the trivial "confessional"
sense, seems to me to put limits on poetry, put
limits on any writer or artist, to make him define his
art in those terms. I don't think some of these
questions really have to be restricted to poetry.
There is a wider process than that and particularly
at this time when possibilities have become open to

us, but I just use poetry to speak about all the arts, whatever the art may be. I use it also for what interests me in religion or in thought in general.

NYQ: *Do you feel that the impulse toward form and toward rhythm and rhyme has gotten lost?*

JR: I think that there was a tendency to forget where all of that had come from, that certain forms, which may have originated from speech, tended to become rigid and frozen, and the exercises operating within those forms became meaningless as poets forgot the origin of this in the spoken language or in an actual mysticism and epistemology of numbers. What we don't speak, anyway, is prose. Molière's character talks about how he has been speaking prose all his life, which is patently absurd. We can't speak prose, we can't tell if it's prose until we see it on the page. Not verse either. This is what we speak, the way I'm speaking now. Because it stops and starts, stops again, starts again. To my mind this is closer to a verse situation. It's the artifice of prose that suggests the possibility of a single unbroken line, although pages can't go on that long. We could unwind a scroll and write across it endlessly, and basically that's the prose concept—that it doesn't matter where the voice breaks or that one isn't concerned with that. Later, we may translate prose into a spoken language, if you want to give it that kind of reading. Ultimately we develop radio speech, where the tendency is to get the voice to go on in an unbroken way. In this, the artifice of prose has come back into a spoken medium.

NYQ: *Have you ever written in a formal style? Using direct rhythm and very obvious rhyme?*

JR: You mean using traditional forms? Yes.

NYQ: *In early work?*

JR: Yes, in early work. Now, occasionally I write small pieces in syllabics. If I can't think of any other way to structure, let's say, found material, it's a sort of obvious shape to put it into. Syllabics. I did write sonnets way back, which was a fairly boring procedure. Now I'm more interested in creating the *forms* than putting some statement within a fixed form, and I find that ultimately when you get the hang of that (fixed form), it's very easy to do. This isn't a question of how well you do it—I just don't find it interesting.

NYQ: *Do you ever use little craft games, devices to . . .*

JR: Yes, but there are many more devices, "little games." There are a lot of games that go on in poetry, but they don't always have to be a game with that rather limited series of forms. So, to my mind, the most interesting possibility for the poet . . . the most formal poet working today is Jackson MacLow. He has a fantastic formal imagination going—always working for the possibility of new structures or, most recently in his work, he is going back to a very closed syllabic kind of impulse. Jackson is a great poet even working in this way. But the most interesting things being done are outside the conventional forms. To close the issue and also to take those forms as being either something natural to poetry or its inevitable development, at least in nineteenth-century evolutionary terms, you would come across absurd statements about other people's not having developed either end rhyme or Western metrics as a formal concept. People who were preliterate or preindustrial had not yet reached this stage of end rhyme! The attitude was a trivialization: a puerile view of form and of human capability.

NYQ: *You aren't teaching now?*

JR: Not this year.

NYQ: *Is teaching something you find helpful to your own work?*

JR: No.

NYQ: *And workshop situations the same?*

JR: Yes. I don't really go in for workshop situations. Maybe others do. This is a highly individual matter.

NYQ: *Some poets feel that they grow with this. You are not one of them, obviously.*

JR: I think that there are many situations where you can learn. For instance, when poets come together at a certain point in their lives and interact with each other. This is obviously equivalent to a workshop. I was a little put off by the formality of a workshop, actually going through a formal teacher who is paid to teach, in that sense. For myself, except in the interplay with other poets, I never went through a workshop. No, at the age of sixteen I was in a workshop.

NYQ: *As a student?*

JR: Yes, and I could well have done without it.

NYQ: *About this interplay with other poets—is this a continuing thing in your life?*

JR: I think it's particularly crucial for many poets, somewhere in late adolescence, to be in the company of those who are going about the same kind of work. And to be able to exchange work and to exchange encouragements. I won't say criticism. Criticism isn't precisely it. It's possible to learn in that way. It's also possible to be badly deflected by the imposition of another's set of interests. We have to learn how to avoid being *wrongly* influenced.

NYQ: *What do you feel about revision in your own work?*

JR: This whole question of revision seems to me to be a matter of overcoming distractions. When I'm not distracted to begin with, when I'm sort of concentrating, experiencing a peak of concentration, then I basically don't have to revise what I write. I do tend to be distracted. In other words my discipline in terms of being able to focus on the work is not so great that I invariably write without revision. So revision is an attempt to return, to make up for that loss of focus. In some sense being distracted by sounds, people on the telephone, all of those things take me off into different directions, and I haven't tended to write poetry in which I can take advantage of wandering off. I am trying to focus. The poetry may have its own gaps, but it's a form of concentration. If I can't get it all together at one time, then I have to get it together over a number of occasions. And sometimes something that starts well enough doesn't come to any conclusion.

NYQ: *You wouldn't revise after something has been published. Some poets, say, go back to an anthology. . . .*

JR: I almost never revise that late along. Sometimes I cut out a line or two if a poem is being republished, say, a line ten years later makes me feel that I shouldn't have done this. But basically no revision after publication.

NYQ: *What are your feelings about poets' involvement in social, political, philosophical questions?*

JR: Well, let's say I prefer human beings who are involved in political, social, philosophical questions —involved in the life around them. So the same for poets in a sense. Of course, how much any specific issues should be a part of a poet's interest depends to a large extent on what the poet is driven by, very often a question of what he is driven by. If I write about the Vietnam war, I would have to write a poem that would satisfy me. But I generally haven't followed through on these things as direct subject. Partly because there were so many poems appearing, and my feeling has always been that if everyone else exhausts a topic, I'm satisfied to say that they express my sentiments. There's too much reduplication in poetry. But to oppose a war, I could appear in public and read something or say something or help to plan out some type of action. Ultimately, part of my personal manifesto is that I write those poems that other poets haven't written for me. I put together an anthology of primitive poetry because there was no anthology of primitive poetry. If someone else had come along and done this, it would have saved me the effort.

NYQ: *Do you find poetry readings helpful in your own
          work, or do you find them a natural outgrowth of
          the spoken word in poetry?*

JR: I think readings in that second sense are crucial,
          and it's part of the actual discovery of what poetry
          is. If all the books in the world disappeared, there
          would still be poetry. About books in relation to
          poetry—in certain instances I almost regret the
          existence of books. Let me give a specific. Recently
          in doing oral translations—oral poetry—from a
          series of Navajo poem songs, my intention was that,
          as the translation of oral poetry, the form should
          work itself out not on the page but in performance,
          that it should remain an oral situation. Now, I can
          carry this out through readings and public
          performances, but I don't know how to
          accomplish its publication in a nonwritten form;
          in other words, to produce it as a recording. It's
          much easier for me to write it down. I have no
          difficulty in finding publication as a writer. But I've
          found it impossible so far to get publishers to even
          insert a vinyl disc as part of a book. There is a very
          firm separation between books and recordings,
          which they seem to blame on the bookstores. A
          kind of inertia about that. And so I ended up with
          publication of these songs in book form, the written
          form of the song, which isn't what it's about.
          Perhaps I should just have held to that resolution,
          not to let them appear in written form, except
          publication becomes a question of circulating the
          work, which I think is important to do. Unless you
          want to keep it as a private situation.

NYQ: *You have written a poem entitled "Poland/1931."
          Could you tell us about the writing of this poem?*

JR: Over the last several years, although the interest
          probably goes back before that, I've been working
          on a series of poems called *Poland/1931,* that I
          describe as an attempt to write an ancestral poetry.
          The *1931* of the title is the year of my birth.
          Poland isn't where I was born—I was born in
          Brooklyn—but Poland is where my parents came

from ten years before that. So, in other words, the
date and place mark that part of my autobiography
that precedes my own birth, or to go back to what
we were speaking about before, this seems to me to
be the most interesting thing about autobiography.
So what I've been trying to do in various ways is to
create through those poems an analogue, a
presentation of the Eastern European Jewish world
from which I had been cut off by birth, place and
circumstance, and to which I no longer have any
way of returning, because it doesn't exist in that
place any longer. I have gone backward toward an
exploration of the reality in general, but through the
terms of an actual collective unconscious (at least a
collective consciousness), the particular terms of a
particular people of which I have some
understanding, although it is something I carry
entirely in my mind. I do use aids to that
understanding, to supplement the imagination and
memory with whatever becomes available to me. I
freely draw out of other sources, literary and so
forth, and collage into that work what would help
to make an actual fullness so that at some point,
presumably, I can either be within it or step back
and see it. And toward those ends recently I've gone
beyond poetry as words, to add visual elements and
other sound elements to the presentation. In other
words, I've been building toward a theatre piece, a
mixed media piece, using slides and tapes, musical
collage and song. Until, finally, I would like to fill
a great room with all the elements of this concept.

NYQ: *Do you think this tremendous interest in your past
in terms of your parents and Europe might have
been an outgrowth of your interest in tribal poetry,
a kind of seeking your own tribe?*

JR: I'm not sure where it all comes from. I think
possibly the circumstances of my own "tribal past"
predisposed me, although I am an alienated human
being, very much locked in the present . . . there is
still a pull back to that collective unconscious
(Jungian and tribal as well), so this is probably part
of the condition of my mind to begin with, that I

have some historical sense that might lead my interests backward in time instead of focusing on my immediate situation. The fact of a separation between past and present, although God knows there is a separation, is not enough, and I find in exploring the old poetry that I come on some of the same possibilities that open up to me as a modern poet exploring possibilities in my own time. It's partly that coincidence between new and old that captured my own interest, that strange coincidences would appear. They're no longer that strange to me, because I think in a sense they're part of what has defined the idea of the modern poet from its first development in European romanticism. This has been precisely, what my friend Stanley Diamond calls "the search for the primitive." A common assumption of all literary and artistic and political avant-gardes, that if there is a kind of thing that you work on in the present and move to in the future, somehow it coincides with some early beginnings. Even, let's say that the communism of the future is a reflection, a parallel in Marxist thought, to the communalism of the past. The political state which took over from the communal kinship organization will disappear in a new communalism. In one sense or another, political avant-gardes have been obsessed by a return to paradise, that garden of the primitive. All of these things have become clearer to me in the process. But I think from the beginning I did tend to see a great connection between present possibilities and those overlooked or despised possibilities of the primitive, tribal world. I think along with my own search for the primitive, I became more willing to explore my ancestral past. This is also part of my present. It seems to me I've discovered that I do have some understanding of the terms in which that can be presented. I have a very strong feeling about the necessity to explore it. It's part of an attempt not to be bounded by the established present. Another thing I knew was that behind the return to *Poland/ 1931* was my reaction to the Vietnam war and the feeling that I had at that point, that I no longer

wanted to buy for myself the inevitability of an
American present as it had then developed. That if
America meant anything to me it was in some
nineteenth-century sense, as a meeting place of the
nations. What America had developed into as a
separate American entity was something that at that
point I felt to be repulsive, and I wanted to, in some
very violent, for me, sense, dissociate myself from
this. And it seemed to me no longer worth very
specifically *not* being Jewish or not being what I
was ancestrally to have a share in the American
present. In other words, it seemed much more
interesting and a much better position morally and
spiritually to dissociate myself, to take my stand
against an American present, and in that sense
it seems to have been done by others (black and
Indian poets, and so on) in other ways. Perhaps
it re-establishes a broken American continuity—of
the country as a meeting place of nations.

NYQ: *How long have you been interested in tribal work?*
        What tribes have you done work with?

JR: With Navajo and Seneca. In two different ways.
        First in *Technicians of the Sacred*. This was
        probably just an outgrowth, making a book out of
        interests that concerned me since I was writing
        poetry in college. They had a fairly decent library
        at the University of Michigan, and I had been
        collecting, copying, typing out these primitive
        poems, and rewriting them from the form that most
        anthropologists had put them into, which was an
        abomination. Until about 1964 I did this, at which
        point several of us did a reading of primitive
        poetry in a few places in New York, and so I had a
        chance to bring together the materials. That gave
        me a short manuscript of the *Technicians* book,
        and when Doubleday agreed to publish that, I
        spent about a year's work bringing it up to the final
        size, and added a commentary, which made a five-
        hundred-page book out of it. Toward the very end
        of the compilation of this book, Gary Snyder
        introduced me to Stanley Diamond, who is
        chairman of the Department of Anthropology at

the New School, and Stanley suggested that, as the
anthropologists do, I go out into the field. He
arranged a visit to upstate New York, to the
Allegheny reservation in the western panhandle of
New York State. I went up a number of times,
particularly in the summer of 1968, and worked in
collaboration with several of the songmen there,
particularly Richard Johnny John, on a translation
of Seneca poetry. In addition to that, I became
friendly with David McAllister, a great
ethnomusicologist, who's with the Department of
Anthropology at Wesleyan University in
Connecticut, and he became an intermediary in the
translation of Navajo poetry. He showed extreme
generosity in presenting materials to me for the
translation. It was with the Navajo poetry that I
made the effort to do actual oral translations, so
that I finally ended up translating everything that
the voice can carry, including a translation of the
so-called meaningless syllables and music.

NYQ: *Does this interest in tribal poetry mean that we are*
          opening up our sense of what poetry is?

JR: In a sense we are opening to the possibilities of
          *inter*tribal life. The whole world is opening to that
          possibility. To rediscover the tribal and, on the
          other hand, to create the great universal powwow,
          the gathering of the tribes, both become possible. I
          wouldn't want to return to that tribalism which
          keeps people apart from each other. That's the
          drawback of tribalism. The danger of tribalism is
          that the tribe can be so self-contained. It is the
          most self-contained form of human existence. To
          come back into isolated tribes is not the point. But
          the power of the tribal is the power of particulars,
          the power of localities, the power of the communal,
          which is fundamentally the experience of small
          groups. But hopefully because of the kinds of
          communication open to us now, the tribes can speak
          to each other. I have most recently been translating
          Indian poetry, including the meaningless syllables,
          word distortions and music, and have been
          exploring ancestral sources of my own in the world

of Jewish mystics, thieves and madmen. I believe everything is possible in poetry, and that our earlier Western attempts at definition represent a failure of perception we no longer have to endure.

NYQ: *How do you yourself work, how do you write?*

JR: Well, if anybody's interested, I write mostly on the typewriter with a pencil close at hand to jot things down. I like to see the poem on the typewriter—I am print-oriented in that sense, but where typing is interrupting the concentration, I'll move over to a place where I can jot things down.

NYQ: *Do you keep a notebook of lines of poetry?*

JR: No. But if something comes out of the blue I reach around desperately for pencil and paper. But I don't tend to carry pencil and paper. I often will try to remember lines. A poem can grow from a line sometimes. I figure if you lose a line, it's not a thing that will cause the world to end. Part of the wisdom of poetry is—can you imagine what a fantastic overproduction of poetry there is? We overproduce everything, even poetry. A good poet can go with a dozen poems for his whole lifetime. That's power enough. Imagine, to have a dozen powerful disease-curing stabilizers that have been dreamed to you. Against which you have this tremendous need to keep producing poetry. In some sense, what do we need it for? Myself, my poetry, if it has any effect that I can see working on the minds of others, it is mostly in a performance situation, and what can I perform but a handful of poetry? Why build up a repertory of poems? I suppose it's part of the whole producing, consuming economy and culture. Poets also have this notion. Particularly today there's a great value placed on being prolific. . . . For some it's a question of their own necessities as a person. So I'm not being completely serious about this. But about losing lines. . . . !?

NYQ: *Do you ever build a poem out of one line?*

JR: Yes, you keep scraps of paper, or worksheets around. In that sense I will go back to it after I abandoned

it, and sometimes to just a single line extracted from
a discarded poem. You sometimes have poems
happen, too. You're looking for something to
engage your attention, and you can be misled by
working on what's not to the point, and somewhere
in the middle of that, there's something that's really
concerning you. After being away for a while, you
can strip all the rest away and this line, this image
embedded in a poem that's otherwise meaningless,
turns out to be what you wanted to explore. This is
the important thing to work through.

NYQ: *What do you do about dry periods?*

JR: I can't think of any ways except to wait. It would
again be like the question of losing lines. True, there
are other things to do with your life besides writing
poems. I would hate not to be able to work out any
more poems, a fear that comes up if I haven't
written for several weeks. That would be
unpleasant. But I don't tend to panic in that sense,
and I'm engaged in making poems at different
levels of concentration anyway, so I can be busy
with informational translation, say, when I'm not
actively doing other things. Knowing that the other
things will happen when they're ready to.

NYQ: *Can you tell us about the magazine you are editing?*

JR: I've done magazines before which were generally
poetry magazines with a particular point of view,
presenting contemporary poetry. Now I've just
gotten the first issue of a magazine I'm coediting
with Dennis Tedlock, a magazine called *Alcheringa*
and presented as "the first magazine of the world's
tribal poetries." The magazine operates as an
ongoing extension of the work I was doing in
Technicians of the Sacred and the point of view
I'll be going on with in *Shaking the Pumpkin*. To
encourage experiments in the translation of tribal
poetries and be a kind of meeting place for people
in different areas who are concerned with that and
who can most profoundly increase our sense of the
possibilities of poetry on the one hand, and help in
combating cultural genocide and its manifestations

on the other. *Alcheringa* is an Australian aboriginal word of great potency, meaning the dreamtime, or the eternal dreamtime or the dream that speaks about the mythological past, both as it was for the eternal beings and as it manifests itself in the present in song and poetry. This is an attempt to explore the possibilities of making immediate such poetries as they exist among tribal people.

SELECTED BIBLIOGRAPHY

Technicians of the Sacred, Garden City, N.Y., Doubleday & Company, Inc., 1969.

Poems for the Game of Silence 1960–1971, New York, Dial Press, 1971.

Esther K. Comes to America, Greensboro, N.C., Unicorn Press, Inc., 1972.

Shaking the Pumpkin, Garden City, N.Y., Doubleday & Company, Inc., 1972.

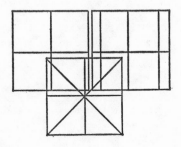

CRAFT INTERVIEW
WITH ALLEN GINSBERG

NYQ: *You have talked about this before, but would you begin this interview by describing the early influences on your work, or the influences on your early work?*

ALLEN GINSBERG: Emily Dickinson. Poe's "Bells"—"Hear the sledges with the bells—Silver bells! . . ." Milton's long line breath in *Paradise Lost*—"Him th' Almighty Power/hurled headlong flaming from the ethereal sky,/with hideous ruin and combustion, down/to bottomless perdition,/there to dwell in adamantine chains and penal fire,/who durst defy the Omnipotent to arms . . ."

Shelley's "Epipsychidion" "one life, one death, one Heaven, one Hell, one immortality And one annihilation. Woe is me! . . ." The end of Shelley's "Adonais"; and Shelley's "Ode to the West Wind" exhibits continuous breath leading to ecstatic climax.

Wordsworth's "Intimations of Immortality"—"Our birth is but a sleep and a forgetting:/the soul that rises with us, our life's Star,/Hath had elsewhere its setting, . . ."—also Wordsworth's "Tintern Abbey" exhortation (or whatever you call it): "a sense sublime of something far more deeply interfused, whose dwelling is the light of setting suns, and the round ocean and the living air, and the blue sky, and in the mind of man . . ."—

That kind of poetry influenced me: a long breath poetry that has a sort of ecstatic climax.

NYQ: *What about Whitman?*

AG: No, I replied very specifically. You asked me about my *first* poetry. Whitman and Blake, yes, but in terms of the *early* poems I replied specifically. When I began writing I was writing rhymed verse, stanzaic forms that I derived from my father's practice. As I progressed into that I got more involved with Andrew Marvell.

NYQ: *Did you used to go to the Poetry Society of America meetings?*

AG: Yes, I used to go with my father. It was a horrifying experience, mostly old ladies and second-rate poets.

NYQ: *Would you elaborate?*

AG: That's the PSA I'm talking about. At the time it was mainly people who were enemies of, and denounced, William Carlos Williams and Ezra Pound and T. S. Eliot.

NYQ: *How long did it take you to realize they were enemies?*

AG: Oh, I knew right away. I meant enemies of poetry, very specifically. Or enemies of that poetry which now by hindsight is considered sincere poetry of the time. *Their* highwater mark was, I guess, Edwin Arlington Robinson, "Eros Turannos" was considered, I guess, the great highwater mark of twentieth-century poetry.

NYQ: *Where did you first hear long lines in momentum?*

AG: The texts I was citing were things my father taught me when I was prepubescent.

NYQ: *Did he teach them to you as beautiful words or as the craft of poetry?*

AG: I don't think people used that word "craft" in those days. It's sort of like a word that has only come into use in the last few decades. There were texts of great poetry around the house, and he would recite from memory. He never sat down and said now I am going to teach you: Capital C-R-A-F-T. Actually I don't like the use of the word craft applied to poetry, because generally along with it comes a defense of stressed iambic prosody, which I find uncraftsmanly and pedantical in its use. There are very few people in whose mouths that word makes any sense. I think Marianne Moore may have used it a few times. Pound has used it a couple of times in very specific circumstances—more often as a verb than as a general noun. "This or that poet has crafted a sestina."

NYQ: *Would you talk about later influences on your work? William Blake? Walt Whitman?*

AG: Later on for open verse I was interested in Kerouac's poetry. I think that turned me on more than anyone else, I think he is a very great poet and much underrated. He hadn't been read yet by poets.

NYQ: *Most people associate Kerouac with prose, with* On the Road, *and not so much with* Mexico City Blues. *Or maybe they differentiate too strictly between prose and poetry.*

AG: I think it's because people are so preoccupied with the use of the word craft and its meaning that they can't see poetry in front of their on the page. Kerouac's poetry looks like the most "uncrafted stuff" in the world. He's got a different idea of craft from most people who use the word craft. I would say Kerouac's poetry is the craftiest of all. And as far as having the most craft of anyone, though those who talk about craft have not yet discovered it, his craft is spontaneity; his craft is having the instantaneous recall of the unconscious; his craft is the perfect executive conjunction of archetypal memorial images articulating present observation of detail and childhood epiphany fact.

NYQ: *In* Howl, *at the end of Section One, you came close to a definition of poetry, when you wrote:*

> *who dreamt and made incarnate gaps in Time &*
> *Space through images juxtaposed, and trapped*
> *the archangel of the soul between 2 visual*
> *images and joined the elemental verbs and set*
> *the noun and dash of consciousness together*
> *jumping with sensation of Pater Omnipotens*
> *Aeterna Deus.*

AG: I reparaphrased that when I was talking about
        Kerouac. If you heard the structure of the sentence I
        was composing, it was about putting present observed
        detail into epiphany, or catching the archangel of the
        soul between two visual images. I was thinking then
        about what Kerouac and I thought about haiku—two
        visual images, opposite poles, which are connected by
        a lightning in the mind. In other words "Today's been
        a good day; let another fly come on the rice." Two
        disparate images, unconnected, which the mind
        connects.

NYQ: *Chinese poets do that. A few issues ago we ran some
        work by Wallase Ting. Is this what you are talking
        about?*

AG: This is characteristic of Chinese poetry as Ezra Pound
        pointed out in his essay "The Chinese Written
        Character as a Medium for Poetry" nearly fifty years
        ago. Do you know that work? Well, 'way back when,
        Ezra Pound proposed Chinese hieroglyphic language
        as more fit for poetry, considering that it was primarily
        visual, than generalized language abstraction English,
        with visionless works like Truth, Beauty, Craft, etc.
        Pound then translated some Chinese poetry and
        translated (from Professor Fenellossa's papers) this
        philosophic essay pointing to Chinese language as
        pictorial. There is no concrete picture in English, and
        poets could learn from Chinese to present image
        detail: and out of that Pound hieroglyph rose the whole
        practice of imagism, the school which is referred to as
        "Imagism." So what you are referring to is an *old*
        history in twentieth-century poetry. My own thing
        about two visual images is just from that tradition,
        actually drawing from Pound's discovery and
        interpretation of Chinese as later practiced by Williams
        and everybody who studied with Pound or who
        understood Pound. What I'm trying to point out is that
        this tradition in American poetry in the
        twentieth century is not something *just* discovered. It
        was done by Pound and Williams, precisely the people
        that are anathema to the PSA mediocrities who were
        attacking Pound and Williams for not having "craft."

NYQ: *In that same section of* Howl, *in the next line, you wrote:*

> *to recreate the syntax and measure of poor human prose and stand before you speechless and intelligent and shaking with shame, rejected yet confessing out the soul to conform to the rhythm of thought in his naked and endless head.*

AG: Description of aesthetic method. Key phrases that I picked up around that time and was using when I wrote the book. I meant again if you place two images, two visual images side by side and let the mind connect them, the gap between the two images the lightning in the mind illuminates. It is the *Sunyata* (Buddhist term for blissful empty void) which can only be known by living creatures. So, the emptiness to which the Zen finger classically points—the ellipse—is the unspoken hair-raising awareness in between two mental visual images. I should try to make the answers a little more succinct.

NYQ: *Despite your feeling about craft, poets have developed an attitude towards your work, they have discovered certain principles of breath division in your lines—*

AG: Primary fact of my writing is that I don't have any craft and don't know what I'm doing. There is absolutely no art involved, in the context of the general use of the words art and craft. Such craft or art as there is, is in illuminating mental formations, and trying to observe the naked activity of my own mind. Then transcribing that activity down on paper. So the craft is being shrewd at flashlighting mental activity. Trapping the archangel of the soul, by accident, so to speak. The subject matter is the action of my mind. To put it on the most vulgar level, like on the psychoanalyst's couch is supposed to be. Now if you are thinking of "form" or even the "well made poem" or a sonnet when you're lying on the couch, you'll never say what you have on your mind. You'd be babbling about corset styles or something *else* all the time instead of saying, "I want to fuck my mother," or whatever it is you want. So my problem is to get down the fact that I want to fuck my mother or whatever. I'm taking the most hideous image possible, so there will be no misunderstanding about what area of mind you are dealing with: What is socially unspoken, what is prophetic from the unconscious, what is universal to all men, what's the main subject of poetry, what's underneath, *inside* the mind. So, how do you get that out on the page? You observe your own mind during the time of composition and write down whatever goes through the ticker tape of mentality, or whatever you hear in the echo of your inner ear, or what flashes in picture on the eyeball while you're writing. So the subject is constantly interrupting because the mind is constantly going on vagaries—so whenever it changes I have a dash. The dashes are a function of this method of transcription of unconscious data. Now you can't write down *everything* that you've got going on—half conscious data. You can't write down everything, you can only write down what the hand can carry. Your hand can't carry more than a twentieth of what the mind flashes, and the very fact of writing interrupts the mind's flashes and redirects attention to writing. So that the observation (for writing) impedes the function of the mind. You might say "Observation impedes Function." I get down as much as I can of genuine material, interrupting the flow of material as I get it down and when I look I turn to the center of my brain to see the next thought, but it's probably about thirty thoughts later. So I make a dash to indicate a break, sometimes a dash plus dots. Am I making sense?—

Saying "I want to fuck my mother"—that's too heavy. It waves a red flag in front of understanding, so we don't have to use that as the archetypal thought. Like "I want to go heaven" may be the archetypal thought, instead of "I want to fuck my mother." I just wanted to get it down to some place that everybody knows where it is. If I say "I want to go to heaven" you might think it's a philosophic conception.

NYQ: *How much do you revise your work?*

AG: As little revision as possible. The craft, the art consists in paying attention on the actual movie of the mind.

Writing it down is like a by-product of that. If you can actually keep track of your own head movie, then the writing it down is just like a secretarial job, and who gets crafty about that? Use dashes instead of semicolons. Knowing the difference between a dash — and a hyphen -. Long lines are useful at certain times, and short lines at other times. But a big notebook with lines is a helpful thing, and three pens—you have to be shrewd about that. The actual materials are important. A book at the nightstand is important—a light you can get at—or a flashlight, as Kerouac had a brakeman's lantern. That's the craft. Having the brakeman's lantern and knowing where to use the ampersand "&" for swiftness in writing. If your attention is focused all the time—as my attention was in writing "Sunflower Sutra," "TV Baby" poem later, ("Wichita Vortex Sutra" later, in a book called *Planet News*)—when attention is focused, there is no likelihood there will be much need for blue penciling revision because there'll be a sensuous continuum in the composition. So when I look over something that I've written down, I find that if my attention has lapsed from the subject, I begin to talk about myself writing about the subject or talking about my irrelevant left foot itch instead of about the giant smog factory I'm observing in Linden, New Jersey. Then I'll have to do some blue penciling, excising whatever is irrelevant: whatever I inserted self-consciously, instead of conscious of the Subject. Where self-consciousness intervenes on attention, blue pencil excision means getting rid of the dross of self-consciousness. Since the subject matter is really the operation of the mind, as in Gertrude Stein, anything that the mind passes through is proper and shouldn't be revised out, almost anything that passes through mind, anything with the exception of self-consciousness. Anything that occurs to the mind is the proper subject. So if you are making a graph of the movements of the mind, there is no point in revising it. Because then you would obliterate the actual markings of the graph. So if you're interested in writing as a form of meditation or introspective yoga, which I am, then there's no revision possible.

NYQ: *Your poem about the sunflower shows remarkable powers of concentration.*

AG: "Sunflower Sutra," the original manuscript in pencil's somewhere at Columbia University Library. In examining it you will see published poem deviates maybe five or ten words from the original penciled text, written in twenty minutes, Kerouac at the door, waiting for me to go off to a party, and I said, "Wait a minute, I got to write myself a note." I had the Idea Vision and I wanted to write it down before I went off to the party, so I wouldn't forget.

NYQ: *Did it dictate the sense, or did you just do it for yourself?*

AG: Observing the flashings on the mind. As somebody said, the craft is observing the mind. Formerly the "craft" used to be an idea of rearranging your package, rearranging. Using the sonnet is like a crystal ball to pull out more and more things from the subconscious (to pack into the sonnet like you pack an ice cream box). Fresher method of getting at that material is to watch mind flow instantaneously, to realize that all that is, is there in the storehouse of the mind within the instant any moment: that's the Proust of eternal recall, remember, the entire *Remembrance of Things Past* came to him just as he was dunking that little bit of madeleine cake into his tea. You know, the whole content of that one instant: that epiphanous instant, working with that instant—the mind then and there. That method I learned from Kerouac and I am interested in. That method is related to other "classical" methods of art composition and meditation like Zen Buddhist calligraphic painting, haiku composition also a spontaneous art, *supposed* to be spontaneous. People don't sit around revising haikus. They are supposed to be sitting around drinking saki, near a little hibachi (charcoal stove) with fireflies and fans and half moons through the window. And in the summertime you are supposed to say, "Ah, the firefly has just disappeared into the moon . . ." Make it up then and there. It's got to come from the perception of the moment. You can't go home the next day and send your friend the haiku and say "I thought of a funny one: the firefly just . . ." That wouldn't be real.

NYQ: *Do you see time used as a unit of structure, as well as a point of view?*

AG: Time of composition is the structure of the poem. That is the subject. What is going on in the mind during that moment is the subject. "Time is of the essence," said Kerouac in very great little essay on writing poetry, one-page set of advice, in back of Don Allen's *The New American Poetry: 1945–1960*, the section is devoted to composition theory. I learned my theory from Kerouac. The preoccupations I have are Hindu, Buddhist, Hassidic—I spend every morning one hour sitting cross legged, eyes closed, back straight, observing my consciousness and quieting my consciousness, watching processions of mental imagery. Someone who isn't into that kind of meditation might find it an unknown territory to go into, chaos, and see it as much too chaotic to get involved with.

NYQ: *You once wrote, I won't write my poem until I'm in my right mind.*

AG: Yes. Of course, *that* poem is like a series of one-line jokes, so to speak. At the expense of the body politic, at the expense of the mass media Hallucination of Being entertained by the middle class.

NYQ: *Does this refer to an attitude of yours about state of mind?*

AG: I'm referring to a nervously comical attitude toward America. It ends "I'm putting my queer shoulder to the wheel." What I'm saying is, my poetry—this particular poem—my poetry in general—shows as such drivel because the United States is in such a state of apocalyptic drivelhood, that we're destroying the world, actually, and we're really destroying ourselves, and so I won't write my poems until I'm in my right mind. Until America gets out of its silly mood.

NYQ: *Would you discuss travel, when you're in different places do you find yourself affected by the prosody of the place?*

AG: I try to learn what I can. I got involved with mantra chanting when I was in India and brought it back to

America. I do a lot of mantra chanting here. Just
because I was interested in it and it had something to
do with poetics, I thought. It also had to do with
vocalization in that it did relate to preoccupations
that I was familiar with in Pound's dictum "Pay
attention to the tone leading of vowels." Sanskrit
prosody has great ancient rules involving vowels and a
great consciousness of vowels or a consciousness of
quantitative versification. Like Pound is conscious of
that too, tried to bring that to the awareness of poets
in the twentieth century, tried to make people more
conscious of the tone leading of vowels and
renounce hyper attention to accentual rhythm. Pound
said that he thought the future America prosody would
be "an approximation of classical quantity," he thought
that would be a formal substitute for iambic count,
stress count. The whole poetic movement of the century
climaxed in what was known as Beat of San Francisco
or Hippie or whatever Renaissance movement was
finally a realization of a new form of prosody, a new
basis for the prosody. Actually I've written a great deal
about the subject. I don't know if you're familiar with
much of it, but some poetics is covered in a *Paris
Review* interview [*Paris Review* ⅂37: Spring, 1966—
Editor]. The relationship between Poetics and Mantra
is gossiped on in a *Playboy* interview. A closer analysis
of stress prosody, that kind of craft, sits in a preface to
my father's book*—where I referred—(in answer to an
earlier question) to one of the books that influenced me
when I was young called *American Poetry,* edited with
Introduction, Notes, Questions, and Biographical
Sketches by A. B. De Mille, Simmons College, Boston,
Secretary of the New England Association of Teachers
of English, Boston, Allyn and Bacon, 1923, Academy
Classic Series. It was, like the high school anthology,
for most older high school teachers who teach now,
their education. It was the standard anthology of the
early twenties and used around the schools. So, they
say in this book . . . I read Dickinson and Poe and
Archibald Rutledge and Whittier and Longfellow and

* *Morning in Spring,* Louis Ginsberg, New York, William Morrow & Co.,
Inc., 1970.

Thoreau and Emerson and John Hay Whitney, all the
bearded poets of the nineteenth century in that book.
This book described accentual prosody as "particularly
well adapted to the needs of English poetry . . . definite
rules, which have been carefully observed by all great
poets from Homer to Tennyson and Longfellow." They
gave as an example of accentual prosody in this book
for teachers and students:

Thŭu tóo/sǎil ón,/Ǒ Shíp/ǒf Státe./

Remember that line? They had it marked: as above.
As you notice they had an unaccented mark for O and
then an accented mark for Ship. When you read it you
will realize that O is an exclamation, and, by definition,
you *can't* have an unaccented mark for that and an
accented mark for Ship. Which means that by the time
1923 had come about teachers of English prosody had
so perverted their own ears and everybody else's ears
that they could actually write down O, as unaccented.
See, it was done like that. Well, what it means is that
nobody could pronounce the line right. They were
teaching people to mispronounce things. It would have
to be: Thou too/sail on,/O Ship of State, many long
vowels. But when you got up on the elementary or high
school lecture platform, they used to say: Thóu tóo/sáil
ón,/Ó Ship/ǒf Státe. Hear? Another example they had
in there was:

Whose héart/-strǐngs aŕe/ǎ lufe

when it quite obviously is: heárt-stfings. So, in other
words, that's where "craft" degenerated. That's why
I'm talking about how do we get out from under that.
Because that was the Poetry Society of America's
standard of poetics. And that's what Pound was fighting
against. And replacing with a much more clear ear.
And of course that's what Williams was working on,
and that's what Creeley, Olsen and Kerouac have
always been compensating for. That's why I'm so mean
about the use of the word "craft." Because I really
wanted to make it clear that whatever people think
craft is supposed to be, that what they've been taught

at school, it's *not* that at all. One had better burn the
word than abuse it as it has been abused, to confuse
everybody.

NYQ: *How does your own teaching affect your work?*

AG: I don't teach too much, I go around and give poetry
readings. When I go around to a college generally I'll
teach a course in like talk. Generally, it ranges oddly
from abnormal psychology courses to psychology
courses, whether I'm discussing drugs or consciousness.
But that also leads into a discussion of letters because
that also concerns consciousness. Sometimes drugs.
Sometimes if there's a course in Blake I'll teach that,
mainly by singing Blake's *Songs of Innocence and
Experience* which I've been putting to music. ("Blake's
Songs of Innocence and of Experience Tuned by Allen
Ginsberg" MGM/Verve FTS 3083.) Learning music
and examining the prosody in Blake syllable by syllable
tonally, making them tunes. I lectured last week at
Columbia Law School, mainly about research that I've
been doing that implicates the CIA in opium traffic in
Indochina. And I'll be lecturing next week at the NYU
Medical School—New York Med. Committee on
Human Rights, the rights of junkies being persecuted
by police, narcotics agents who themselves are peddling
dope. A lot of teaching or lecturing but it's scattered all
over and up and down and it's not all poetry.

NYQ: *You have been giving readings with your father.*

AG: We've done about four a year since 1965. We started at
the PSA. But we don't do it often. It would get to be
too much of an act or something. Generally we do it
when there's some sentimental or aesthetically
interesting occasion. Like at the PSA, that was
interesting aesthetically. At the Y the other night,
that was interesting because it is the traditional place
for "distinguished poets" to read. I do it because, partly,
to live with my father, because he's not going to be
here forever. Nor am I. As a poet I'm interested in
living in the same universe with him, and working in
the same universe with him. We both learn something
from it, get a little bit into each other's souls, the world
soul. A father can learn a son's soul and a son can

learn a father's soul, it's pretty much knowing God's soul, finally. It's like a confrontation with my own soul which is sometimes difficult. But it usually winds up pleasurable. Sometimes I have to see things in myself or face things in my father that are quite hideous. Confront them. So far this has turned out to reconcile us more and more.

NYQ: *Do you think things are getting easier?*

AG: As the world slowing draws to its doomy dead ocean conclusion in the 2000th year, it gets harder and harder. You know the *Times* editorial said that the oceans will be dead as Lake Erie in the year 2000. It was in the paper today! "Reputable scientific evidence" says that given the present rate of waste, the world's oceans (where Leviathan has already been extincted) will be dead as Lake Erie. Which is what I was thinking when I was coming here. The poetic precedent for this situation is like Ezekiel and Jeremiah and the Hebrew prophets in the Bible who were warning Babylon against its downfall. Like Eldridge Cleaver is using the Poetics of Jonah. They were talking about the fall of a city, like Babylon, or the fall of a tribe, or cursing out the sins of a nation. But no poets have ever had to confront the *destruction of the entire world* like we have to. No poet has ever had to confront an editorial in the New York *Times* that says the oceans will be dead as Lake Erie in the year 2000. It's so incredible as a subject that you can't even go back to the biblical prophets for a model to say "Well, I think I'll write a poem like Jeremiah now, or I'll tell these people at *The New York Quarterly* I'm working in the tradition of Jeremiah." But really, no, because not even Jeremiah had to confront a subject as immense as what I and you have to deal with, which is the end of the habitable human world. It is a possibility. Or the millennial salvation of the human world. If we make it past 2000. Talking in terms of craft, the easy way would be to say let us model . . . I think I'll come on with a big con . . . "I'm modeling my recent work after Jeremiah." I'll go back and read the Bible and model all my latest, a whole bunch of electronic poetry about the oceans being polluted. I'd just make a lot of images. You know:

"Woe on thee, New York." But the whole thing is much too serious and vast that you can't go back because it didn't work. Jeremiah didn't save Babylon or wherever he was trying to save, I forgot. This is a life and death matter for the entire world. So the old craft, the old images and the old examples, even as deep and profound as the Bible, don't provide the model that we can faithfully copy or project from in order to save our souls and our skin now. The poet is now confronted with all human history to date, the accumulation, the ecological chain reaction of all human history from the Magdalenian cave painting forty thousand years ago to the end of this century. All the bad vibes and good vibes put together. All human consciousness now totaled up in the libraries and on microfilm and on tape available, all the paintings ever done available in museums, music, all ever written down and available on tape machines, cassettes, hi fi systems, all human conceptual consciousness that could have been formulated available in the British museum and the New York library. And simultaneously, apparently, the end of the world approaching, not as a poetic image, but as an absolute fact reported in the newspapers. So I think that actually comes to affect one's sense of poetics. For instance, I begin to wonder what's the point of writing poems down on paper and printing them, when neither paper nor print nor electricity nor machines nor newspapers nor magazines will survive the next thirty or forty years. Wouldn't it be best if one were interested in what would survive, wouldn't it be best just if one were to deal only in those forms which are memorizable and singable and which could survive beyond the printing press, if one were interested in "immortality." If one were interested in art which is perennial, endurable, that is useful in caves, if people have to live in caves, from that point of view, for that reason, there would be only music.

NYQ:　　　*Did you ever study music? Take up an instrument?*

AG:　　　No, I began doing mantra chanting and studying Indian music, and doing repetitive mantra chanting and developed out of that, together with the Blake work. Mantra chanting involved just one chord. Hare

Krishna, Hare Krishna, Krishna, Krishna, Hare, Hare,
etc. all done in a C chord, C major. Then I got to some
variations. I've put most of Blake's Songs to music
now, I think I've got thirty-five out of the forty-five.
There's a record out of half of them, I'll finish that
up this year, it's quite a project, a huge project.

NYQ: *Have you ever taught the poetry of Blake?*

AG: Well, I teach him by singing him. Because Blake sang,
you know. That's why they're called *Songs of Innocence
and Experience.* He was a literal poet.

NYQ: *What was his own music for the songs like?*

AG: Nobody knows. They are not written down. There
were some scholar musicians according to biographers
who heard him but didn't notate. Probably similar to
what I'm doing, so I'm told by Foster Damon, who was
a great Blake scholar, and who was a musician too.
What I'm doing is sort of in the style of the hymns of
Isaac Watts and people of that time.

NYQ: *Why do you suppose you feel a kinship for Blake, for
exalted works?*

AG: I think I mentioned earlier "Intimations of
Immortality," "Tintern Abbey," that pantheistic
nature, the specific line I quoted, "a sense sublime of
something far more deeply interfused, whose dwelling is
the light of setting suns, and the round ocean and the
living air, and the blue sky, and in the breast of man, the
spirit that impels all thinking things all objects of all
thought, . . . and rolls through all things." So I quote
that as a psychedelic statement, "mind-manifesting,"
fit for classical meditators and modern dope fiends.

NYQ: *Was pantheism behind your starting your own farm?*

AG: As reflected in a poem called "Wales Visitation" in
Planet News book, which is a poem written on LSD.
When I get onto LDS or psylocybin Mexican
mushrooms now the vision trips I get on are mostly
like Wordsworthian common daylight, connected with
the symmetry of the thistle or the emptiness inside the
lamb's eye. So the last time I took LSD it was in Wales,
when I wrote that poem and that turned me on to the

possibility of actually altering my immediate environment and living in that world permanently. Which I do now.

NYQ:	*Did you find yourself?*

AG:	It helped. I don't do it too much because I'm on a commune. A couple of acres with organic gardening and we have our own cow for milk and we get our own eggs from our chickens and there's a pet pig. Have a vegetarian table, have a horse, goat milk, and goats, ducks. Lots of dogs and cats. Anywhere between seven and twenty people. It's ecologically inadvisable to be eating meat from here on out, meat is wasteful of the acreage.

NYQ:	*What do you do with the pigs then?*

AG:	We're having spiritual communion with the pigs, discovering the personality and the emotions of the pigs, pigs are the smartest of the barnyard animals, they are also extremely emotional. Ducks are pretty dumb. They keep sitting on rotten eggs all the time.

NYQ:	*You read the "Wales Visitation" poem on the Buckley TV interview?*

AG:	Yes—"Wales Visitation."

NYQ:	*Is this your favorite poem?*

AG:	Of my most recent poems, this is, like an imitation of a perfect nature poem, and also it's a poem written on LSD which makes it exemplary for that particular modality of consciousness. It's probably useful to people as a guidance, mental guideline for people having bum trips because if they'll check through the poem they'll see an area which is a good trip. An ecologically attuned pantheistic nature trip. Also it's an example of the fact that art work can be done with the much maligned celebrated psychedelic substances.

NYQ:	*Didn't T. S. Eliot say that he didn't believe in that?*

AG:	Yeah, but Eliot was not a very experienced writer, he didn't write very much, he didn't write very much poetry. Anyhow there's a tremendous amount of evidence that good work can be done in all states of

consciousness including drugs. Not that drugs are
necessary. It's just that it's part of the *police* mythology
that nothing can be done, that LSD leads only to
confusion and chaos. That's nonsense.

NYQ: *In nondrug states, do you ever work half asleep?*

AG: Yes, as I said I keep a notebook at my bedside for
half-conscious, preconscious, quasi-sleep notations.
And I have a book out now called *Indian Journals*
which has such writing in it, including poems emerged
out of dreams and remembered in half waking, long
prose-poetry paragraphs, using double talk from a half
sleep state.

NYQ: *That seems a very relaxed and vulnerable kind of
writing, as opposed to what you spoke of before, where
you tried to get everything into the mind.*

AG: They're both related to consciousness study. Take it as
part of a tradition going back to Gertrude Stein who
was a student of William James at Harvard, whose
subjects were varieties of religious experience and
alterations of consciousness. That was James' big subject
—the pragmatic study of consciousness, the modalities
of consciousness. She applied her Jamesian studies and
her medical studies to the practice of composition and
saw composition as an extension of her investigations
into consciousness. That's the tradition that I would
like to classify myself within, and I think that's a main
legit tradition of poetics, the articulation of different
modalities of consciousness, almost, you can't say
scientific, but the *artful* investigation or articulation of
extraordinary states of consciousness. All that rises out
of my own preoccupation with higher states of
consciousness on account of, as I said over and over,
when I was young, twenty-four or so, some poems of
Blake like "The Sunflower," "The Sick Rose" and
"The Little Girl Lost" catalyzed in me an extraordinary
state of mystical consciousness as well as auditory
hallucinations of Blake's voice. I heard Blake's voice
and also *saw* epiphanous illuminative visions of the
rooftops of New York. While hearing Blake's voice.
While reading the text of "The Sunflower," "The
Sick Rose" and "The Little Girl Lost." This was

described at great lengths in other occasions. But I
want to go back to that just to reiterate that I see the
function of poetry as a catalyst to visionary states of
being and I use the word visionary only in these times
of base materialistic media consciousness when we are
so totally cut off from our own nature and nature
around us that anything that teaches nature seems
visionary.

NYQ: *Don't you feel that is changing?*

AG: No, I feel it's getting worse and worse. We are getting
more and more enraptured in our robot consciousness.
Robot consciousness itself is beginning to break down,
so there may be a change in the sense that the young
people are aware that something has gone wrong with
human nature, in America at any rate. We don't know.
It says in the *Times* that we have until the year 2000
when the oceans will be dead as Lake Erie. That's a
sense of doom. I mean no generation can change that.

NYQ: *The* Times *may not be right.*

AG: Well, underground papers for years have been saying
that the ecological catastrophe is a world-wide thing
that's coming soon, and scientists have been saying it
for years. Finally it's gotten around even to the
newspapers even though the *Times* isn't necessarily
right. So it's something that has to be taken seriously,
someone has to start believing it. It is really certainly
going to be right. Unless people accept that that *is* the
state of things, nobody is going to have the energy or
the decision to change it. If everybody merely accepted
the fact that we had till the year 2000 there would
have to be changes. They would have to be
instantaneous. Every single air-conditioning unit would
have to be turned off beginning this month, December
1970. It means every single automobile has got to be
stopped. Every new highway has to be stopped. It
means people have to instantly boycott every
nonreturnable bottle.

NYQ: *But maybe people would rather die.*

AG: Apparently people would rather die. "To be or not to
be, that is the question."

NYQ: *What do you feel about a poet's duty to protest, his responsibility to speak out?*

AG: I'm hoping to save my own skin. I was hoping to live to the year 2000. I'm going to be seventy-four in that year and the oceans are going to stink like the garbage heap of the Passaic River. I've already given up the idea of having any children. I don't want to have children, definitely not, into this situation. That old poem of Dylan's you know? "You're hurled the worst curse that could ever be hurled afraid to bring children into the world." I won't have children but *I'm* going to have to suffer through this. We'll have to face whatever apocalypse there is with our own bodies. We'll all have to. Everybody who expects to be living another twenty years is going to face the Great Squeeze.

NYQ: *But people who should be reading protest poems, don't read them. What then?*

AG: Try to maintain the same prophetic consciousness, which isn't very hard to maintain, all you have to do is read the editorial in the New York *Times,* they say the oceans will be dead in our lifetime. And at the same time try to find some medium for penetrating ordinary human consciousness with that awareness, which is what I'm doing. As the ship sinks. But the young people already know, there's a latent inclination toward apocalyptic awareness in young people, which is why their behavior is so amazing. It's mostly the older people that don't begin to account the consequences of their own deeds. Which is partly why I read with my father, to try to communicate with older people, too. It's a desperate situation. Also, I think the game is lost anyway. It's a question of preparing others how to die, how to enjoy the apocalypse, how to go through it without too much panic. Ride out the bum trip. The other side is like the great white void. I just don't think it would be a good idea if everybody died painfully, resentfully, kicking and screaming. So if people can learn to die properly they might learn to live.

NYQ: *What do you mean, learn it quickly?*

AG: Well, we've got about twenty years. It's amazing how much people have learned, the generation changes are so vast, just from the point of hair style, could you imagine long hair with beards ten years ago? It would be unthinkable, the things that people are putting up with now, as normal change. Things like legalizing grass, just about on the verge of that now, reducing punishment for possession. Because these are such minor tiny things, it doesn't really amount to very much. I don't think anything will happen until the New York *Times* and television and everybody get panicked. Looking to save their skins.

NYQ: *Could you comment on very specific details of your writing patterns?*

AG: Like?

NYQ: *Do you ever write with music on in the background?*

AG: Musical background imposes a rhythm, has its own rhythm. And I am sort of articulating my own body rhythm, body mind pulsations. So I don't consciously turn on, like Hart Crane, to a jazz record before I write. Kerouac used to do a lot of writing with St. Matthew's Passion in the back. His B minor Mass.

NYQ: *You once said you were a worry wart. Yet you have such a sense of joy and freedom, in reading, and in writing, too.*

AG: Ideally, the ambition, my childhood desire, is to write during a prophetic illuminative seizure. That's the idea: to be in a state of such complete blissful consciousness that any language emanating from that state will strike a responsive chord of blissful consciousness from any other body into which the words enter and vibrate. So I try to write during those "naked moments" of epiphany the illumination that come every day a little bit. Some moment every day, in the bathroom, in bed, in the middle of sex, in the middle of walking down the street, in my head, or not at all. So if it doesn't come at all, then that's the illumination. So then I try to write in that too. So that's like a rabbinical Jewish Hassidic trick that way.

So I try to *pay attention all the time*. The writing itself, the sacred act of writing, when you do anything of this nature, is like prayer. The act of writing being done sacramentally, if pursued over a few minutes, becomes like a meditation exercise which brings on a recall of detailed consciousness that is an approximation of high consciousness. High epiphanous mind. So, in other words, writing is a yoga that invokes Lord mind. And if you get into a writing thing that will take you all day, you get deeper and deeper into your own central consciousness.

NYQ: *And does this lead you to a greater reality?*

AG: A greater attention. Not attention, more *feeling* emerging out of that. So you walk down the city streets in New York for a few blocks, you get this gargantuan feeling of buildings. You walk all day you'll be at the verge of tears. More detail, more attention to the significance of all that robotic detail that impinges on the mind and you realize through your own body's fears that you are surrounded by a giant robot machine which is crushing and separating people, removing them from nature and removing them from living and dying. But it takes walking around all day to get into that state. What I mean is if you write all day you will get into it, into your body, into your feelings, into your consciousness. I don't write enough, actually, in that way. *Howl, Kaddish* and other things were written in that way. All-day-long attention. My writing now—I don't spend enough time writing. Partly I'm spending my energy, my time on other things. One thing is learning music, so I find I spend more time composing music and working at the Blake than I do in composing my own poetry. I also find that answering letters from people—there being maybe twenty letters a day—diverts me from what I should be doing, so I wish people would stop writing me letters: I try to answer and every letter I answer takes me away from my own poetry. I'm also involved in a project for the P.E.N. Club—I'm a member of their Executive Board and Freedom to Read Committee, in which I'm surveying the government's attack on what amounts to 60 per cent of the underground newspapers: bombings of their offices—arrests of vendors of the underground papers—narcotics arrests in which drugs are planted in the offices—obscenity accusations and prosecutions—FBI visits to printers and distributors warning them off: so I'm compiling files several feet thick for a "White Paper" that they're putting together. I'm also involved in a research project investigating dope peddling by the Narcotics Bureau and the CIA involvement with traffic of opium in Indochina, and I am working on documentation of that now. So I got my attention split into too many areas to be very effective as a poet. So I'm going to withdraw from it, and hereby as a signal I'm making an appeal for people to stop writing me letters.

NYQ: *Maybe you could delegate these things.*

AG: I just do it because there's nobody doing it. Sixty per cent of the underground papers have been busted and there is nobody in the middle class that has taken on this situation. Certainly the *Times* doesn't do it. The P.E.N. Club didn't do it. Authors' Guild didn't do it. Libraries didn't do it. The Little magazines didn't do it. It's a responsibility.

NYQ: *Everybody is trying to stay away.*

AG: Everybody's busy. A total proliferation of signals in every direction and photographs. Nobody can read or keep track of everything any more. At one point I found that Mafia people had gotten involved with one of the larger defense contractors, and I thought that was, like, a Big Headline type story for the Washington *Post*. I talked with a *Post* reporter named Nick Von Hoffman, he said yeah, he knows about that particular story "but there's so much shit going down in Washington" that it's just one of many ripples as the entire world collapses. What difference does it make, one little problem about Little magazines or if the CIA is peddling dope or the oceans are being poisoned and the atmosphere is poisoned and the overpopulation is outleaping itself, and every newspaper that reports it is a further drain on the tree life and using all these batteries to discuss it is a drain on the electric power, and every time you switch on a recording machine the flowers burn, and every time you pick up an issue of the New York *Times* to denounce pollution, sixty thousand trees go down and pollute the waterways. So maybe every time I open my mouth it's polluting the environment. It's hard to know what to do.

NYQ: *You can always write poetry.*

AG: Only way out is grow your own food, and compose in an art form which doesn't require material consumption. In other words, compose in a poetry which is memorizable, that might be the way out: bypass both print and television and radio, if somebody could come up with an interpersonal art form that would completely eliminate the power of the mass media electricity-consuming network.

NYQ: *That's the oral tradition all over again.*

AG: Right, back to Neolithic, which is what Gary Snyder has been suggesting all along: An art just requiring our bodies. Everybody's practicing that except middle class Americans. Any indigenous scene where you don't have the giant electric media to divert our consciousness into electronic simulacra there are still interpersonal "primitive" shamanistic religious, communal art forms.

NYQ: *Perhaps children could be made aware of this.*

AG: Right now I just came from Paterson, New Jersey, and the kids around there were raking up leaves to burn. I'm told that in China at the age of two, kids are propagandized to plant trees: "Plant trees, plant trees, plant trees." The same problem. I have that same problem. How do you do something which requires attention if the phone rings all the time? I answer it. Lately I've been sitting every day for an hour in the morning, so I've just been sitting through and letting it ring. It's disturbing to think that other people are beginning to lose hope. In the possibility of a connection. Finally lose hope. It's terrible to be involved in the collapse of a network, an overextended network, all those failed hopes. Salesmen dying.

NYQ: *Would you talk about the concept of the catalogue, in poetry?*

AG: Catalogue serves a lot of different functions, one function is to simply log all the processions of thoughts in the mind, one way of *linking together* the mind's thoughts. This was done by Christopher Smart in his catalogues: *"Rejoice in the Lamb (Jubilate agno)."* Just a method of free association, and a method of freeing associations. For associational *processions,* just like a mnemonic trick. Loosening the mind, associating. For catalogues, the "who" catalogue in *Howl* seemed to me to exhaust that form. And so in "Sunflower Sutra" I moved on to get a rhythmic pulsation going through the entire poem that would not depend on cataloguing. Nor depend on "who" at the beginning of each line. "Sunflower Sutra" is an example of trying to get beyond the catalogue: syntactically balanced, a giant sentence which will include the whole associational mobile. Also the catalogue has another function which is the old Bardic lyric instrumental pulsation at the beginning of each line as you stroke the lyre and say: Blom—Leif went forth merrily into the ocean and then, Blom—Naiads came up out of the rocks and waved to him. Blom—And then old Neptune showed his horned hair above the grey water, and Blam—The porpoises danced about the ship. When you have a catalogue and you say "and" or "who" or "for" as Smart did, you have that lyric tone like the chord struck by the finger. It sets up a rhythmic pulsation. Religions use the same technique, the litany form, church uses the same technique, really an articulation of body movement. Religious forms like litany exploit the same physiological body potentialities that Christopher Smart's litany did.

NYQ: *Do you think that long lists within a single line is trying to get past something?*

AG: Getting past something but also including everything that you've been thinking about. Try to include everything and come to a conclusion. Include everything that you thought of all day long, so you list them all within a line, a litany, any way you can put them down, and say, all right, now what does all this mean?

NYQ: *Is there no sense in eliminating things?*

AG: If it was something I really wanted to eliminate, I just wouldn't include it. If it were that boring or that insignificant . . .

NYQ: *What about the Old Testament writers, is it the same reason, the natural breath line?*

AG: Yes. Because I don't know Hebrew, so I don't know what . . . Or Aramaic, so I don't know what their literal motifs might have been. You know, all that stuff might have been rhymed. So, God knows. But we know the English thing, and the English version seems to satisfy the needs of present prophetic versification, or got near to it anyway, or be a basis on which to begin, that form, including litany. So getting back to our original splenetic denunciation of the use of the word "craft": The problems confronted in attempting to graph the operations of the mind in language and the problems confronted historically at this apocalyptic-end-of-history time are so complex and so new and previously unexperienced by any culture that we have within memory—(this might all have gone before but all recollection was destroyed with the apocalypse, last time) the forms are so new as far as human history is concerned that no previous models of speech forms are sufficient, and we have to invent our own, just as no previous models of life style within memory are sufficient, and we're going to have to out of our own native genius invent our own, out of our own imagination, as Blake and Whitman proposed. The old poetic task is we have to invent our own lives, make our own miracles. Which is the beauty of our situation, as well as its misery: the fearful aspect but it's also the most beautiful aspect. Whatever survival, if we survive, is going to come because we decided to. If we're magnanimous enough to continue, to wish to continue to work with each other to survive. And if we find a poetry adequate to that, it's just that we will have taken a realistic estimate of our bodies, of our breath, and of our machinery and our history, and imagined it—a beautiful enough prophecy with such exquisitely penetrant prosody that the hardest hat will vibrate with delight.

SELECTED BIBLIOGRAPHY

Howl & Other Poems, San Francisco, City Lights Books, Inc., 1956.

Kaddish & Other Poems, San Francisco, City Lights Books, Inc., 1961.

Empty Mirror, San Francisco, City Lights Books, Inc., 1961.

Reality Sandwiches, San Francisco, City Lights Books, Inc., 1963.

Planet News, San Francisco, City Lights Books, Inc., 1968.

Indian Journals, San Francisco, City Lights Books, Inc., 1970.

The Fall of America, San Francisco, City Lights Books, Inc., 1973.

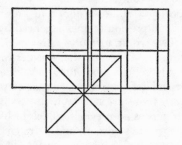

CRAFT INTERVIEW WITH DENISE LEVERTOV

NYQ: *What stories or poems from your childhood reading do you remember particularly? Which ones do you think may have had an influence on your development as a poet?*

DENISE LEVERTOV: Well, it's always difficult to know what did and what didn't affect your work later. My mother read aloud to me a great deal when I was a child, even after I was reading to myself. She read Beatrix Potter, whom I consider a great stylist, the Andrew Lang fairy books, Hans Andersen. She read aloud very well, and she read not only to me, but to the assembled family, consisting of my sister, my father, and myself—all of Dickens, all of Jane Austen, and most of George Eliot, most of the nineteenth-century classics. It was a somewhat nineteenth-century household, I think, in that in the evenings we would sit around listening to reading out loud.

NYQ: *Your name is often linked with the names of the Black Mountain poets, with William Carlos Williams, Ezra Pound and H.D. Who are some of the other poets, early or contemporary, whose work has significantly affected your own?*

DL: As a child, when I started reading poetry, I read Keats
and Tennyson and Wordsworth. Then I also read the
younger poets, the kind of avant-garde ones in England
during my childhood—Auden and Spender and Eliot. I
read lots of Elizabethan poetry as a child—lots. When I
was growing up, people in England were really very
ignorant of American poetry. I really did not know
many writers, and the ones I did know were not reading
Pound. I did not read him until about a year before I
came to America. Williams was totally unknown to me
until that time. H.D.—of course, one always saw the
Imagists' stuff, but I didn't know the latest. There is a
lot of H.D. which was published in England which has
never been published here. Stevens I began to read in
Paris, the year before I came to America. I read, you
know, the English people who were just a little older
than I was, and who were being published in England
when I was first publishing. And well, I'd read some
French poetry at that time—a little Rimbaud and
Baudelaire, nothing much else, really.

NYQ: *The words "dance," and "dancing" appear regularly in
your poetry, but only in your most recent collection,*
Relearning the Alphabet, *is there a poem about the
experience of dancing itself. Are there ways, perhaps in
the area of rhythm, where your having been a dancer is
reflected in your work?*

DL: I have come to feel that there definitely are. You see, I
studied very strict ballet when I was intending to become a dancer. I was sort of pushed into that by my
sister, and when I quit I had a revulsion against it and
didn't even like to think about it for a number of years.
Then I danced again, just for pleasure. I did some
modern dance in New York with a friend, Midi Garth,
who is a very fine dancer; and when we lived in
Mexico I found a ballet class which I went to a couple
of times a week for a year, and I got quite good again,
and began to enjoy the dancing for itself. I had looked
on it as something with such a rigid technique, as
something that did not seem to connect at all with what
I became interested in—in writing and the other arts.
But I came to feel that my experience dancing had
definitely given me some sense of internal rhythm, and

of gesture as it translates itself into language, of pace, of energy, of things like that, which possibly I wouldn't have felt if I'd never danced. So it was a rather obscure influence . . .

NYQ: *What about the kind of self-discipline a dancer has to learn? Do you discipline yourself in your writing—write at certain regular times, in a particular place?*

DL: No. I don't really believe in anything that rigid and that imposed from without. I feel that classic ballet with its rigid discipline is a very very narrow medium— it doesn't have a wide or deep range of expressiveness. It can be very beautiful, I enjoy seeing it, but I think of it as decorative and relatively superficial, among the art forms.

NYQ: *Do you feel differently about modern dance?*

DL: Well, theoretically. Actually, I have very rarely seen modern dance that seemed to reach the kind of depth and subtlety and have the range of language arts or music. The dancer I spoke of, Midi Garth—I've seen some performances of her solo works, her own choreography, that did seem to me to be very high art, but I've rarely seen modern dance that deeply satisfied me.

NYQ: *You encourage your students to keep writing notebooks. Do you do that yourself?*

DL: Yes, I do.

NYQ: *What is the relationship between the look of your notebooks, and the collection of material in your "Notebook" poem?*

DL: It's really something of a misnomer. That was just a sort of handle, to refer to the poem by. The part that you've seen, in *Relearning the Alphabet,* has been augmented, and it will be part of a book called *Staying Alive.*

NYQ: *When will that be published?*

DL: There's a slim chance that it may be out in the fall, if we have a lot of luck in getting it together and get a printer to do it in time, but otherwise it will be out next spring. New Directions doesn't have a winter list.

I'd like very much to have this book out in the fall, if it's humanly possible, because I have a certain sense of urgency about it—both because of its nature, and because one feels urgent anyway, at this time. Everyone feels somewhat apocalyptic, I suppose—one feels in a hurry to get things done and to speak to one's brothers and sisters while there's still time.

NYQ: *The new book continues the revolution theme?*

DL: Yes.

NYQ: *What effect has your teaching had on your writing?*

DL: I think it's had a mixed effect. Often it definitely takes time and energy away from writing. On the other hand, it's had a profound effect on my life in bringing me into contact with the student generation and with political activism on the various campuses. If I hadn't been teaching I might easily have found myself very isolated politically, and perhaps would not have developed. I feel I have learned a lot through teaching which I wouldn't have learned without it. And in some cases, like last year at MIT and the year before at Berkeley, especially, I experienced a marvelous sense of community with my students at times, and I'm glad not to have missed that. Of course I've always felt it with individual students, but I've twice felt it—not all the time, but some of the time—with a group of students. I think that was a very important human experience.

NYQ: *Are there areas in which you have generally found American students to be well equipped when they come into a poetry writing class, or places where they are often deficient?*

DL: Well, I can't compare them with, say, English students, because I was never a student in England myself, and I've never taught anywhere but in America. But I'd say that most American students are grossly deficient in their reading background and general knowledge. There are lots of people with lots of natural talent, and very very few with any sort of useful background.

NYQ: *Do you partly blame television for that?*

DL: I don't blame any single factor for it, but I certainly

don't think that television has helped. It is definitely a
generation of spectators, and I don't know that this
affects student *poets* particularly, but it does affect
students in the classroom. My students this year, for
example, tend to want to be entertained, I think. They
want me to put on a performance for them in which
they can sit passively back and not participate. Of
course, the more politically conscious students are, the
more they really try to participate in discussion and in
everything else that's going on in the class. They want
to create their own education. The students I have this
year are politically very backward, an economically
elite group, I would say, and it's very difficult to get
to each other. They don't have a sense of collective
possibilities. Students, and people in general in this
country, have less and less of a common culture. Even
if you get a bunch of people aged about twenty together
who have all read a fair amount and looked at some
paintings and had other experiences in the arts, there is
very little likelihood of their having read the same books
or looked at the same paintings, and the only thing that
they can count on for sure is usually certain TV
programs, such as "Captain Kangaroo," which they
watched when they were little. And that's the common
currency, which is a very low grade of common cultural
currency, the only dependably shared element. I think
that's a pretty sad state of affairs, to put it mildly.
However, as far as poets are concerned, it's very hard to
say what is good or bad for a person of real talent. It's
such an individual matter.

NYQ: *You've written about helping your students to
experience a poem as a sonic entity, apart from its
meaning. How do you go about that?*

DL: By trying to get them to listen to the poem, to hear it a
number of times over, before launching into discussion
of it. A lot of students—I would say the majority of
students—have somehow picked up the idea that a
poem is a problem to be solved, and that one reads a
poem efficiently by making a paraphrase of it while
reading it, and by this process of paraphrasing you
somehow *obtain* the poem. Then you can forget it, and
go on to the next one. But they don't listen to music
that way. Of course, if a person is a serious student of

music, he will learn about musical form, he will be interested in it, and he will recognize when a theme is transposed into another key, or when it recurs played by another instrument, all those little things that take place in the structure of a piece of music. But certainly the average person who cares to listen to a piece of music isn't constantly doing that, he doesn't regard that as the only way in which he can really get the music. It's a direct experience which is accepted as such by most people. Poetry presents complicated surfaces of denotative and connotative meaning as well as of sound patterns, and it's natural that people want to feel that they have understood what has been said, and sometimes a certain degree of interpretive paraphrase may be necessary if you want to talk about a poem. But you can receive a poem, you can comprehend a poem, without talking about it. Teachers at all levels encourage the idea that you have to talk about things in order to understand them, because they wouldn't have jobs, otherwise. But it's phony, you know.

NYQ: *Do you think the fact that memorization has gone out of fashion has anything to do with the modern reader's having trouble reacting to a poem as rhythmic sound? Poetic rhythms aren't established in his head, in his ear . . .*

DL: I don't know. It's an interesting theory. I've never been able to memorize anything myself, but I think I have a strong sense of rhythmic structure. I remember a French teacher I went to when I was a kid being quite impressed with me because I read aloud a French poem in a metrically correct way, and she said she very rarely had a student who did that. I think that's because I picked up very quickly on the rhythmic structure of the poem, but it certainly wasn't through memorization, so I don't feel I'm in a position to pass judgment on that.

NYQ: *You have done direct translation, knowing the other language well yourself, you have also translated using a linguist, as you did with the* In Praise of Krishna *poems. Do you find the experiences very different in the degree to which you are able to reach the heart of the original poem?*

DL: There's certainly a degree of difference. However, in
        those Indian poems, my collaborator was himself so
        deeply into the poems and was able to give such fine
        explanations of any questions I had, and his own
        versions which I worked on were so good, that in some
        cases I really changed very few words. In others I
        changed quite a lot. The degree of difference was not as
        great as it can be when you have a less sensitive
        collaborator. I once did that, and it just didn't work out.
        The big difference is that translating from a language
        you don't know at all, you have actually no idea what
        it sounds like. With the French, although I didn't try
        any sort of elaborate imitations of sound and structure,
        I did of course know what it sounded like and was
        influenced in my versions by the sound of the original.

NYQ: *Where, on a scale that ran from literal translation to
        adaptation, would you put your translations of the
        Guillevic poems?*

DL: The Guillevic ones, with few exceptions, are very close
        to the original, I think. I noted the places where I knew
        that I had departed, and there are many places where I
        just goofed. With those exceptions, they're not
        adaptations. They are translations, but I tried to make
        them stand up as poems, and therefore it's not a line-by-
        line thing. You'll find some stanzas are longer, or
        possibly shorter, in mine than in the original because
        I broke the lines differently with the idea of English-
        American rhythms. With some translators, if a stanza
        has five lines in the original they have five lines, quite
        rigidly. I didn't stick that closely, but I never
        deliberately changed an image, added an adjective,
        except as noted in the text.

NYQ: *There are clear similarities between your poetic style
        and Guillevic's style. Do you feel one poet can
        successfully translate the work of another whose interests
        and methods are radically different from his own?*

DL: I would think it would be very difficult. I myself would
        not be very interested in attempting it. I have to feel a
        certain affinity to be drawn to translate something.

NYQ: *Why do you do translations?*

DL: It's to—to really get deeper into the poem. One of the
        things one is doing in writing poems at all is grasping
        one's own experience by transmuting it, one is
        translating experience into language, one is apperceiving,
        one is finding out what it is that one knows. So with
        poems in another language, I tend to feel that if I'm
        attracted to a poem I want to absorb it more deeply by
        the act of translation. It's already a verbal experience,
        but it isn't absolutely distinct from that basic impulse
        to grasp experience in language that a poet has anyway,
        I think. It's just an extension of it.

NYQ: *You've said you try to help each of your students find
        his own voice. When you came to this country to live,
        what impact did meeting the American idiom have on
        your poetic voice?*

DL: Well, it certainly made a difference. Of course, it's
        impossible to predict what my development might have
        been if I'd stayed in England. I have always felt that I
        would not have developed very far because it was not
        a good time for English poetry. It was really in the
        doldrums, and I think I might have found it stultifying.
        I presume that I would have gone on being a writer
        because I can't imagine being anything else; and you
        know I had started writing very young and had had a
        book published before I came here. I think it was very
        beneficial for me to come to America at a time when
        American poetry was in a very live period. But, although
        it seemed so at the time, in recent years I've come to
        realize that it wasn't a dramatic break. My early poems
        are very kind of wish-y romantic poems, the ones in my
        first book, but they have in them the seeds of everything
        that I've done since, actually. Hayden Carruth pointed
        out to me that in the poems about my sister, and in the
        ones in which I am writing about my childhood, my
        diction becomes quite British. It was an unconscious
        thing, but in fact my language has always moved back
        and forth between English and American usage. It leads
        to problems for the reader, because there are ways I
        have of saying things, if I'm saying them in an English
        kind of way, that the American reader doesn't pick up
        on. As for the English reader, the English reader doesn't
        know how to read American poetry anyway, because

the whole pace of American speech is very different.
Of course, this has changed somewhat in the last ten
or fifteen years because there is much more interest in
American literature now in England, and people have
seen so many American movies they're probably getting
the feel of the American idiom. I feel that I am
genuinely of both places, and that has simply extended
my usage. I'm glad to have a foot in more than one
culture.

NYQ: *To what extent do you feel a poet can use words in his
writing that are not part of his normal vocabulary?*

DL: He can, if he's not doing it for pretentious reasons, but
because really, in looking for the accurate word, he
comes upon a word which, in its meaning and sound,
makes him say, "Aha! This is the word I need for this
thing that I'm saying." At that moment that word
becomes a natural part of his vocabulary. After all,
the whole thing was once unknown territory to each of
us. Our vocabulary grows as we grow. So I wouldn't
exclude words that a person finds because he's looking
for them. But the sort of deliberate showing off—
occasionally you find somebody actually looking through
the dictionary for abstruse words and sort of saving
them to be used in some poem—I think that's just
childish.

NYQ: *When a new poem begins in your head, do you start
writing immediately?*

DL: It depends on what is coming into my head. If it is a
sort of vague feeling that somewhere in the vicinity
there is a poem, then no, I don't do anything about it,
I wait. If a whole line, or phrase, comes into my head,
I write it down, but without pushing it unless it
immediately leads to another one. If it's an idea, then
I don't do anything about it until that idea begins to
crystallize into some phrases, some words, a rhythm,
because if I try to push that into being by will before
the intuition is really at work, then it's going to be a
very bad beginning, and perhaps I'm going to lose the
poem altogether. So there is some feeling of when to
begin writing, but it's really rather hard to describe,
especially since it's somewhat different with each poem.

There is often a kind of preliminary feeling, a sort of aura—what is it? An early warning?—which alerts one to the possibility of a poem. You can smell the poem before you can see it. Like some animal . . . Hmmm, seems like a bear's around here . . .

NYQ: *Do you usually hear a poem's rhythm from the beginning?*

DL: Well, if it was the smell of a bear, you know, you might begin to hear it kind of going . . . pad . . . pad . . . pad around the house; but if, let's say, it was a kind of a rustle in the bushes, which might be a bird or a snake or a squirrel, it might start to go blipblipblipblip . . .

NYQ: *Do you revise a good deal?*

DL: That again depends on the individual poem. Of course, the longer the poem, the more revision. The kind of poem that comes out right the first time is almost always a very short poem. When poems emerge full-blown, I feel that there's been lots of preliminary work done on them, at a preconscious level.

NYQ: *Since you write in nontraditional, free forms, what determines the physical shape a poem of yours will take? For example, what most often decides stanza divisions for you?*

DL: I've written about this in an article called "Some Notes on Organic Form," which has been published in a number of places. It was first in *Poetry Magazine,* and then it was reprinted in a *New Directions Annual,* and it's been reprinted again in an anthology called *Naked Poetry* which Bob Mezey and Stephen Berg brought out about a year ago. I think of there being clusters of perceptions which determine the stanza. Of course, sometimes the stanza breaks in the middle of a sentence, syntactically, but the perception cluster, nevertheless, did pause there for a moment.

NYQ: *What do you consider in deciding the length of a line?*

DL: I regard the end of a line, the line break, as roughly equivalent to half a comma, but what that pause is doing is recording nonsyntactic hesitations, or waitings, that occur in the thinking-feeling process. This is where the dance comes into it. You can't get this onto your tape, but I can sort of demonstrate it for you [*stands, and moves to the center of the room*]. You see, in the composition of a poem, thinking and feeling are really working together, as a kind of single thing, although they often get separate in other areas of one's life. We don't want to call the movement of that process thinking-feeling, it's too clumsy; and we don't want to call it thinking—it's more than thinking—and we don't want to call it feeling—it's more than feeling—so let's call it perception, as perhaps a not totally accurate, but usable, term. That process does not go on at a steady walking pace [*walking*]. It doesn't constantly dance around, either, but it may kind of hurry forward [*little fast steps*], and then it will stop [*stop*], and then it will walk more slowly, and it has definitely an almost dancelike movement to it, not constantly skipping and jumping and running, but a varied motion. For instance, when one is simply conversing, with feeling, with a friend, even if one tends to think and speak in rather complete sentences, nevertheless, there are pauses in one's speech which are expressive pauses—sometimes for emphasis, sometimes because one has rushed forward to a certain point [*demonstrating*], and one doesn't really know what the next word that one is going to say will be. These are not syntactic pauses. The sentence is there, in back of them. Sometimes the sentence becomes broken, sometimes the sentence is never finished, often the sentences are complete. But articulations—in the sense that our bones, our fingers, are articulated, right? they have joints, they can bend— occur. These occur within the rationale of the syntax, and the line break is a peculiarly sensitive means of recording those things. So that one can pick up all the rhythm of feeling, all the rhythm of experience, in ways which prose is perhaps not as well equipped to do. Of course, good prose is rhythmic, too, but it doesn't depend quite so heavily as poetry does on the finest adjustments of rhythm and even of typographically indicated intonation.

NYQ: *There is a remarkable variation in the speed with which your lines can be read—sometimes there are several speed shifts within one short poem, such as "The Singer"; and sometimes the change comes between sections of longer poems, as happens in the one called "Six Variations."*

DL: It's never directly stated in that poem, but the six variations are about language and what it can do. You know, it mentions Gertrude Stein's dog Basket, and how she learned what a sentence was. The section with the long rhymes, with the ashcans and the children on the street, demonstrates the speed of polysyllabic lines— the lines are longer, but there are lots of polysyllables in them, and the movement is a sort of fast, rippling movement. And then there's a section with many monosyllables that moves very slow and is about ". . . heavy heart and/cold eye." So they are variations almost on how the syllable works, variations on the theme of the function of the syllable? That's not quite accurate, but . . .

NYQ: *You control line speed, then, by the length of the lines, and the number of syllables, and—*

DL: Not the number of syllables so much as the kind of syllables, and whether the consonants are sufficiently harder to enunciate so that they help to slow things down, too. However, when one talks about these matters, it tends to sound as if the poet were extremely deliberate and conscious, but in fact it is something that becomes second nature so that you're doing it instinctively. When you're revising you may find places where you've botched it, your instincts were not working well, and then you may deliberately try to achieve an effect by those means which you know will help to achieve it. But in the first instance one is working pretty unconsciously, I think.

NYQ: *Can you say generally, in deciding between several words for a particular spot in a poem, if you put more importance on sound or on sense?*

DL: Well, the sonic effect would be the more important, but it's never a factor entirely separable from other things

about the word. If you wanted a word that had
something sort of thick about it, let us say, you might
find a word which had that sonic quality and yet the
associations of that word, or the fact that it was a
homonym and the associations with the word that it
sounded like, were all wrong, would prevent your using
it. Let's say you have a choice of adjectives, and one
has an onomatopoeic quality which you want, but it also
has a couple of "s's" in it, and the rest of the line, or
the line just before it, is already pretty sibilant, but you
feel that that line is right. You might have to forgo the
word that you've just found and keep on looking,
because you can't have all those "s's" jammed up
together. There's almost never just one factor to be
considered. You always have to weigh the one against
the other.

NYQ: *In your more recent poems you seem to be indenting*
less than you did in the earlier ones. Is there a reason
for this change?

DL: Lately I've been doing it quite a lot again, I think.
When I indent, I'm trying to do two things. One is very
obvious. If I have something that approximates a list, a
number of things mentioned in succession, in different
lines, which form a kind of category, I sometimes like
to indent them and line them up. They're like a
subsidiary clause. And that's for reasons of clarity. But
the other reason for indentation is that if the eye is
going from the end of one line all the way back to the
margin, it takes infinitesimally longer than if it goes
only to the beginning of an indented line. Sometimes
one feels that the next line *is* another line, it's not just
part of the line before it, yet it is in some way intimately
connected with that line in a manner which makes one
desire to have that little extra speed for the eye, which
transmits itself to the ear and the voice.

NYQ: *It's a psychological adjustment.*

DL: It's a psychological adjustment which, however, is also,
I think, a neurological one. I don't know if they have
instruments which measure that—I daresay they do—
but it's something one feels, one doesn't need an
instrument to measure it. I'm pretty sure that it works

because I have had the satisfaction of hearing people read poems of mine aloud who are not simply imitating me, because they haven't heard me read them, and they've read them right. The way I've deployed them on the page has been an accurate indication of how they're supposed to be read. Now just Wednesday, I had a sort of argument with some students who were objecting to that much direction by the poet. I defend it, absolutely, because I feel that it's exactly like the writing down of music. When music is written, it allows a considerable amount of interpretation to the performer, and yet it is always definitely that piece of music and no other. You get twenty competent pianists playing a Beethoven piano sonata, and each performance will be different. But it is recognizably the same piece of music. One may take the whole thing faster than another, one may make the loud parts louder and the quiet parts quieter, but the composer has indicated that here it's allegro and here it's adagio, or here it's fortissimo and here it's pianissimo. That is his privilege, and although we don't have such a generally accepted system of notation for the nuance, I see no reason why the poet shouldn't have the same privilege, and by that means obtain as fine results as composers have done. I don't feel that it is an imposition on the reader. It still allows him lots of freedom, and without that much care about the structure of a poem, I think what you have is a lot of slop.

NYQ: *How concerned are you about the way the entire poem looks on the page?*

DL: What happens visually produces a certain psychological effect, there's no doubt about it. When you look at a piece of music and the score is very very black with notes, you get a kind of crowded, agitated, perhaps even busy feeling. And a poem that fills up a page has psychologically for some people, or perhaps for all people at some moments, a somewhat intimidating effect. You're not sure if you can get into it. A poem that has two-line stanzas and lots of space tends to attract the eye. But I think these are very secondary effects. They're not essential where one is considering

the nature of the poetry. The written poem is the
written notation of a sonic effect. Which doesn't mean
that the best way to receive poetry is to hear it and not
see it at all. I think it's a question of eye-ear
coordination. I'm not fully satisfied with poems that I
only hear at a reading or on a record and never get to
look at. I have to look at them, too. But by the same
token, I want to *hear* a written poem, and I will either
read it aloud to myself if I can't hear the poet read it,
or even if I'm not actually reading it aloud I'm
sounding it out in my head. I think the two things
are equally important. Sometimes a poem will look
absolutely, delightfully decorative on the page, but I
think when that *takes over*, it's a mistake. They were
doing it, of course, in the seventeenth century—wings
and crosses and things—and sometimes it works out,
but I don't think it's really a main direction for poetry.
To hell with what it looks like, you know. Some poems
that do sort of get all over the page, like some of Olson,
or some of Duncan, I've actually heard objected to
because they looked so messy. That's not the point.
Never mind if they do look messy! They're indicating
rhythm and pace, and all sorts of sonic values.

NYQ: *You often repeat words or themes in your poems. Do*
you have any theories about the value and effect of
repetition?

DL: Do you mean, throughout all my poetry the same things
come up, or within one poem?

NYQ: *Within one poem.*

DL: Oh, well, there is the impulse to tie things together. If
one feels them to be at all tied together, one wants to
get that into the structure, instead of things flowing
along to the point where they slip out of your fingers.
Maybe it sounds a little compulsive, but in other works
of art which I value I often see echoes and
correspondences. I see the curve of the bushes in the
corner of that painting by Howard Fussiner, echoed by
the curve going the opposite way of the armchair down
in the lower left-hand corner. I see the uprights of the
delphiniums out the window, there, and the trunk of a

tree in the distance, and the vase—they're all related
to each other as uprights in that picture. It's the
compositional sense, it's the impulse to create pattern
or to reveal pattern. I say "reveal," because I have a
thing about finding form rather than imposing it. I
want to find correspondences and relationships which
are there but hidden, and I think one of the things the
artist does is to reveal. That's the principle on which
I've worked.

NYQ: *It's interesting that you mentioned Gertrude Stein
earlier. Repetition was so important in her writing.*

DL: Well, think of any work of art that you really value.
Can you think of one in which there are not such
things?

NYQ: *But sometimes there is more repetition in one work than
in another, sometimes the repetition is especially
obvious, and its effect is easy to feel . . .*

DL: Where there's more of it, in any particular artist's work,
I think it indicates that that artist has a feeling for
denseness of texture; and where you find it very little,
he is perhaps after a kind of transparence, an almost
waterlike, flowing thinness of texture. For example, the
very unstructured work of Gary Snyder, whose poetry I
like very much. Read his statement in that anthology,
Naked Poetry, and compare it with mine. You'll see
two very different sensibilities, in regard to form,
operating there, and I think the differences in our work
run naturally out of that difference in the way we want
things to be. What pleases him is something more
loosely formed, spread out. I certainly seem to have
inherent in my nervous system more of a liking for
pattern, not exactly symmetry, but I want to gather
things together and see them in their juxtapositions.

NYQ: *Since your poems are such physical wholes, is the need
to divide the longer ones up into pages a problem for
you, when you put them into books?*

DL: No, but I have had one typographical problem.
Sometimes, if I have a long line, and it's wider than the
page permits, then of course the last few words have to
be sort of tucked under. And since I do so much

indentation for structural reasons, it bugs me very much when I have to have a line broken up that way, because the reader might well think that that is an indentation. It's sometimes a little hard to make sure it looks like what it is. I have wished that poetry books could be different dimensions, as some published by small presses are, but my publisher tells me that it's very hard to change the dimensions of books. Bookshelves are designed to hold books of certain dimensions, booksellers don't like to handle books that are odd shapes, and distributors don't like to distribute them, so one is stuck . . .

NYQ: *Many of your poems reflect an experience of reality and of the present moment that is extraordinarily clear and deep. In "The Coming Fall," for instance, you speak of "A sense of the present," and ". . . a shiver, a delight/ that what is passing/is here . . ." Are you able to maintain this awareness for long periods?*

DL: Oh, that's a hard question to answer. Not very often, I would say, and perhaps rarely when not engaged in the writing of poems. But sometimes, as something distinct from writing, I've experienced it, too.

NYQ: *You often use the word "joy" in describing those moments. Once you say "terrible joy," and in the poem called "Joy," you say, ". . . glad to the brink of fear." What is that fear?*

DL: "Glad to the brink of fear," is actually a quote from Emerson, where he speaks of crossing either the Boston or the Cambridge Common on a cloudy, raw sort of evening (I'm paraphrasing now, because I can't remember the exact words) with nothing very special about it, and being seized with "joy to the brink of fear." Well, I suppose joy is a passion, and all passionate things are perhaps very close in nature to their opposites. Joy, pain, fear—there comes a point, perhaps, where one no longer knows which is which. I think that is what he was talking about, and I guess that is what I am talking about, too. What people call ecstasy is more like terror than it is like contentment, isn't it.

NYQ: *Some poets today are using drugs to reach a state of
        heightened consciousness in which they then write
        poems. Have you any feeling about this practice?*

DL: Well, I smoke grass—I smoke it as a social pleasure and
        in order to relax, but I don't use it in order to work up
        poems. In fact, I don't smoke very much. It's kind of
        hard to get! I like to drink, but it's not something that I
        use in relation to writing, and I haven't taken any other
        kinds of drugs such as acid, mescaline, any kind of
        psychedelic drug. I've had experiences without the
        benefit of any such thing that I feel have been so close
        to what people describe having with drugs that I feel
        I don't want to disturb the peculiar balance of my
        imagination and my associative language. I feel that if
        others need to loosen up this way or that, well, that's
        their way of doing it. And I have felt a certain amount
        of fear of spoiling what I have got. It would seem kind
        of greedy. But if I came to a point in my life where I
        felt dried up and out of touch with my unconscious,
        with my imagination, then I guess I would try whatever
        seemed to be a good way to shake myself up again.

NYQ: *Your poems contain many religious words, such as
        "hymn," "psalm," "communion wine," "pilgrimage."
        You speak of ceremonies and rites. You often use the
        word "light" in a Quaker sense. There is a sense of joy
        like that of the Hassidim. In your love poems there is
        frequently a kind of devotional feeling along with a
        sensuous one. And, throughout your books, one
        recognizes themes that recall the Quaker, Jewish and
        Zen emphasis on the importance of the present moment.
        What does the word "religious" mean to you?*

DL: The impulse to kneel in wonder. . . . The impulse to
        kiss the ground. . . . The sense of awe. The felt
        presence of some mysterious force, whether it be what
        one calls beauty, or perhaps just the sense of the
        unknown—I don't mean "unknown" in the sense of we
        don't know what the future will bring. I mean the
        sense of the numinous, whether it's in a small stone or a
        large mountain. I think at this particular point, that
        sense of joy which you've mentioned in my poems, and

which I think is very real to me, and has been, is at a
very low ebb. I think of my poem called "Living," which
says:

> *The fire in leaf and grass*
> *so green it seems*
> *each summer the last summer.*
>
> *The wind blowing, the leaves*
> *shivering in the sun,*
> *each day the last day.*
>
> *A red salamander*
> *so cold and so*
> *easy to catch, dreamily*
>
> *moves his delicate feet*
> *and long tail. I hold*
> *my hand open for him to go.*
>
> *Each minute the last minute.*

There's a certain apocalyptic sense in that, but there's
also a kind of joy in the marvelousness of that green
fire in the grass and leaves, and in the beauty of the
little salamander. My feeling this winter, like many
peoples', is so doom-filled, the sense of time running
out is pretty much squashing my sense of the beauty of
the ephemeral being ephemeral. I've always hated
artificial flowers unless they were just flagrantly and
beautifully, sort of brassily, artificial. But the good
imitations, the ones that you think are real until you
get up to them, and then there's that awful dead plastic,
are really vile. And the reason why I think they're so
vile is because so much of the beauty of a flower is in
its very perishableness. One doesn't want it to last
forever and accumulate dust. And so there is joy in the
very sense of mortality, in a way. But facing not just
the mortality that we have always had with us, but the
annihilation of all life, which is every day more and
more a real possibility, one's feeling of anguish and
despair certainly takes over.

NYQ: *Speaking of social protest, W. H. Auden has said, "I*
do not think that writing poems will change anything."

*Many people disagree with him, and you are one of
the poets who, over the last five years, have written
many poems of protest against injustice, particularly
against the Vietnam war. That situation is worse now
than it has ever been. What do you feel, at this point,
a poet can do?*

DL: To confine it to America of the last five years, let us
           say, I think the poetry of protest, indignation, anger
           and so forth, that has been written by many, many poets,
           has helped to awaken many people to the situation.
           There were the Vietnam Poetry Readings that Robert
           Bly and other people organized, where slides of
           Vietnam, of napalmed children and also of beautiful,
           still untouched villages—sort of alternations of terrible
           destruction and of what the country looked like before
           it was blasted—were combined with the reading of
           poems. Those things, back in 1966, stirred up quite a lot
           of people to become active in the antiwar movement.
           And the antiwar movement itself has grown very much
           and is becoming a more revolutionary movement in
           which people no longer see stopping the war as a single
           issue which can be divorced from racism, imperialism,
           capitalism, male supremacy. There are increasing
           numbers of people who understand, or are beginning to
           understand, the connections between all these things.
           And the poets have played some part in this
           consciousness-raising. There's a lot more going on in the
           way of organizing and educative work in local
           communities than there was two years ago. A lot of
           people who were activists in college, who have now
           graduated or dropped out, instead of also dropping out
           of the movement (which is the way it used to be) have
           gone further into it, but you don't hear so much about
           them because they're working in very sort of
           unspectacular, local ways. This is something about
           which in itself I'm not despondent. I don't think that
           the movement is a failure, and hasn't achieved anything,
           and so forth; but the fact is that we're working against
           time. And the factors, including ecological ones, against
           which people on the revolutionary side are working are
           so tremendous, they're such tremendous, heavy forces,

that one just doesn't know whether there's going to be *time* for this new kind of patient, consciousness-raising work to produce its effect before a disaster is brought about by the other forces.

NYQ:

As for your own activities—do you feel differently now from the way you did in 1966 and 1967 about what you should be doing? Certainly you are now more concerned than you were then about time running out.

DL:

Yes, well, all we could think of to do in 1966 was to have big, peaceful demonstrations, which got bigger and bigger. People as astute as, let us say, Chomsky, feel that those demonstrations did have a deterrent effect, that the United States might have gone further, might have used nuclear weapons by this time, if there had not been a strong, growing, antiwar movement in this country. So you don't measure the results of those demonstrations by positive results, you have to measure them by sort of negative ones, which is very hard to do. Now, most people feel mere demonstrations, mere massing of people, is no longer enough. There has to be definite civil disobedience action, and the spearhead of the movement is those people who have done sabotage, who have destroyed files—not only draft files, but the Dow Chemical files, and so forth—all those sorts of actions. If there are going to be more moratoriums, they're going to have to take a different form. I think there are a lot of people who are still back in 1966 in their political development, and they need to experience big demonstrations, which do have a radicalizing effect. When they get tear-gassed, and they see police beating up people with clubs at a demonstration, either they cop out and never go to another one (in which case they wouldn't have been very useful people anyway), or, step-by-step, it radicalizes them. What I personally am trying to do at this point is very, very mild, because I find myself teaching at a school which is back in 1954, I would say, and I'm trying to organize a teach-in. I think that the right speakers at a teach-in could stir those people up, and it would be a beginning for a lot of them, at least.

SELECTED BIBLIOGRAPHY

The Jacob's Ladder, New York, New Directions Publishing Corp., 1961.

O Taste and See, New York, New Directions Publishing Corp., 1964.

The Sorrow Dance, New York, New Directions Publishing Corp., 1969.

Relearning the Alphabet, New York, New Directions Publishing Corp., 1970.

To Stay Alive, New York, New Directions Publishing Corp., 1971.

Footprints, New York, New Directions Publishing Corp., 1972.

The Poet in the World, New York, New Directions Publishing Corp., 1973.

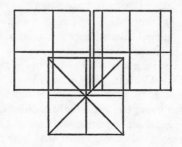

CRAFT INTERVIEW
WITH GALWAY KINNELL

NYQ: *In our craft interviews we have tried to be as objective as possible, and not get too involved with feelings and emotions about things, but stay with craft and style.*

GALWAY KINNELL: All matters I don't know anything about.

NYQ: *Could you tell us something about your method of writing—revision and that sort of thing?*

GK: Only that I usually do revise a very great deal.

NYQ: *And what about beginning to write at a certain time of the day, music, etc.*

GK: No, I have no habits, no habits.

NYQ: *What about revising something that has already been published?*

GK: Yes, sometimes after a poem has been published in a magazine I might change it a bit here and there before putting it into a book.

NYQ: *And your translations—your translations of François Villon—what function do you feel that translation has for a poet?*

GK: There are people for whom translating is a way of making clearer to themselves the kind of poetry that they would like to be writing themselves. But for myself translating has just been a way of getting under the skins of poems I liked. I don't think it has played any important role in my own writing.

NYQ: *What about your recommendations regarding translations?*

GK: For a person with time and energy to spare, translation is a marvelous thing to do. For one of a more plodding disposition, it can rob you of the strength you might put into your own work. Also, translation can be an escapist activity, for in translating there is much of the "fun" of writing and little of the responsibility and risk, the real excitement of writing. It's therefore a tempting activity. While you are engaged in translating it's easy to think you are doing something splendid and important, but at the end the true joy turns out to be missing. I have myself given up translating, because it takes me such a long time and my life seems so filled now I can't afford that time and energy.

NYQ: *How do you feel about teaching in terms of what it does for your own work?*

GK: I don't think that it does anything for my own work. Teaching is exciting and interesting, and it is an honorable profession. But I don't think it nourishes a writer. Many of the people you are talking to are too much like yourself: it's too much like a conversation going on inside your own head. It would be much better if one could find a work by which you could enter a new world, a world different not only in its kinds of people, but also in its materials and terminology. As yet I haven't found for myself such a work.

NYQ: *Do you think this would bring you more reality experiences?*

GK: Yes, I think it would keep you in relation with a wider world and help prevent academic atrophy.

NYQ: *What about workshops? Have you participated as a student?*

GK: No, I never studied in a workshop.

NYQ: *How do you feel about them from the point of view of the new writer?*

GK: All I can say is that I never met a writer who thought he had learned much from a workshop. On the other hand, many seem to have enjoyed the association with other writers and feel that the excitement generated in workshops brought forth more from themselves than a life in isolation might have.

NYQ: *What about poetry readings?*

GK: I do quite a lot of them. They can be awful. There are few things more depressing than reading poems you have read many, many times, to people who aren't terribly interested in hearing them, who attend the reading because they regard you as a curiosity. The only way to survive such an evening is to read to yourself. But then it happens you meet an audience that seems at one with you: reading to them gives you a rather beautiful sense not so much of sharing your own feelings as of being the voice of everyone there. This can be thrilling for one who has lived much of his life alone. Furthermore, if you've just recently written a poem there is a matchless excitement in reading it to others. The great moment is when you become one with the poem and create it anew as you read it.

NYQ: *You were active, I understand, in setting up the University of Chicago Adult Education program, and the program at NYU. Could you comment on that in relation to your poetry? Was it all part of the same thing?*

GK: It was a separate compartment. I would not be able to do the same thing now. I had a lot of energy at that time, enough to maintain compartments.

NYQ: *What was it you did in terms of the program?*

GK: We tried to figure out what would be the education we would like to have had and to organize that kind of education into a program of courses. I don't think it's quite the kind of education I'd like to have now. Now I don't think I would do it in quite the same way.

NYQ: *What about adult education in this country and the relationship between poetry and education? Is there enough poetry in it?*

GK: I don't think the way poetry is treated in colleges—whether for adults or undergraduates—is really the right way to treat it. Of course, I wouldn't like it *not* treated in colleges either. And yet the thing about poetry is that if you're moved by a poem you might not wish to say anything at all. You might wish to live with that poem in silence for a while. If you're not fully able to understand it, maybe if you just read it to yourself again and again, get it by heart, you will come around to understand it—and understand it in a way we don't have terms for expressing. In a class, however, they want you to analyze the poem, say exactly what it means, clear up the difficulties. You have to commit two sins: eradicate the mystery of the poem and talk about it on demand, which is to say in someone else's critical language. But the university lives on talk, and so apparently that's the way it's got to be.

NYQ: *Would there be another way to present poetry to a class?*

GK: Ideally, only ancient poetry should be studied in universities. The function of the study would simply be to compensate for all the time that has gone by. Contemporary poetry would be so available, so much part of one's life, that to "study" it would be superfluous. Of course this isn't the case. I don't think the solution is to submit contemporary poetry to the same objective scrutiny as ancient poetry, as universities now mostly do. Rather we perhaps should try to discover a whole new function for the teaching of contemporary poems. Perhaps we shouldn't teach them directly at all, but use contemporary poetry as pretexts for getting students to look into their own inner lives—their own deepest experiences—and to meet each other rather openly at this level.

NYQ: *Do you think we have failed to create an audience for poetry—in the basic education system—not just the colleges? Do you think it should be a spontaneous thing—and if not created do you think it should just die?*

GK: I don't think the responsibility ultimately rests on the teachers. They themselves have been betrayed in regard to poetry—and all that mysterious life that poetry seeks to express—not by their own teachers but by the whole technological culture in which we live. The reason poetry is returning into the lives of young people is their revulsion against technology and technological alienation. We have all become a little clearer about what human life is.

NYQ: *There was an evolution from interest in the arts to becoming more pragmatic, an interest in the dollar, etc. Do you think this is a further evolution to the way back—the way it used to be?*

GK: I think it will take a new unpredictable turn. We'll just have to see what happens.

NYQ: *Could you comment on your use of invented words— neologisms—"Crucible" and "Body Rags," the word regarding the porcupine "spartles across the grass."*

GK: I have invented a few words but not many. What I have done more is to try to rescue certain ancient words.

NYQ: *Is it despair at finding a traditional word that makes you want to rescue?*

GK: I think there is a danger our language will get too mental. We are discarding some of the great sensual words in favor of more electric words, whether astronaut language, hip slang or advertising talk. I would simply like to see as rich a vocabulary as possible available to us. English is a fantastic poetic language, and to lose any of its gorgeous words seems a waste. I guess we use the words which correspond to our feelings about reality. As we become more mental and technological, we discard the words which evoke mysteries, that don't interest us any longer.

NYQ: *You say you have no habits, but how do you write?*

GK: Well, I never write on a typewriter. Sometimes I keep notebooks, but since I tend to lose them I manage with scraps of paper.

NYQ: *Do you carry around a fragment or a line for ages until you use it in a poem?*

GK: Sometimes I do.

NYQ: *Is that your usual way of starting a poem?*

GK: You see, I don't really have a usual way. I have started poems that way, but other times I have written the whole poem out from the beginning to the end.

NYQ: *About six years ago there was a photograph in* Life *magazine with regard to your involvement in civil rights. How do you feel about involvement in any political activity for a poet?*

GK: As poets are freer than most people to engage in such activities it's rather wasteful of them to decline. In the case of the protests against the Vietnam war, very few poets didn't take part in some way. No other profession or group was so overwhelmingly opposed to the war and so active in opposing it. As to whether they should or shouldn't: I only think that if they hate the war they should, if they don't hate the war they shouldn't.

NYQ: *In terms of enriching your poetry, do you feel involvement has any bearing on that?*

GK: I think involvement in the effort to alleviate pain in the world, whether a militant cause or just caring for a sick person, any involvement at all which seeks justice and brings you into a feeling of love and community is purifying and is bound to be nourishing —and this is true whether you are a writer or not.

NYQ: *I note in a brief biographical sketch about you in* A Controversy of Poets (*Paris Leary and Robert Kelly, editors; Anchor Books, Doubleday, 1965*) *that you have spent some time in France and in Teheran. What about living away from this country—what effect do you feel it has had on your work?*

GK: I was a rather backward person, I think, and living in France especially opened up worlds for me that probably would have remained closed if I had stayed in Chicago, where I had been living. I guess that's good for one's poetry. Traveling itself isn't particularly useful; it's what happens to you. I guess it can happen anywhere.

NYQ: *What about your poems "The Bear" and "The Porcupine"? Bill Packard sees them as rather unique nature poems. Do you agree with his interpretation of them?*

GK: As for the term "nature," I think we have to revise our understanding of it in regard to poetry. The "nature poem" as opposed to, say, the poem of society or the urban poem, doesn't have much future—and not much past, for that matter—we have to get over that notion we carry from the Old Testament on down that we are super beings created in God's image to have dominion over everything else—over "nature." We have to feel our own evolutionary roots and know that we belong to life in the same way as do the other animals and the plants and stones. Then a nature poem wouldn't be a matter of English gardens, of hedgerows and flowers. It would include the city too: if the beaver dam is a work of nature, so is the city a work of nature. The real nature poem will not exclude man and deal only with animals and plants and stones; it will be a poem in which we men refeel in ourselves our own animal and plant and stone life, our own deep connection with all other beings, a connection deeper than personality, a connection which resembles the attachment an animal has for an animal. We're going toward that sense of ourselves and we're going away from it simultaneously. Now, for the first time in a long time, there is a kind of countermotion toward the natural, toward connection with the life of the planet.

NYQ: *So it isn't a totally new development?*

GK: No. Thoreau was doing precisely this 125 years ago. He had a kind of allergy to technology, an instinctive reaction to it—it made him break out in spiritual hives. Yet even he, because of the terminology available, kept making the fast distinction between man and nature.

NYQ: *He was the first?*

GK: No, I wouldn't say so. I suppose that in all human societies from the beginning there have been both a drive to control and dominate nature and a hunger to be one with nature. These contended in some kind of balance. Only since the Renaissance did the drive to dominate overwhelm the other. Only in the twentieth century have we seen the catastrophic result.

NYQ: *What do you do about dry periods? Do you have them?*

GK: Yes, dry periods, of course, but I don't think of them that way—more as complications of life—practical and emotional complications—which produce in me depressions, and when, therefore, I can't write.

NYQ: *So you wait as you simplify and it just levels off? Then you write again.*

GK: So it's been true in the past. I can't say for the future.

NYQ: *What of your early influences?*

GK: I had a teacher in college, Charles Bell, who was a powerful influence on me. Aside from him, really no one I knew. As for poets I read, when I was young Eliot influenced me much, later Yeats, Whitman and Rilke.

NYQ: *What about poets now? Do you read for influence or just because you like them?*

GK: I read because I like them. If any contemporary poet influenced me at all I think it was Allen Ginsberg, in *Howl.*

NYQ: *Do you think it is necessary for a poet to go through form and then break out of it?*

GK: No. That was what happened to my generation— almost all of us began writing in strict forms and almost all of us gave it up. I don't think this will happen in the future. Those who say you have to "learn the rules in order to break them" are probably extrapolating from their own experience, and that experience was probably a historical quirk. I doubt it's necessary. I don't see any young people interested in form and I see them writing a lot better than we were writing at their age. I doubt that there will be a return to form even as an exercise.

NYQ: *Do you ever set up a form and try to write within it as a challenge?*

GK: No, never.

NYQ: *Your long poem "The Avenue Bearing the Initial of Christ Into the New World"—was it your intention at that time to write a long poem?*

GK: Yes. When I began writing it I understood it would be a long poem. I can't even say I experienced much difficulty, it rather wrote itself and it surprised me that it came out as whole as it did.

NYQ: *Everything works so beautifully in the poem, the words, the specificity—did it just happen that way or was it predetermined?*

GK: There was something terribly exciting about that neighborhood—those people, those things. Whatever poem came out of it flowed from that excitement. I don't think I set out to be specific; it happened.

NYQ: *You lived there or you just observed it?*

GK: I lived there a couple of years.

NYQ: *What about young writers—is there any person or set of persons writing that you would feel the young writer should be aware of?*

GK: I think the atmosphere is such today that young writers don't have any problem in discovering their kinsmen among writers of the world. I only think young poets should read the poets they love. Twenty-five years ago certain poets were kept secret, so to speak. There weren't too many people who knew of Neruda, for instance. Things have changed so much, there are so many translations available, word of mouth conveys so much, I don't think people have trouble finding friends among writers.

NYQ: *Do you think this was a purposeful thing in the past?*

GK: No, it was due to the provincial quality of American letters. We were very Anglophile and a little Francophile—and that was it. Not too many people were doing translations and not too many publishers were interested in turning them out.

NYQ: *Whom do you read now?*

GK: With some shame I have to say that in the last three years, while I've been working on my new long poem, I've hardly read any poetry at all, except poems by students and friends. Now that my own poem is finished I hope to read again.

SELECTED BIBLIOGRAPHY

What a Kingdom It Was, Boston, Houghton Mifflin Company, 1960.

Body Rags, Boston, Houghton Mifflin Company, 1968.

Book of Nightmares, Boston, Houghton Mifflin Company, 1971.

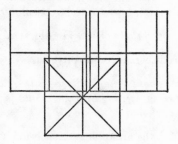

CRAFT INTERVIEW
WITH JOHN ASHBERY

NYQ: *When did you first start writing poetry?*

JOHN   When I was in high school. As a kid I was more
ASHBERY: interested in painting and wanted to be a painter; in
         fact I did up until I was about eighteen. It overlapped
         with poetry and I found that I was able to say better
         what I wanted to say in poetry than in painting,
         which I subsequently lost interest in.

NYQ: *We understand you always begin with a title. Does
         that mean you have the title before any conception of
         the subject matter or the form?*

JA: I don't always do that but what happens is that a
         possible title occurs to me and it defines an area that I
         feel I'll be able to move around in and uncover. It's
         not that I feel necessarily that titles are important in
         themselves. I remember hearing Aram Saroyan
         telling students in Indiana what was happening in
         New York and one of the things he said was "Titles
         are out, man." This may or may not be true, but in
         any case it seems to me that the title is something that
         tips the whole poem in one direction or another,
         doesn't it? I mean a satirical title can give a different
         color to a poem that might be very different if it were
         titled something else. As I say, I feel the title is a very
         small aperture into a larger area, a keyhole perhaps, or
         some way of getting into the poem which I suppose is

my thoughts at any particular moment, which I find I can then organize by this means.

NYQ: *Do you find the beginnings of your poems in your immediate surroundings? notes or recent conversations? dreams? reading? painting?*

JA: I'd say in all those, yes. I often begin writing a poem with a collection of odd notations that have come out of conversations, dreams, overheard remarks on the street and these, again, are a further definition of an area that I'm hoping to explore. Very often I throw out these beginning notes once I've finished the poem; but again they are devices which enable me to get at something I don't already know. I can't tell you why a certain overheard remark seems significant and another one doesn't except that when I'm in a state of attentiveness, waiting to write a poem, I can tell intuitively what's going to help me to write it and what isn't.

NYQ: *You always want a poem to explore unknown territory?*

JA: Yes, that's what a poem is to me; I think every poem before it's written is something unknown and the poem that isn't wouldn't be worth writing. My poetry is often criticized for a failure to communicate, but I take issue with this; my intention is to communicate and my feeling is that a poem that communicates something that's already known by the reader is not really communicating anything to him and in fact shows a lack of respect for him.

NYQ: *You talked about an especially attentive state. Could you tell us about that? Is that something akin to inspiration?*

JA: People often ask do you sit around and wait for an inspiration or do you just sit down and write. I think when I first began writing poetry I had the idea that one sat around and waited for the muse to descend; but now I have to program myself in order to find time to write since I have a job, and I've also gotten so much in the habit of writing critical articles and reviews for my work that I don't seem to have to wait any more. All I need is the time and a not too depressed state of mind to be able to start concentrating attentively in order to pick up whatever is in the air.

NYQ: *You have a constant accumulation of things waiting to be written?*

JA: I hope so. I go at them one at a time; I can't look too far into the future. One never knows of course. Very often there isn't anything there but you have to proceed on the assumption that something is, otherwise you don't write.

NYQ: *We understand that for your writing you keep a tape recorder by your bed. What is it useful for?*

JA: I did that for a while but I haven't used it lately. I had one of those pocket kinds and I thought if I kept it by my bed I might wake up in the middle of the night with some great line that I'd be too lazy to write down, and I did this a few times. I've since found that those lines are usually not too memorable once daylight comes. I used to carry it around with me—I waste a lot of time before writing by going for long walks—and occasionally I would take this pocket tape recorder along, fish it out of my pocket and mutter something into it, getting strange looks from people; but I found a pencil and paper are really just as good. I jot down little phrases and ideas on pieces of paper, dig them out of my pockets and keep them around as I'm starting to write. And then as I say I get away from these once the writing takes over.

NYQ: *Do you actually compose at a typewriter?*

JA: Yes. I used to be able to write only by hand and about ten years ago I'd become so used to typing that I began writing poetry that way. I think it was while I was writing "The Skaters," which has very long lines in it; I found that I would often forget the last part of the line before I got a chance to write it down and the typewriter was more efficient for this. Now I use it all the time.

NYQ: *To go back a little, to what you were saying about eliminating the initial phrases, what is it about them that makes this necessary?*

JA: They often stick out like sore thumbs even though they were what prompted me to write what came after them. As I say, they are devices and sometimes that's all they seem to be; they often don't fit into the texture of the poem; it's almost like some sort of lost wax or other process where the initial armature or whatever gets scrapped in the end.

NYQ: *In '69 when you appeared in Bill Packard's class at NYU you said you usually write listening to the radio or record player. Is the music a direct stimulus or a partial distraction? How does it work?*

JA: The thing about music is that it's always going on and reaching a conclusion and it helps me to be surrounded by this moving climate that it produces— moving I mean in the sense of going on. I find too that I suddenly get into, as they say, a certain composer's work which seems to me to be a very good background for what I'm thinking about while I'm writing a particular poem.

NYQ: *So you actually choose people to work by sometimes?*

JA: Very often. While writing one of the three prose poems which is in my book that's coming out I got to listening to Brahms' first sextet and it seemed to be the only piece of music that would work for this particular poem but it's hard to say anything very meaningful as to why. Poetry is mostly hunches.

NYQ: *What other composers have you used?*

JA: I have very eclectic tastes in music as in most other things: Couperin is often very good. I played Elliott Carter's Concerto for Orchestra a lot while I was writing "The New Spirit." Mostly however I would say my tastes run to nineteenth-century music for purposes of poetry.

NYQ: *Traditionally a poet's craft or the way he wrote a poem was contained within a fairly fixed set of*

*conventions: meter, rhyme, the most obvious. As a
modern poet, do you have anything analogous to that
kind of craft?*

JA: Not any more. When I was younger I investigated the
various forms and meters; I reached a point I think
where I felt, if called upon, I could write a sonnet
that had a beginning, middle and end and would say
what a sonnet is supposed to say. And my early
attempts to do without these traditional structures
were not very successful. I feel that I've had to get a
great deal of practice in the kind of free poetry that I
write in order to be able to do it I hope successfully,
and now it's something that I simply don't think
about any more; I sit down to write without any
questions of form or anything like that although it's
not that I ignore them; I feel I've digested them for
my purposes and can concentrate on the more
important aspects of poetry.

NYQ: *With regard to revision, you've said that you
"absorbed from Cage and Zen that whatever way it
comes out is the way it is." Was it difficult for you to
accept that idea?*

JA: I don't know that I would make that statement now
because I do a certain amount of revising, although I
do less of it now; I used to go over every poem and
change things constantly until often there wasn't very
much left of the original, but this is something that
comes with practice. Young people in universities
always ask the question "Do you revise very much?"
because, I suppose, they're going through the same
period that I did. I don't any more and yet I
wouldn't say that whatever comes out is all right; it's
just that I've, I think, trained myself not to write
what I'm going to discard later on. I do a lot of small
revisions but I think I've moved away really from the
total freedom I thought I had when I was beginning to
experiment with very free, almost unconscious poetry.

NYQ: *In what book?*

JA: A lot of these poems I've never published and there
are a lot in *The Tennis Court Oath* which are really

like automatic poetry, which no longer interests me very much. For instance, the poem "Europe," the long poem in that book, is one that's no longer very close to me. At the time I wrote it I was baffled as to what to do in poetry; I wasn't satisfied with the way my work was going and I felt it was time to just clear my head by writing whatever came into it and that's very much the case with that poem; and I think it helped me along but I don't value it as much as ones I've written since.

NYQ: *Your poem "The New Spirit" appeared in the* Paris Review, *Fall 1970, and will be included in* Three Poems *("The New Spirit," "The System" and "The Recital") to be published by Viking in February 1972. In "The New Spirit," there still seems to be operative some extension of this notion of acceptance that you described as coming from John Cage and Zen, the way you refer to there being many ways and how you choose or get pushed into one way but they're all valid.*

JA: That's something that's part of the content of the poem which is a little different. Yes, that's an idea that probably keeps cropping up in my work but as far as the actual writing of the poem it doesn't have much to do with it.

NYQ: *Would you say you usually write a poem at one sitting?*

JA: Shorter ones, yes, but long ones like the ones I've done lately I only work perhaps an hour at a time— it's very hard to write poetry for much longer than that—and so these are things that take a period of perhaps several months and it's something of course quite different from a poem written all at once because one's mind changes during the course of the writing; these changes are reflected in the poem, give it a diversity that the other wouldn't have.

NYQ: *Do you ever discard something you've written because it seems insufficiently poetic?*

JA: I don't know exactly what poetic means.

NYQ: *We were just thinking that you might have some notion in your own mind, if not necessarily one to define at the moment, but some sense that something didn't fit within your notion of what is poetic.*

JA: That I would certainly do but as I say the word "poetic" is one that we of course all use, but I'm not really sure of what it means and it often has a pejorative sense. So in this case I would probably say unconsciously to myself that that doesn't work or that's no good or that doesn't fit; the concept of its being poetic doesn't occur to me in the process of writing.

NYQ: *Would you agree that you sometimes deliberately work to maximize content over subject matter?*

JA: Yes, that's a very accurate phrase as far as my poetry goes, I think. My poetry doesn't have subjects. Not in many years have I sat down to write a poem dealing with a particular subject and treating it formally in a kind of essay. My poetry, as I indicated in what I said already, has an exploratory quality and I don't have it all mapped out before I sit down to write. I do have a very general idea which it would be very difficult to tell anybody about before I had written the poem; it would simply make no sense to another person and yet I know myself enough to know that it's probably going to lead to a poem.

NYQ: *What techniques do you use for staying away from subject matter?*

JA: I'm not sure that I use any techniques to stay away from subject matter. I guess I feel that subject matter is, might well be, some tributary part of a poem; because I think when there is a poem—take a poem of the past, for instance, a poem by Hardy or Dover Beach or something like that where the meaning is perfectly clear, the subject matter is common knowledge and it's the other things that get included into the poem that raise it to the level of poetry and which are therefore the vital elements in the poem. I suppose one might say really that subject matter is a kind of structure which gets transformed in the

process of the poem's being written so that it becomes
something quite different, and I guess what interests
me in poetry is the difference, the ways in which the
prose sense of a poem gets transformed in poetry and
this I think is the area that I write in to the exclusion
of a formal theme or topic. I find one can say very
much more by advancing immediately to the poetry in
the poem.

NYQ: *The poetry consisting mainly in the fluidity of thought
        rather than objects of thought?*

JA: Yes, I think I'd agree with that.

NYQ: *Memory, forgetfulness and being are simultaneously
        present in much of your work, which prompts us to ask
        what tense do you like to work in?*

JA: You mean a verbal tense? Well, I guess in all of them
        simultaneously since these three things that you
        mention imply different tenses and they're certainly
        things that are happening in our minds all the time
        which I'm attempting to reproduce in poetry, the
        actions of a mind at work or at rest.

NYQ: *What is your fascination with dreams and daydreams?
        Do you try to reproduce dream qualities or techniques?
        Do you find they are truer than ordinary consciousness
        to man's relation to space and time?*

JA: I don't know; maybe the dream aspect of my poetry
        has been overemphasized. I think in fact that the
        conscious element in my poetry is more important than
        the unconscious element, if only because our conscious
        thoughts are what occupy us most of the day.
        Unconscious memories, dreams that suddenly recur
        and seem to have an explicable signification or
        meaning all of a sudden also come into my work just
        as they come into our thoughts, but I would say that
        my poetry is really consciously trying to explore
        consciousness more than unconsciousness, although
        with elements of the unconscious to give it perspective.

NYQ: *It seems that your relationship to confusion has
        changed as described in "The New Spirit." Do you
        think that's so? You remarked in Packard's class about*

some of your poems being barrages of words and, in that earlier work, not wanting people to follow things item by item but to get a swarm effect; that's one way, and another way is related to your use of surrealist techniques.

JA: I don't know, I never thought of myself as having a relationship to confusion; every moment is surrounded by a lot of things in life that don't add up to anything that makes much sense and these are part of a situation that I feel I'm trying to deal with when I'm writing; and yet I don't want to feel that in my poetry I've set up a standard of confusion that I'm either reacting to or trying to abolish. I guess what I'm doing is merely starting with the disparate circumstances that as I say are with us at every moment; maybe that's why I begin with unrelated phrases and notations that later on I hope get resolved in the course of the poem as it begins to define itself more clearly for me.

NYQ: *We have tried to get a sense of your geography by going through "The Skaters" to see where it takes place. It seems that you are indoors near a piano but your mind will travel as far as a label on a wine bottle, a painting or a postage stamp will take you, back and forth across a placeless abstract area, and the voyages are as imaginary as that narrated in "The Instruction Manual." What is your relation to these imaginary voyages now? And did you at one time recognize your propensity toward them and make a deliberate decision to utilize the mileage they might give your poetry?*

JA: First of all, to begin with "The Skaters," that poem is a meditation on my childhood which was rather solitary. I grew up on a farm in a region of very hard winters and I think the boredom of my own childhood was what I was remembering when I wrote that poem —the stamp albums, going outside to try and be amused in the snow. I don't know whether that's what you mean by geography. Also an imaginary voyage prompted by the sight of a label or a postage stamp was again a memory of childhood—and also I guess of certain of Raymond Roussel's poems such as "La Vue," an epic-length poem describing a scene viewed inside the hollow handle of a paper knife.

NYQ: *What is your fascination with the repetition of words for time and its divisions?*

JA: Will you give me an example?

NYQ: *Day seems to be your favorite, and afternoon, we'd say, would be your second favorite, and then months, and night.*

JA: I hadn't realized that before. Day of course does appear very commonly in my poetry and I think all these things could be explained by the fact that the poems are setting out to characterize the bunch of circumstances that they're growing out of and a day might be said to be the basis for a poem, that one sits down to write a poem on a particular day and that's the beginning of the poem—the fabric of it—and afternoon and night are further aspects of day that moves on, and then it gets collected into months and weeks.

NYQ: *Is your work primarily about the sense of time, motion, change: is it, as Lawrence Alloway says, "continuum poetry"?*

JA: Yes, I would accept that, I think, and that might again be another reason for the importance of music to me which is something that takes time and which actually creates time as it goes along, or at any rate organizes it in a way that we can see or hear and it's something that's growing, which is another aspect of my poetry, I think; it's moving, growing, developing, I hope; that's what I want it to do anyway and these things take place in the framework of time.

NYQ: *Have you been specifically influenced in terms of a certain sense of indirectness, randomness, sense of time, by relativity, quantum mechanics or thermodynamics?*

JA: No, not at all, I know absolutely nothing about physics; I never took it in high school, I took chemistry instead. My maternal grandfather who had a great influence on my growing up was in fact a

physicist and the head of the physics department at
the University of Rochester so perhaps through
osmosis some physics has come down to me.

NYQ: *What about philosophical ideas?*

JA: Philosophy hasn't directly influenced my poetry but
the process of philosophic inquiry certainly has; again,
sitting down to somehow elucidate a lot of almost
invisible currents and knocking them into some sort of
shape is very much my way of doing, but as for specific
philosophical concepts I don't think they play any
role in my work.

NYQ: *In reference to communication it's often said that as
randomness increases, meaningfulness decreases.*

JA: In the last few years I have been attempting to keep
meaningfulness up to the pace of randomness. I don't
feel I've succeeded in doing this in poems such as
"Europe" and the others I was speaking of before; but
I really think that meaningfulness can't get along
without randomness and that they somehow have to
be brought together.

NYQ: *Is randomness more a methodology or is it more a
subject for you?*

JA: More of a content perhaps; but a methodology too.
As has been pointed out by Richard Howard, among
others, my poems are frequently commenting on
themselves as they're getting written and therefore the
methodology occasionally coincides with the subject.
They are a record of a thought process—the process
and the thought reflect back and forth on each other.

NYQ: *With regard to time, you seem to be aware of the end
of something even before it has begun and that one is
apt to experience something not necessarily when it
does happen but later; as if nothing—no incident,
thought or feeling—can ever be located in time, until
perhaps "The New Spirit." What seems to go along
with this is a nearly perpetual sense of something
missing or a frequent overcast of regret or nostalgia.
Would you comment on this?*

JA: Awareness of time and regret and nostalgia are
         certainly important raw materials for poetry because
         they are things that I, and I think everybody,
         experience constantly. In a way the passage of time is
         becoming more and more *the* subject of my poetry as I
         get older.

NYQ: *You said in '69 that you wanted "to stretch people's
         brains a little." What was the rationale behind that?
         And would you still put it that way?*

JA: That actually I borrowed from John Cage whom I
         once interviewed for the *Herald Tribune* in Paris
         when he was having a new work done and said that he
         wanted to stretch people's ears a little so that they
         could hear a little bit more and this little is actually a
         lot, really, provided that the process keeps on going the
         only way it can keep on going. I suppose what I mean
         was to make people receptive to a more all-embracing
         or a little bit more all-embracing kind of poetry than
         they were before. That's my hope at any rate.

NYQ: *Are you interested in the occult?*

JA: Not particularly.

NYQ: *You do use astrological signs and, for instance in "The
         New Spirit," those Tarot card figures.*

JA: Yes, but those were really almost decorative elements
         in that poem and I think probably were there because
         they're something that young people today are
         involved in and were a way of situating the poem in
         the present—it is called "The New Spirit"—but I
         don't have any very deep interest in them for myself.
         The occult is not mysterious enough.

NYQ: *You once expressed an interest in having no external
         references within a poem. Why? And what does the
         elimination of such references do to what happens
         within a poem?*

JA: Because I want the reader to be able to experience the
         poem without having to refer to outside sources to get
         the complete experience as one has to in Eliot
         sometimes or Pound. This again is a reflection of my
         concern for communicating which as I say many

people don't believe I have—but for me a poem has to be all there and available to the reader and it of course is very difficult to decide at certain moments what the ideal reader is going to know about and what he isn't going to know about; one has to do this by intuition as the cases come up.

NYQ: *Do you think of your poems as being autobiographical?*

JA: Only in a general way. When I was talking about "The Skaters" a little while ago as being a kind of autobiographical poem in the sense that I was writing about childhood memories, I didn't want them to be specific ones that applied to me but only ones that anybody would use if they were thinking autobiographically; they were just to be forms of autobiography rather than special elements that applied to my own life and in fact many of them are made up things, not things I experienced as a child.

NYQ: *The islands, the ships and cruises and so on are the made up part?*

JA: Oh, it would be hard for me to tell you which ones are and which ones aren't; those certainly would be made up since I never took a boat until I was much older. But those passages in "The Skaters" are no longer much related to childhood; it's mostly the first section which deals with that kind of imagery.

NYQ: *Would you describe the ways in which you see the personal pronoun, especially the word "you"?*

JA: The personal pronouns in my work very often seem to be like variables in an equation. "You" can be myself or it can be another person, someone whom I'm addressing, and so can "he" and "she" for that matter and "we"; sometimes one has to deduce from the rest of the sentence what is being meant and my point is also that it doesn't really matter very much, that we are somehow all aspects of a consciousness giving rise to the poem and the fact of addressing someone, myself or someone else, is what's the important thing at that particular moment rather than the particular person involved. I guess I don't have a very strong sense of my own identity and I find it very easy to move from one person in the sense of a pronoun to another and this again helps to produce a kind of polyphony in my poetry which I again feel is a means toward greater naturalism.

NYQ: *What was your early interest in elaborate forms? You say you really don't think about form in that sense any more.*

JA: I wasn't really thinking of elaborate forms which I used in my early poems when I spoke of forms before because they are highly artificial and arbitrary ones which are not the conventional forms we think of in connection with "form," even the sonnet is not that artificial or elaborate. And I think when I spoke of forms before I was thinking of building a poem with elements that one had very clearly in mind, and using them to construct a poem in the traditional sense. These forms such as the sestina were really devices at getting into remoter areas of consciousness. The really bizarre requirements of a sestina I use as a probing tool rather than as a form in the traditional sense. I once told somebody that writing a sestina was rather like riding downhill on a bicycle and having the pedals push your feet. I wanted my feet to be pushed into places they wouldn't normally have taken; that's why I used these particular forms which I don't do much any more, perhaps because I don't like to repeat myself and also perhaps because I feel I don't need these props any more.

NYQ: *What determines the lengths of lines and stanzas in your poems?*

JA: That's difficult to say. I use a very long line very frequently in my poetry which I feel gives an expanded means of utterance, and saying a very long thing in place of what might originally have been a much shorter and more concise one is an overflowing of the meaning. It often seems to me to have almost a sexual quality to it in the sense that the sexual act is a kind of prolongation of and improvisation on time in a very deep personal way which is like music, and there's

something of the expansiveness of eroticism in these
lines very frequently for me, although that's by no
means a conscious thing that I undertake in writing
them. And for stanzas the ultimate look of a poem on a
page is something that I visualize in advance. Again
it's the box, the framework, which is going to contain
the poem and which is arranging it for the viewer. I
think very much of the way that the poem will look,
not just the lines, the stanzas, but even the form of
the letters, all these are things that come into one's
experience as one is reading poems which I, insofar as
it's possible, try to take into account.

NYQ: *You're not influenced particularly by the notion of*
open field or projective verse techniques?

JA: It's nothing that I've ever codified or set up as a
standard in writing poetry but I guess I certainly do it.
I don't see very much relation between my own poetry
and what is called projective verse although it seems to
me that in fact that's what I'm doing.

NYQ: *But it came naturally rather than being an idea you*
picked up some place?

JA: Yes, I hadn't read Olson or his essay at the time I
began doing it myself.

NYQ: *Why did you choose a ten-line stanza for "Fragment"?*

JA: That again was the way I decided the poem was going
to look before I wrote it; it wasn't that I felt it had any
particular significance but that was going to be the
form in this particular case. Also I had been reading
Maurice Scève, the sixteenth-century poet who wrote
in dizains and I was impressed by the fruitful
monotony of his form, as over and over again he says
very much the same thing in the hundreds and
hundreds of ten-line stanzas, constantly repeating the
form and yet adding something a little new each time,
and the ultimate cumulative effect of these additions
is something I was aiming at, although I didn't use the
ten-line stanza with any very definite aim in mind or
desire to imitate Scève particularly. It also seemed like
a good in-between length; lacking the in-the-round
effect of a sonnet and longer than a quatrain; a

purposely stunted form which is ideal for these
repetitions with minimal variations.

NYQ: *What criteria do you use in deciding between writing*
         a free verse or a prose poem?

JA: I don't think I have any criteria. It's what seems
         suitable at the moment and I can't say any more than
         that. The prose is something quite new: I had written
         one or two prose poems many years ago and not
         found it a particularly interesting form and then it
         began to creep into a couple of poems in *The Double*
         Dream of Spring and then suddenly the idea of it
         occurred to me as something new in which the
         arbitrary divisions of poetry into lines would get
         abolished. One wouldn't have to have these interfering
         and scanning the processes of one's thought as one
         was writing; the poetic form would be dissolved, in
         solution, and therefore create a much more—I hate to
         say environmental because it's a bad word—but more
         of a surrounding thing like the way one's consciousness
         is surrounded by one's thoughts. And I was also very
         attracted by the possibility of using very prosy
         elements, conversation or journalese, what libraries
         classify as "nonfiction"; to extract what's frequently
         poetic and moving in these forms of communication
         which are very often apparent to us and which
         haven't been investigated very much in poetry.

NYQ: *It's still something that's quite unique in English, the*
         prose poem, whereas it's become fairly standard in
         French.

JA: That's true, but there's something very self-conciously
         poetic about French prose poetry which I wanted to
         avoid and which I guess is what I found disappointing
         in my earlier prose poems; it's very difficult to avoid a
         posture, a certain rhetorical tone.

NYQ: *In "The New Spirit" you say, "In you I fall apart, and*
         outwardly am a single fragment, a puzzle to itself. But
         we must learn to live in others, no matter how
         abortive or unfriendly their cold, piecemeal renderings
         of us: they create us." I wonder if this has any
         bearing on your long poem "Fragment" and its title?

JA: The title "Fragment" for that poem was a kind of a joke because it's very long and yet like any poem it's a fragment of something bigger than itself. And it is a single fragment and a puzzle to itself as it is to others.

NYQ: *You don't have any Shelleyesque notion, do you, of individual poems being part of one great, grand poem?*

JA: Oh, I suppose so, sure I do. I don't know as I'd use the word grand, but maybe great. As I say, each one is certainly part of something larger than itself which is the consciousness that produced it at that moment and which left out all kinds of things in the interests of writing the poem, which one is nevertheless aware of in the corners of the poem.

NYQ: *Would you have anything to say about the content of "Fragment"?*

JA: I don't remember it very well. I think what I said before about its taking up again and again a single situation and repeatedly developing and then in a way casting aside what has been developed to start over again is the content in this particular case. I think it's like maybe all of my poems, it's a love poem; Scève's "Délie" was a long cerebral love poem; and the actual situation isn't apparent in the poem, but it's what is behind it and is generating these repeated re-examinations and rejections and then further examinations.

NYQ: *You seem to have an increasing interest in longer poems. What do you aim for in them that you feel you can't achieve in short one- to two-page poems?*

JA: I'm frequently asked this question. It seems quite obvious to me that one is given much broader scope to work with and as I said before the time that it takes to write and the changes in one's mood and one's ideas enrich the texture of the poem considerably in a way that couldn't possibly happen in a poem written all at once. And they are in a way diaries or logbooks of a continuing experience or at any rate of an experience that continues to provide new reflections and therefore it gets to be much closer to a whole reality than the shorter ones do.

NYQ: *In your* Art News Annual *article on "The Invisible
         Avant-Garde" you said, "Most reckless things are
         beautiful in some way, and recklessness is what makes
         experimental art beautiful, just as religions are
         beautiful because of the strong possibility that they are
         founded on nothing." Do you feel you have been
         reckless with poetry? Where?*

JA: I think there's something quite reckless about my
         poetry in general; I think for many people it's quite
         debatable whether it is poetry or not, and it is for me
         too. And I can never be certain that I'm doing the
         right thing by writing this way which nevertheless
         seems the only right way of writing to me. I think the
         poignancy of this position gets into the poetry too and
         intensifies it. I could read you a passage from one of
         my recent poems which might clarify this: "You know
         now the sorrow of continually doing something that
         you cannot name, of producing automatically as an
         apple tree produces apples this thing there is no name
         for," which I guess is one of the places where my
         work is commenting on the work itself, and yet I
         should caution against reading my poetry too much in
         this light. When it is commenting on itself it's only
         doing so in such a way as to point out that living,
         creating is a process which tends to take itself very
         much into account and it's not doing so with any
         attempt to explain the poetry or explain what poetry
         ought to do.

NYQ: *What types of diction are you aware of incorporating
         into your poetry?*

JA: As many kinds as I can think of. In "The System," for
         example, there's an almost pedantic, philosophical
         language and a lecturing quality and the poetry keeps
         running afoul of clichés and pedestrian turns of
         phrase; again these are the result of my wish to reflect
         the maximum of my experience when I'm writing;
         these are ways in which one finds oneself talking to
         oneself or to someone else.

NYQ: *You do seem to use parody and certain types of diction
         or jargon, really, in a wry way. There is a humorous or
         satirical aspect to things that you write.*

W. H. AUDEN

PAUL
BLACKBURN

ANNE
SEXTON

STANLEY KUNITZ

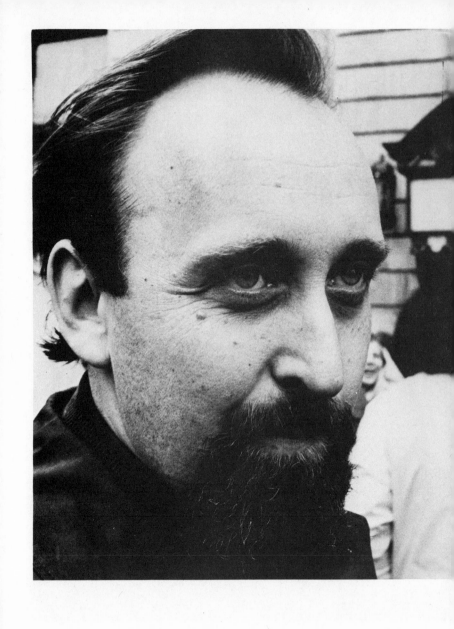

JEROME ROTHENBERG

ALLEN GINSBERG

DENISE LEVERTOV

GALWAY KINNELL

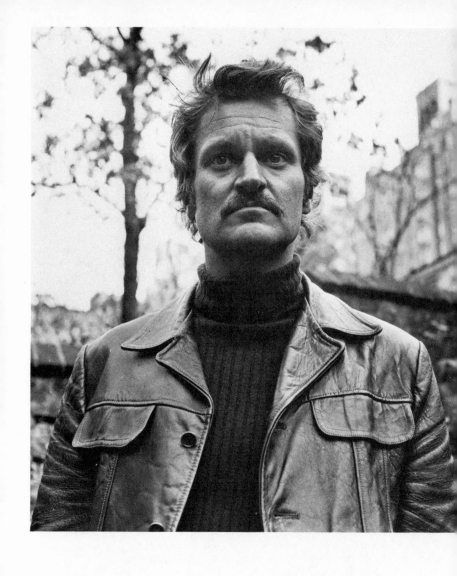

JOHN ASHBERY

JA: Yes, but it's not so much satirical as really trying to revitalize some way of expression that might have fallen into disrepute. Again, just because it's a way that we frequently have of speaking it deserves our attention and we should find out what it is that makes us talk that way and why it is that we do that, there's a good reason I think each time.

NYQ: *And the same thing would apply to parody?*

JA: Yes, I don't think that parody as such is my aim when writing this way; it's not to ridicule.

NYQ: *What about lyricism? Do you think of yourself as being lyrical or trying to be lyrical sometimes?*

JA: That's a word like poetic which I don't really understand; I guess romantic in the sense of romantic poetry I would understand and agree to; all my stuff is romantic poetry, rather than metaphysical or surrealist.

NYQ: *We've mentioned this before but how has writing journalistic prose on a regular basis affected your poetry?*

JA: I did that mostly during five years of my living in Paris when I wrote weekly articles in the *Herald Tribune*. I don't think the way I was writing had very much effect on my poetry but the fact of having to sit down and do it for a deadline without really having much time to think about what I was going to say certainly made me less intimidated by the idea of sitting down and writing a poem and in that way I'm certain it was very helpful. On the other hand, my reading of newspapers, which is something I'm addicted to, has certainly surfaced in a recent interest in discovering new poetry in what would ordinarily be considered prose.

NYQ: *Having written several plays and a novel as well as five books of poems could you give us some idea of what it is that makes you turn to one form rather than another?*

JA: I think you're somewhat exaggerating the extent of my writing; the novel was written in collaboration

with another poet, James Schuyler, and we began it
really as an amusement for ourselves and never
expected to finish it or that it would be published.
And that is a work quite apart from my other writing.
And the plays I've never really been very satisfied
with; I've always meant to go on and do something
more with writing for the theatre because I feel that
writing for a number of different voices is something
that I am equipped to do and I would like very much
to do it for the theatre. I have some ideas about that
but most of the things of mine that I think are the
most important to date are poems.

NYQ: *You have said that for you and your friends*
          contemporary painting was at one time more
          important to you than contemporary poetry. Is this
          still so? Do you read much poetry?

JA: I don't remember saying that; it never has been for
          me. But certainly at one point the most interesting
          experiments were being done in painting and therefore
          one wanted to keep up with them if only to have an
          example of what one might try to do in one's own art;
          but as far as painting itself goes, although I know I'm
          an editor of *Art News,* I don't feel that the visual
          part of art is important to me, although I certainly
          love painting, but I'm much more audio-directed.
          And I don't read very much modern poetry. I'm quite
          ignorant of what's being written now; the poetry I
          read is mostly poetry of the past, from the nineteenth
          century back.

NYQ: *You say you wrote the French poems in* The Double
          Dream of Spring *in French first with the idea of*
          avoiding customary word patterns and associations;
          and we've mentioned Scève and Roussel; could you
          tell us about some of the ways in which involvement
          with the French language and perhaps particular
          French writers has influenced the way you use English?

JA: I think French poetry on the whole hasn't influenced
          me in any very deep way although I have mentioned
          Scève and Roussel; I think those particular instances
          of influence were not really profound ones for the

poems. I don't know that the French language has influenced me very much; of course it does have a mathematical clarity to it which I might occasionally use in a poem for a change in tone that I might feel was expedient at a particular point. Sometimes in my poetry I feel a sense of things that we don't have in the English language like genders of nouns or the past historical tense; I think in fleeting moments I get an idea of a structure that doesn't exist in English, nothing very central to my poetry.

NYQ: *There is a general effect in a lot of your poems of talking things out, of trying to say things in a lot of different ways. Perhaps in "The New Spirit" the effect of it is new.*

JA: Yes, "the madness to explain" that I mentioned in one poem. And not only the talking things out but also the hopelessness of actually doing this.

NYQ: *Is one impulse of "The New Spirit" an effort to live through and out of the* Waste Land *consciousness?*

JA: What do you mean exactly by the *Waste Land* consciousness, you mean that everything is desert and with the decorative elements Eliot used?

NYQ: *Yes.*

JA: Maybe, although that wasn't a conscious thought when I wrote it. Most people would agree that *The Waste Land* is a pessimistic poem; I think that my most pessimistic moments in my big poems are optimistic, in fact there's a line in "The New Spirit" which might be used to illustrate this: ". . . just as the days get whittled down to more and more darkness at the end of the year without one's wishing to be back at midsummer, for this is somehow a higher ledge though a narrower and bleaker one, so time running out does not make this position less worthy or any of the individual instants of light darker." I think also what you might feel about that poem I covered a little before when I talked about the fact that somebody is being born; in other words at the end a person is somehow given an embodiment out of those proliferating reflections that are occurring in a generalized mind which eventually run together into the image of a specific person, "he" or "me", who was not there when the poem began. In "The System" I guess you might say that the person who has been born as "he" has taken over in the first person again and is continuing the debate.

NYQ: *Are you working on anything now beyond "The Recital" that you'd care to talk about?*

JA: I am but I don't like to talk about my work in progress; I never do.

SELECTED BIBLIOGRAPHY

The Tennis Court Oath, Middletown, Conn., Wesleyan University Press, 1962.

The Double Dream of Spring, New York, E. P. Dutton & Co., Inc., 1970.

Three Poems, New York, Viking Press, Inc., 1971.

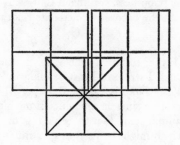

CRAFT INTERVIEW
WITH JAMES DICKEY

NYQ: Deliverance *got us to thinking about the poet's writing novels—*

JAMES DICKEY: Almost every poet feels like it's incumbent on him to try to write at least one. That was my situation.

NYQ: *When did it start?*

JD: *Deliverance?* Or do you mean poets generally?

NYQ: *Poets generally.*

JD: If you take enough time to try to write poetry, and you're serious about it, you build up an enormous linguistic skill. The poor human creature, the poet, cannot help thinking that, in a culture that rewards written things as it does the works of certain novelists, it might be possible for him to subsidize his poetry-writing out of the proceeds of a successful novel. For example, Karl Shapiro just has a new book called *Edsel,* and I think this is one evidence of the tendency I'm describing. Hart Crane, in a letter somewhere, when somebody asks him why he doesn't write fiction, says, "I've just never been able to think of anything with a plot." Neither have I, except *Deliverance.* It just seemed to work out.

NYQ: *Do you feel it as an extension or another dimension of something you might have begun—*

JD: Well, I would say this about my own relationship to the English language: Poetry is kind of the center of the creative wheel: everything else is actually just a spinoff from that: literary criticism, screenplays, novels, even advertising copy. If you keep that part of your work steady, and you recognize it yourself as being central to what you're trying to do—then the other things can be done as well. For me, poetry has got to be the center of everything, but also the kind of options and word choices and things that poetry makes you attend to are additionally useful in other kinds of linguistic forms.

NYQ: *Was there any shift in adapting to a different form?*

JD: No, it was fascinating. What I missed at first was what I had depended on as a resource for a long time, it was the poetic line. You don't have that in prose; you have the sentence and the paragraph. But you don't have the rhythmical continuity of the line. And I missed that for a while. But then you get interested in the other resources, the prose resources, and what the paragraph can do, for example. You carry your poetic, your word-choice ability into that, instead of into the line; it is interesting to do.

NYQ: *Is there anything on the adaptation from novel form to screenplay form to cinema that gave you trouble?*

JD: One thing only. The difficulty was a lot of the novel is interior monologue; for instance, what the narrator thought or said to himself as he was climbing the cliff, and so on. You have to find a way to objectify these things in cinematic terms and show what in the novel you did in an interior monologue. When Ed is climbing the cliff in the novel, he's thinking about how to ambush this guy. He thinks it out, in other words. But you wouldn't know, in the film, exactly how he is figuring on going about what he's getting ready to do if you didn't have some way for the form to let you know that. So we do two things: We have him not think it out to himself but talking to Bobby about it before he starts. And we also have him talking to himself all the time. Which seems to work out pretty good.

NYQ: *Now if we can go over to some other roles a poet has, aside from pure poetry—his working as critic, or as*

teacher. As critic, you said: "I am for the individual's
reaction, whatever extraneous material it includes, and
against all critical officialdom." (Preface, Babel to
Byzantium) *This was '65, '66—do you still feel the same*
way?

JD: Exactly. There are some things in *Babel to Byzantium*
that I was absolutely and dead a hundred per cent, 180
degrees wrong about, but that wouldn't be one of them
—yes, I do feel exactly like that. I was wrong about some
of the poets I talked about. I've changed around about
a good many of them.

NYQ: *Is it something new that a critic is able to be so much*
more open about something like that now?

JD: I think it is. And I think that *Babel to Byzantium* had
something to do with this. At least I hope it did.

NYQ: *Yes. We couldn't imagine certain critics in the postwar*
period making such a statement.

JD: No. You have, of course, a literary critic like Yvor
Winters, for example, and you know that this fellow
feels that he cannot afford to be caught contradicting
himself. I think that's a lot of shit. I think you should
have different opinions at different times. The whole
thing should be open and fluid, and not locked into
some strait jacket of a self-imposed critical system.

NYQ: *The function of criticism has changed, because—*

JD: I hope it has.

NYQ: *—because that was a pretty dogmatic and tight attitude.*

JD: It used to be more so than it is now.

NYQ: *Now criticism seems to be more trying to—what? See*
into the poetry?

JD: Why is it a critic can't say about a book or a poet, "I
loved it last week; this week I dislike it"? Or, "I disliked
it last week, but I'm crazy about it now." You know?
Of course you can't have any system, but there's
something about the human mind that insists on being
dogmatic and systematic. I think it's a terrible mistake.

NYQ: *We don't seem to have any people now who are trying for any kind of definition of poetry.*

JD: No.

NYQ: *What poetry is.*

JD: No. Nobody will ever know what it is.

NYQ: *You also mentioned, in that Preface, Auden's idea of a "censor."*

JD: Yeah.

NYQ: *Which you describe as—*

JD: But he changes, too.

NYQ: *Yeah?*

JD: I don't mean Auden, but the censor.

NYQ: *Along with the censor, you develop this idea: "the faculty or indwelling being which determines what shall and what shall not come into a poem, and which has the final say as to how the admitted material shall be used." You said that was derived from—Coleridge?*

JD: Or something.

NYQ: *Is this—*

JD: Yeah, that's what he calls, what Coleridge calls the "architectonic" faculty.

NYQ: *Is this something that can be taught? Or trained or conditioned?*

JD: It can be trained to some extent, and conditioned to a large extent. But taught? I'm not sure about that. I'm a college professor, as so many of my generation are, and I work with students every day of my life, and I've never been able to decide that.

NYQ: *No?*

JD: I think there are some sensibilities that a teacher of creative writing of a certain kind can be extremely good for. There are also certain ones that you can be death and destruction for, even though you're doing the best you can. You can turn out to be the worst possible

influence they could ever have come onto. You know?
And I've been both ways, lots of times. The teacher
really isn't God, all he has is his own opinions—and as
I say, they change.

NYQ: *The younger generation now are teachers—*

JD: But I've been an awful lot of other things besides a
teacher. I was an Air Force career man, I was a
professional guitar player, I've been an awful lot of
different kinds of things. But as somebody said
somewhere, "The main problem for an American writer,
or indeed for any writer, is to find a way to survive and
get his work done and take care of his people." The
university, for me, worked out badly at first. It works
out badly at the lower levels, for the writer. But at the
upper levels, where they let you have your way, it's good.
But as a teacher of freshman English, controlled by the
syllabus, supervised all the time—that's humiliating, and
that's why I got out.

NYQ: *This business of poetry workshops is, historically, a fairly
modern thing. What do you feel is the value for a young
person in going into a workshop to study under a known
poet? Did you, looking back now on workshop
experiences you may have had, feel they were very
formative for you?*

JD: I never was in one. I've taught them, but I've never
been in one. I have a feeling it would have been bad for
me.

NYQ: *Bad for you? Did you ever have the experience of a
formal structure of criticism by your peers?*

JD: No, none at all. I developed completely in the dark, and
very haphazardly.

NYQ: *Do you feel there's too much emphasis now on group
criticism?*

JD: Yes, yes, I do. I do it, but I do it because so many people
are doing it badly and destructively, and I figure that if
it's going to be done at all—I mean, it's the same reason
that I would take a position, say, as the chairman of the
Pulitzer Prize Committee. Because if I didn't, they
would get somebody in there like Robert Bly, and he

would get somebody up there to make a political speech. That's doing poetry no good.

NYQ: *Your saying that raises the question about rivalries and the wonderful feuds that can go on in the world of poetry. Sometimes it seems to be a very healthy thing.*

JD: Well, it is, but there's so many sick people doing it, we live in what I would call a kind of Age of Moral Blackmail.

NYQ: *Yes?*

JD: So that if you were a poet, and if you didn't agree with me on Vietnam, I would say then that your poetry was no good.

NYQ: *Yes.*

JD: It's that kind of thing is what's going on now, all the time: political opinions substituting for talent.

NYQ: *Yes.*

JD: And that's wrong. That's wrong for us all.

NYQ: *In some ways, though, even back in the more tight academic periods when aesthetic theory was the vogue, there were feuds then, but they were more submerged.*

JD: Yeah. Right. But there was not nearly so much name-calling. I mean, they had decorous articles attacking each other's opinions about Aristotle—in the back pages of the *Kenyon Review!* It was that sort of thing. Now it's all political.

NYQ: *We'd like to shift now to an article you wrote in 1965, called "Barnstorming for Poetry." That article described the poet as public reader, and we're curious to know how much you feel that experience may have had a subtle effect on the work you're doing now.*

JD: None.

NYQ: *None at all?*

JD: None. I write an awful lot of poetry that's not suitable for public readings, and I don't write anything just to be able to get up there and read it.

NYQ: *Do you feel the word placement in the poetic line has been at all altered by oral reading?*

JD: No. No. I'm a very good reader, I'm told. But I don't do it for the money at all, and never would. If I ever did that, I'd get out of it. I've given my life to poetry—I wrote it on troopships, and in airplanes. I wrote it going on business trips. I wrote it in American business offices. I wrote it on weekends and vacations—simply for one reason: I love it. It's been the central concern of my being and my character all my life.

NYQ: *You imply there are a lot of traps in the economics of poetry readings.*

JD: Plenty.

NYQ: *And in the frenetic pace which some poets might not be up to sustaining.*

JD: Well, it's killed a lot of them.

NYQ: *Yes. And altered their style.*

JD: Yes.

NYQ: *To what extent do poetry readings actually complement the center of a poet's concern?*

JD: Well, I've never really taken the time to think about that.

NYQ: *You never feel nervous.*

JD: I tell you, yes I do feel—did you say menaced?

NYQ: *Nervous. But menaced also.*

JD: Menaced, yes!

NYQ: *At times you feel you might be getting—*

JD: Yes, yes!

NYQ: *—a little further away—*

JD: Yes, yes.

NYQ: *—from writing poetry.*

JD: Yes, I do, I do, because it's fatally easy to fall into this business of doing nothing but going around giving readings, and I've been quite guilty of that—

NYQ: *And then—*

JD: Because after you've gotten up to a certain level, like
        Lowell and Berryman maybe and a few others, where
        you can get these enormous fees, you not only figure
        that you really don't have to write any poetry any more,
        you figure that it's better if you don't.

NYQ: *Yes?*

JD: Because the reputation that brings in this dough is
        already there, and if you write more stuff, you're just
        giving somebody a chance to bust you.

NYQ: *Hemingway had that problem . . .*

JD: Sure he did.

NYQ: *You have to keep the images straight, and see yourself
        basically as poet.*

JD: The only thing that's going to save you is the basic love
        of *das ding an sich,* the thing itself: poetry. That's the
        only thing that's going to save you. All this publicity, the
        dough, the women—especially them—are fatally easy to
        come by.

NYQ: *Yes.*

JD: And a certain type of person is going to settle for that.
        Me, I won't. I won't do that.

NYQ: *If we can shift a bit. You use a phrase, a concept you call
        "presentational immediacy"—*

JD: That's a phrase of Whitehead's.

NYQ: *Well, you describe it as "a compulsiveness in the
        presentation of the matter of the poem that would cause
        the reader to forget literary judgments entirely and
        simply experience." Does this have to do with the oral
        presentation of the poem?*

JD: No, no, I don't mean it in that sense. In fact, I'm using
        it in a different sense from Whitehead. No, I don't mean
        the presentation, say, from a reading platform. I mean,
        for words to come together into some kind of magical
        conjunction that will make the reader enter into a real
        experience of his own—*not* the poet's. I don't really
        believe what literary critics have believed from the

beginning of time: that poetry is an attempt of the poet to create or re-create his own experience and to pass it on. I don't believe in that. I believe it's an awakening of the sensibilities of someone else, the stranger. Now if I said the word "tree," you and I would not see the same tree, would we?

NYQ: *We're not sure.*

JD: What would you see—just as an experiment, what tree would you see?

NYQ: *A very gnarled old oak tree that's been blasted by lightning.*

JD: Yeah. That's right. I'd see a pine tree!

NYQ: *Yeah.*

JD: So if I use the word *tree* in a poem, this would be something that would bring out your gnarled oak tree to you, you know, when that wouldn't have been what *I* had in mind at all. It's an awakening of the sensibility of someone else. It's giving *his* experience to *him*. It's revitalizing his experience, rather than trying to pass yours on to him. You see what I mean?

NYQ: *Yes. "Presentational immediacy," then, would be in the composition. It would also carry over into the performance, into the reading of it. You mentioned, about 1965, you said, "Of late my interest has been mainly in the conclusionless poem, the open or ungeneralizing poem, the un-well-made poem."*

JD: Now you know I didn't know what the hell I was talking about! It sounded good at the time! Well, I think what I did mean in that—the open, conclusionless poem— was that I was brought up on poetry that came essentially out of criticism. I was educated in the era of the New Criticism, and the neat poem with the smashing ending.

NYQ: *Yes.*

JD: I think maybe we can do something else now. You know, you have to keep moving around. There's a certain type of poet who was young in the '40s, James Merrill was one, Wilbur was one, Anthony Hecht was one—fine writers, fine poets—but they got sold on that neat kind of poetic construction, and it turns out that the only work they've ever done that's good, that's remarkable, is what they've done to transcend what they were initially so good at.

NYQ: *Yes.*

JD: You getting some stuff into that machine?

NYQ: *Well, we hope so.*

JD: Well, we *hope* you are, but are you?

NYQ: *You did say before we began taping that* The New York Quarterly *was the best poetry magazine in the country, didn't you?*

JD: Yes. Yes, I'd say. Yeah, it is. Sure it is. It's very well edited.

NYQ: NYQ *began as a reaction against a lot of what you were talking about, the university periodicals, quarterlies which were too entrenched. But we were talking about "presentational immediacy."*

JD: I've got to make a Whitehead reader out of you! If *you* can understand him, please tell *me!* He's the most difficult philosopher I've ever read.

NYQ: *What about Heidegger?*

JD: Oh but Whitehead's got so much more to him than Heidegger. When you read Whitehead, you know there's something going on up there, if you could just rise up to it. You just feel about Heidegger and his *dasein* and all of that business, that it's just philosophical jargon. Whitehead and Russell take a whole thirty pages of the beginning of *Principia Mathematica* to define what unity is—in other words, what is involved when you say "one." I would have thought that would be fairly simple, but it isn't, apparently. Oddly, I was a philosophy major in college.

NYQ: *Really?*

JD: My major professor was a disciple of Wittgenstein, named Christopher Salmon, who was an Englishman, and a very, very good teacher. But my minor was astrophysics.

NYQ: *Great.*

JD: I didn't really get into English until I went into graduate school.

NYQ: *Was that on the conviction that you did not want to be exclusively English literature department?*

JD: Probably. I didn't want the kind of officialdom that that entails. Yeah, at Vanderbilt I had the best teacher that I ever—the two best teachers—the three best teachers I ever had. Old Salmon was one, who died this hideous, agonizing, humiliating death of cancer, rectal cancer. He was one of the three best, and another one was Monroe Spears—I don't know whether you know his work—he's an American literary critic, eighteenth-century scholar—he just had a book last year called *Dionysius and the City*. It is very good, extremely good. And the other one was my astronomy professor. His name was Carl Seifert. He was killed in an automobile accident, a couple of years after I left there. But he opened me up to the magic of the universe. He's the only person that I have ever encountered who had feelings about the universe. Most of us, you know, we just take it for granted. Carl Seifert was fond of quoting Edwin Arlington Robinson's line from one of his letters: "The world is a hell of a place, but the universe is a *fine* thing!"

NYQ: *Did you continue an interest in astrophysics?*

JD: Not as much as I wish I could. I always feel like I could get it back. I don't know if I could get the math back, but I could get some of it back. I used to do a lot of spectroscopy work, and analyzing calcium lines.

NYQ: *Could we look at an example now of "presentational immediacy." There's an image in "The Lifeguard," two lines:*

> *Beneath me is nothing but brightness*
> *Like the ghost of a snowfield in summer.*

> *Is this the beginning of what you would call "magical conjunction"?*

JD: Well, I would like to think so, but I couldn't say that myself. It would have to be said for me. Yeah, a moonlit lake would be like a disappeared snowfield. You know how pure a field of snow is, not even a track on it, no, nothing to disturb its purity—that's what I tried to get, anyway. The ghost—it's disappeared, it's gone, it's not a lake, the snow's all gone, in summer, it's all melted—but if it were there, if it existed, it would look like this.

NYQ: *Is there anything in its absence?*

JD: Yeah, also. I hope.

NYQ: *Can we look at another image, in "The Movement of Fish," in these eight lines:*

> *Yet suddenly his frame shakes.*
>
> *Convulses the whole ocean*
> *Under the trivial, quivering*
> *Surface, and he is*
> *Hundreds of feet away,*
> *Still picking up speed, still shooting*
>
> *Through half-gold,*
> *Going nowhere. Nothing sees him . . .*

> *This reads like onomatopoeia, as if you had actually re-created the sudden disappearance of the fish.*

JD: Yeah, you've seen fish do things like that, you don't know what's scared 'em, they just jump and they run like hell. There's nothing bothering 'em . . .

NYQ: *So much of that seems to work through what you've done with the placement of the lines, that suddenly the fish is gone.*

JD: Yeah, well I don't really know. You see Buckley and me the other night talking on "Firing Line"?

NYQ: *No.*

JD: to the life of the imagination and the sensibility, and We were talking about poets. As poets we're committed almost everybody wants to be that kind of a person. But what's really doing us in psychologically is exactly the effort to be like that. It's being oversensibilized, and overimaginative, and above all, overanalytical.

NYQ: *You mean that all you have to do is observe the fish accurately and try to see the way the fish actually moves.*

JD: Yeah, right. What we are doing to ourselves is that we've made it so that we can't peel an apple without self-consciousness. We can't do the simple things that used to give such pleasure to people who were able to do them without excessive self-consciousness about it. But the paradox is that poets are dedicated to excessive self-consciousness. You know what I mean?

NYQ: *Yes.*

JD: And everybody wants to live fully and be creative and imaginative and intelligent and so on. But some of the happiest people I've ever known in my life were dumb, stupid people. They didn't have any of the hang-ups that the intelligentsia has got. An excessively cultivated sensibility killed Randall Jarrell, it killed James Agee, it killed many another—

NYQ: *Hart Crane?*

JD: Hart Crane, especially him. And now it's killed John Berryman.

NYQ: *Could we look at another image, this one from "The May Day Sermon," just a part of a line, the one describing the young man starting the motorcycle, and it's divided into units:*

> *. . . he stands up   stomps   catches   roars*

Here the space units work in re-creating the physical act of starting the motorcycle. Is this an example of what you couldn't do when you went over into prose, you couldn't try to re-create the river using unit phrases?

JD: No, no, it wouldn't work. You know, I see that split line stuff that I've done, I'm not doing it any more, but I see it in almost every book of poetry that I pick up in bookstores. It's sometimes very effective, it's just like any other device, it's good when it's used rightly, and it's bad when it's used wrongly.

NYQ: *Do you feel that about any theory of placement, like breath line or variable foot?*

JD: Well, it also has to be used with tact and intelligence. To get back to Coleridge, to get back to what we call the architectonic quality, you've got to know when to do it, and how to do it, and when not to do it.

NYQ: ˙ *How long did the composition of "The May Day Sermon" take?*

JD: I could go on record as saying that's the best thing that I've ever written. A lot of people like "Falling," but it's too much of a *tour de force*. If I can do more poetry like "The May Day Sermon," I'll be very happy with my life.

NYQ: *How long did it take you?*

JD: Oh, years and years. Years and years. I'm doing another long thing I've been working on for ten years, called "The Stepson," which is about work, the relationship between sex and work. It's about working in a candy factory, as a dropout. I used to work for Tom Huston Peanut Company, making candy bars. And there's a very real relationship about workers and what they do and their sexual life that I don't believe I've ever seen anything written about.

NYQ: *"The May Day Sermon" doesn't seem cinematic, because it's so telescoped—there are so many images working at the same time. There's the sermon to the women, and the whipping of the girl, and the previous action of the sex with the motorcyclist—there are these several realities going on at the same time, it doesn't seem like it could be cut down to one plane for cinema.*

JD: Yeah, if anything could be said good about that poem the best thing that I would like to have said about it is that in it, especially toward the end, there is an authentic frenzy.

NYQ: *You seem to be a part of all of it.*

JD: Yeah, and the fog and the motorcycle, I'd love to *do* something like that, I'd like to be the guy on the motorcycle, I'd like to be the girl and the father, I'd like to be the chickens and the snake—

NYQ: *The poem seems to be like Jeffers' "Apology for Bad Dreams," in that it begins with such a strong image, in the "Apology" it's the whipping of the horse—*

JD: Which is tied up by the nose or something like that—

NYQ: *—but the Jeffers poem is more on a lineal plane, like he gives you the image, and then he gives you the meditation on the image, and then he gives you the statement.*

JD: You know, he's very underrated, isn't he? Jeffers. I'll tell you why I think so; I think he's one of the few American poets we've ever had who had an authentic sense of grandeur. Beside Jeffers, the poets that are paid so much attention to now—Anne Sexton, for example, or Sylvia Plath—they're just so many scab-pickers, you know? They concentrate on their little hang-ups, and bitch about them. If I have to read one more poem of Anne Sexton's about middle-aged menstruation, I'll blow my head off! Those things exist, of course—but those gigantic schools of fish and those flights of birds, they also exist, in Jeffers' imagery! Marvelous *big* imagery, galaxies, oceans.

NYQ: *Jeffers was writing out of a locale, a region, and you're also writing out of a specific locale and region. Is this some new kind of regionalism, different from Sandburg's and Frost's?*

JD: Well, in a way, I don't know—people say so, but I don't really know. The fact of being a Southerner, as far as that conditions you as a writer, or conditions me as a writer, is simply an accident. I don't have anything doctrinaire to feel about it. I would not, for example, as the people who taught me did, like Donald Davidson and Allen Tate and Red Warren—people who were agrarians and had a political stance based on being Southerners, and a poetic stance, and a sociological stance—I would not have anything like their orientation. I'm not like that. My southernness or my regionalism or whatever you choose to call it is simply an accident. Now Wendell Berry is a fine poet, but he's much more of a Southerner than I am and attached to a locale, and so on. Isn't he *good*, though, Wendell Berry's awfully good! We need somebody like him, who really is rooted in the land and believes in it and lives on it and loves it and writes about it. Wendell Berry's the kind of writer that Jesse Stuart should have been, you know. But we need him, because the land is disappearing, and we're not going to do anything from now on except live in places like New York, those huge metropolises of chromium and glass.

NYQ: *You once wrote: "To be a white Southerner in the mid-20th Century is to realize the full bafflement and complexity of the human condition."*

JD: Damn right! It is.

NYQ: *So that it becomes less a hard regionalism than an existential predicament.*

JD: Yes, that's essentially what it is. You cannot transcend your origins, no matter how much lip service you give to political ideas. You cannot, no matter what. If I see a Negro with a white girl at a party, it's offensive to me. It's not my fault, it's not his fault, it's not the girl's fault. That's simply the reaction that's aroused. There's nothing to be done about it. I could go over and talk to them, he's probably a terrific guy, you know, and yet that first gut reaction—you have it, no matter what.

NYQ: *And the poet is—*

JD: He's a creature of gut reaction, he has to be, he certainly does. Now, see, your background is not my background. You might not feel what I feel. But with all the business now about race, and so on, that black pride and black power and all of those things: the blacks should have those things. No man wants to feel helpless. Every man should have his pride.

NYQ: *What about black poetry?*

JD: I wish there would come along some really good black poet, but I haven't found him.

NYQ: *Do you feel that political statements, or social statements, are concerns which are not the immediate business of the poet?*

JD: I think you must be eternally wary of poetry that has newspaper value, topical value, don't you think? Great poetry has been written, as we all know, out of the heat of public occasions, like Yeats' poetry, "Easter 1916," and those things. But the tendency now, with Robert Bly and some of these people like him, and Ginsberg, who's really not a poet at all, is simply to use poetry as an occasion for making Bohemian speeches, which is a terrible, terrible mistake. People who go to those readings, and who seek out these authors on that basis, really don't care anything about poetry. If you go to a reading by Ginsberg, one of these awful group readings, and so on, you hear all this applause, say, where he works in material about Bobby Seale and the Chicago trial and the political conventions and that sort of business—and the audience applauds wildly—they're not applauding the guy's poetry, they're applauding themselves for holding the current fashionable social and political opinions that this guy gets up and tells 'em about. That has nothing to do with poetry.

NYQ: *We'd like to get into some very practical aspects of being a poet. We gather your work takes gestation time before you actually start writing it down.*

JD: Yeah, if I have one principle, rule of thumb, I guess you could say, as a writer, it's to work on something a long, long time. And try it all different ways. I work as a writer—let me see if I can come up with a metaphor or analogy—on the principle of refining low-grade ore. I assume that the first fifty ways I try it are going to be wrong. I do it by a process of elimination. No matter how backbreaking the shoveling is and running it through the sluices and whatever you have to do to refine low-grade ore, you have the dubious consolation that what you get out of it is just as much real gold as it would be if you were just going around picking up nuggets off the ground. It's just that it takes so damn much labor to get it.

NYQ: *Is this labor in actual drafts or worksheets?*

JD: One after the other, yeah. I tell you what you can do, and it might be interesting for you to do. Washington University Press has my papers, and they've got these huge stacks of three, four, five hundred pages of work on a single poem, and you could see what I did from that.

NYQ: *A poem like "The May Day Sermon," we imagine, would have gone through a tremendous amount—*

JD: Two or three hundred. And that's typing it out laboriously time after time.

NYQ: *Most of your work is done at the typewriter?*

JD: Yes, yes.

NYQ: *How much work is done in longhand or pencil?*

JD: I do it any way. I attack the problem any way, with hands, typewriter, feet, teeth, everything else, everything I can get!

NYQ: *On your travels, you spend so much time on the road, do you carry a notebook?*

JD: I do, I don't use it very much, though. I also carry one of those tape things.

NYQ: *Do you compose into the tape?*

JD: No, I do other kinds of writing on the tape. I have a new book out, I did that way. It's called *Sorties,* which is a lot of journal entries and things taken off of tapes and also some new essays. It's called *Sorties.*

NYQ: *What about dry periods, when you just are not able to get going?*

JD: No, there's never one of those, no! I've got so many ideas, I've got stacks of ideas and new projects and so on, enough for twenty lifetimes! Most of them will never be written. There's a sense in which you assign priorities: One is the poem that I just can't keep my hands off, that's the one I do.

NYQ: *You never experience any blockage—*

JD: No, no, it's the opposite, I just don't have the time, enough time. You think you about got what you want?

NYQ: *On the interview? Just about, yes.*

JD: Well, let's end up with one thing that I would like to
        make in a statement, a very simple and a childish and a
        naive kind of a statement, What you have to realize
        when you write poetry, or if you love poetry, is that
        poetry is just naturally the greatest goddamn thing that
        ever was in the whole universe. If you love it, there's just
        no substitute for it. I mean, you read a great line, or
        somebody's great poem, well, it's just there! I also
        believe that after all the ages and all the centuries and
        all the languages, that we've just arrived at the
        beginning of what poetry is capable of. All of the great
        poets: the Greek poets, the Latins, the Chinese, the
        French, German, Spanish, English—they have only
        hinted at what could exist as far as poems and poetry
        are concerned. I don't know how to get this new kind of
        sound or this new kind of use in language, but I am
        convinced that it can be done by somebody, maybe not
        by me, but by somebody. I feel about myself as a writer
        like John the Baptist did, when he said, "I prepare the
        way for one who is greater than I." Yeah, but look who
        it was!

SELECTED BIBLIOGRAPHY

Buckdancer's Choice, Middletown, Conn., Wesleyan University
Press, 1965.

Deliverance, Boston, Houghton Mifflin Company, 1970.

Eye Beaters, Blood Victory, Madness, Buckhead and Mercy,
Garden City, N.Y., Doubleday & Company, Inc., 1970.

Babel to Byzantium, New York, Grosset and Dunlap, Inc., 1971.

Sorties, Garden City, N.Y., Doubleday & Company, Inc., 1971.

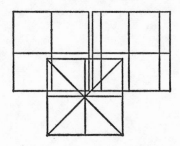

CRAFT INTERVIEW
WITH
MURIEL RUKEYSER

NYQ:	*When did you begin writing poetry?*
MURIEL RUKEYSER:	Since I was a child that's what I did—that's all I did as a matter of fact.
NYQ:	*Just rhymes?*
MR:	Yes. "Tis winter" on the first winter day.
NYQ:	*Then what particular early influences led you to become a poet? Did you have any home background which was conducive or did certain poets you admired influence you? Or a teacher perhaps?*
MR:	It was otherwise. It was the silence at home. It was the river to which I have just come back and didn't realize how much I needed. Books were the Bible and the Book of Knowledge. It wasn't a reading family. They were busy building up New York. It was very much that. No. I ask people now how old they were before they knew there were living poets. How old were you when you realized there were living poets?
NYQ:	*(You're asking me?)*
MR:	Yes.
NYQ:	*I was pretty old, although I did begin when I was a child to write little verses and I had a little family*

newspaper, which included poems. I wrote a play when I was in high school—all rhymed verse—

MR: High school. I was reading then. But writing for the first time—the poems get into one before one has language. I was reviewing some Mother Goose books the other day, and these are the things that happen before one is in language. They say it comes with the beginnings of language, but it's before that. You point to a toe and say, *"This* little piggy went to market . . ."* Collingwood said that's how we learn "toe." And I think after you have *"this* little piggy went to market" then contemporary poetry just follows.

NYQ: *And then you came to the winning of Yale Series of Younger Poets at the age of twenty-one with the collection* Theory of Flight.

MR: I had been writing before this. The poems in that first book start in the second year of college.

NYQ: *Did that affect your poetic career—winning that prize?*

MR: Well, of course it did. The way it was published affected me. It was turned down the first time, and Stephen Vincent Benet, who was then editor, wrote to me when he turned it down. He said there were two manuscripts that had come in that year. One was James Agee's and one was mine. And he was going to publish Jim's and he thought mine could go to a trade house. He wrote three letters, to publishers and an agent, one of which I used, and after that the book was turned down by eleven publishers. Then Mr. Benet did something extremely generous and out of line. He asked for the manuscript back. And he said of course it would have to go in with the rest, and that's how it was published. And a lot of that is in the general form of things for me. The no first, and then the yes. If I've been able to go on writing during times when everything does not go well. At my parents', it meant that there were cigarettes on the dining room table.

NYQ: *Do you think there are any poets who influence the body of your poetry?*

MR: All sorts of influences come in, I think. People always expect the answer to be in terms of poets, and last night I was giving a reading of Blake, and thought how Blake came in for me, and the Bible. When you asked for first things, they were silence, the river and the Bible. Yes, Blake and Keats and Donne, although Donne was not read. I went back to look at the high school anthology that was used, and Donne was not in it. It was a different day. The great poets are the bad influences. Anybody coming too close to the method of Whitman falls into a pit.

NYQ: *An imitator?*

MR: Yes.

NYQ: *Do you find that certain physical conditions are conducive to your writing?*

MR: Yes, but I don't know what they are. They can be anything. A lot of this is unknown to me. I've written under all sorts of conditions. This place feels very good to me. Airports feel good. I've written—you know, the question of a large space directs thoughts to oneself— in relation to space—or a small space like a telephone booth.

NYQ: *Have you actually written poems in a telephone booth?*

MR: Yes—and in an airport. The telephone booth poem was a very short poem.

NYQ: *How about an elevator?*

MR: No, although elevators are good because there's nothing about money in them.

NYQ: *Well, then you don't necessarily discipline yourself by regular hours?*

MR: Not about poems—prose is a different fish. But there is a feeling of a poem arriving—a pressure of a poem that one has not been able to come to that has almost presented itself. There is quite different work after the poem is down on paper and the critical work is there. But I don't know—I couldn't say what conditions— a lot of this is unknown to me. I know I do work all through the night, the further into the night the better. But I think this is about a long stretch. If I can get a twelve- or fourteen-hour stretch I'm better off in anything I do.

NYQ: *Without any interruptions?*

MR: Well, without any interruptions that I don't fall into.

NYQ: *Do you keep a notebook?*

MR: Yes. I carry a little notebook around with me. Some poems come out of it. The big poems in which there are many meeting places come out of those.

NYQ: *Do you have a method of filing them then? I find that notebooks can be quite baffling.*

MR: Very baffling. I can deal with that kind of baffle, though. I thrive on that. This is one of my notebooks and I carry one just like it in my pocketbook at all times. I certainly do.

NYQ: *Is it even by your bedside?*

MR: No, scraps of paper, envelopes, things that I sometimes can't read in the morning.

NYQ: *Do you wake up sometimes and perhaps put down a line that has occurred to you?*

MR: Well, I began that way. That's how I knew in the beginning, because in high school I had a friend, a best friend, in high school who wrote very well and played the piano very well. She seemed to me marvelously making in all things. There was some kind of quarrel—I don't remember what it was about— and she said to me, "Stop writing poems or I'll never speak to you again." Now the "never speak to me again" was a terrible threat to me. That was a punishment at home. The silence. That was only part of the silence that I mentioned. That was a real threat, and I promised that I would never write another poem. A promise is an absolute for me. For four weeks I didn't think of anything, and then a poem began; but I had promised, and for two weeks and two days that went on, then in the middle of the night I got up and wrote the poem. The next morning first thing I went to her and said, "I'm sorry, but I haven't been able to keep that promise." And she said, "What promise?" I knew at that moment. It was nothing as far as she was concerned, but I knew what it meant to me. I knew at that point.

NYQ: *We're glad you did. Galway Kinnell said in an interview with* NYQ *that the complications of life both practical and emotional brought on for him periods of depression during which he could not write. Do you have such dry periods, or what produces your dry periods?*

MR: I have terrible periods. Depression is a mild name for it. Sometimes it means not being able to write. Sometimes something will pierce through a period like that, and then it will go on strangely. That is, I can't tell you the rules. I know that the pit is frightful, and what I find myself doing is translating because I like to have something I care about out in front of me, and not have to send everything out of myself. To have a wonderful poem and do that folly, folly on a madness on a stupidity—translation, I like.

NYQ: *That is just what Paul Blackburn said about translation, that it fills in his dry periods.*

MR: Well, it's the reservoir and one goes to it. And one finds the poets one loves in that way.

NYQ: *Do you find that your teaching or your readings or your lecturing have helped you in your poetry?*

MR: I don't know. I don't teach now. I found that I didn't write when I taught. I wasn't able to. I don't think it's about energy either. I think it's something about the quickness with which one gets a response in the teaching. And one goes away and does not write a poem that day. It's a response that never comes or that comes years later, in writing—that comes out of the silence in which the poem is made—and the teaching seems to crowd that very much. I admire the people who can do it. Well, for instance this year in January, I was asked to come back to the college where I have worked right along, and I said I wouldn't come

back for teaching in the scheduled year, but I would
come back in the week between semesters, and I would
read poems with people, not just with undergraduates,
but with students and faculty, and with people who
worked in the plant. The man who ran the bookstore
was there, and the head of the nursery school. We
read poems every afternoon and every evening, all
week, having conferences in between. And a great deal
came out of that, out of not letting go.

NYQ: *That wasn't exactly teaching.*

MR: No, I don't know what to call these things. I can't
         answer some of your questions because I don't know
         these answers. I've heard people jeer at the word
         "workshop," but I know what I do is and is not
         teaching. I think of it as reading poems with people.

NYQ: *You give readings before audiences too, do you not?*

MR: I read Blake last night and Wednesday I'm reading at
         Cooper Union. I like to read.

NYQ: *Do you read your own poems at any of these times?*

MR: Yes, that's what I've been doing.

NYQ: *Does this have an effect on your work in progress?*

MR: It postpones it, I think, and I think that is the sin
         against the whole thing. And talking about Blake last
         night I reminded them and myself that Blake's patron
         had said, "Postpone your epic and support your
         wife." And this is one of the curses—or three of the
         curses right there.

NYQ: *Rilke said in his* Letters to a Young Poet, *"Nobody
         can counsel you, nobody. There is only one single way.
         Go into yourself." Do you agree with that statement
         or do you seek the advice of other poets in regard to
         your work? The classic example, of course, being Eliot
         and Pound.*

MR: I think it's the ultimate way. I think though there are
         moments in relationships. I don't think of advice, but
         I think with another person something can be struck
         like the thing that is struck between two elements in

a haiku. It is a bringing together that is in all of poetry.
This is in one's relation with another person, and out
of that clash comes either half a line in a poem or
sometimes the instigation of the poem—I think it
comes almost as much in relationships as it does in
going into oneself. Although the going into oneself is
a curious relation with something else. Going diving.
It seems to me that the awful poems are written from
someplace into which the poet has not dived deep
enough. If you dive deep enough and have favorable
winds or whatever is under the water, you come to a
place where experience can be shared, and somehow
there is somewhere in oneself that shares. And I know
with the poems that I thought were most private,
most unsharable, the ones I would not show, would
certainly not print, later when I have shown them, they
were the ones that people have gone to.

NYQ: *You said that at the Barbizon Plaza. You read a*
poem you were working on, and you wondered if it
would ever be printed. Do you happen to remember
what poem that was? Was it the one that was
published in NYQ?

MR: Yes. Yes, it is. That was one that I simply put in with
the pile of worksheets.

NYQ: *We were speaking about translations and how you do*
translations. Your poems have been translated into
many languages.

MR: Yes, I've been lucky.

NYQ: *Have you been satisfied with the way you have been*
translated?

MR: The word doesn't come into this life, not with the
poems one writes or the poems one translates. I don't
know—I stumble very much in other languages and
sometimes the translation of poems is a way into
another language. But I don't know about being
satisfied any way in life. I get very happy somehow
almost every day for a moment. As far as satisfaction
in what one does, one is—it's always the poem one is in
at the moment.

NYQ: *You collaborated with Octavio Paz.*

MR: There was some back and forth with Octavio Paz in
        translating two books of his. We are reworking one of
        those books now.

NYQ: *Another area—the games that many beginning poets
        play, such as anagrams and found objects and
        acrostics. In your collection* The Speed of Darkness
        *you have three poems from a section called games:
        "The Backside of the Academy," "Mountain: One
        from Bryant," "The Flying Red Horse." Would you
        like to tell us something about your conception of
        these poems as games and the techniques you used in
        developing them? Each seems different.*

MR: Yes, I selected those out of many that I wouldn't print.
        I've been doing this, all along. I did serious poems
        based on a principle that started as a game. One
        thought of the sounds of a poem as climbing up all the
        way to the last breath of a poem—doing the
        modulations of one sound, and I call that "held rhyme"
        and have printed some of those. But no one ever
        noticed that anything was in them. When one writes
        sonnets one doesn't think of them as sonnets. We all
        do that. I've published sestinas and a sonnet of mine
        has found its way into the Jewish prayer book, which
        astonishes me. It is absorbed into the prayer book
        all in Hebrew and English and without signature. One
        feels that one has been absorbed into the line and it's
        very good. In the games in *Speed of Darkness,* Bryant
        is simply run backwards, and it's almost as if one ran
        a film backwards. A very curious poem. The
        "Academy" one: I was living on the street in back of
        the academy and my son played there. And it is the
        back side, which I am very interested in—the back
        side of houses. I have a poem called "Despisals"—a
        new one—which is about the backs of things, of all
        things—people too, especially, and what they think of.

NYQ: *Have you ever done a poem on the motion of people?*

MR: Some of that, I think, is in the "Outer Banks." There
        was a question about verbs. You said there are very
        few verbs. I've made a list for you. The quality that I

was trying for in that group of poems was the shifting of things, and the shifting of the sand bars. And I tried to hold it and to get to the main verb in each poem, and that's what happened. I was very glad you picked that up.

NYQ: *Do you think that a poet should begin early to submit work and to enter contests, and do you advise him to slant his submissions for certain markets?*

MR: I don't know how to slant my own submissions. The advice that I have asked for is not like that at all. I think of something that I go back to—the question of a black woman student who met me after class and said, "I thought poets were all universal people. Who is the universal poet?" That's an unborn poet, of course. Of course, hatred and dealing with hatred may be possible in a solving man or a solving woman. It isn't a question of no hatred shown. It's the use of all the emotions, it seems to me. But as far as sending things, I get things back from magazines now. I advise people to make wastebaskets out of their rejection slips. There is something very comforting about throwing something away in a wastebasket which is covered with rejection slips. I have made such wastebaskets for friends of mine. But I tell people, if it breaks them to be refused or refused for no reason or for reasons one knows are nonsense, to get a friend to send out the poems for them. I don't know how much can be learned from the refusals, but surely something can be derived. But, as far as method, I have no idea what makes magazines or publishers move or not move. I don't want to stop it with an answer like that because one does send—I think there is something wrong with the word "submit." I'm perfectly willing to give or offer or sell them, but I don't like to submit. There is something very curious about that. Although I am willing to submit to many things.

NYQ: *You use a great number of rhetorical devices but you rarely use the simile. Is that correct?*

MR: I tacked up before me for a long time the saying "Poèsie farcie de 'comme.'" "Poetry stuffed with like," and I have tried to discipline myself to avoid my

faults that became very evident to me. And Horace
Gregory helped me with this very much. He helped me
with the elimination of a kind of running start which
I used in the beginning, in which, say, the first two
lines were simply getting going and could be thrown
away. And anything that can be thrown away in a
poem must be thrown away. There is no possibility of
marking time or even the use of the rest as in music,
although you can space it certainly on the line, on the
page. But anything that does not absolutely belong
must be got rid of. And very often the "like" and the
"as" that are made in identifications. One wants the
correspondence and resemblance but if I can get to
the unmediated relation, I like to be able to do away
with the "like" and "as" and similes.

NYQ: *You also use repetitions?*

MR: I also use repetitions.

NYQ: *In your poem "Orgy" you used the lines ". . . and he
then slow took off his tie, and she then slow took off
her scarf" and you repeat these phrases throughout the
whole poem. And then in the "self-portrait" section of
the poem "Kathe Kollwitz" you used the words "flows
into" repeatedly and both of them come out as musical
refrains.*

MR: Thank you. They are my rhymings. People ask me
why I don't rhyme, and I find it impossible to answer.
Because I rhyme, and go beyond rhyme. The return
once is not enough for me. I will carry a phrase
through. Or a sound, that may not be at the end of the
lines, but I try to carry any sound that is important
in the poem so that it comes back many times. I find
returns very romantic in all things. I love the coming
back at different times of all things, including sound,
including words.

NYQ: *Are you a musician as well as a poet?*

MR: No. I wish I were. I was sent to a music teacher as a
young girl, a very skilled piano teacher, who worked
with concert pianists before they performed. I was
awful. What I really wanted was to study harmony. I

brought an exercise book to him; he said I would go home playing eight more bars of Chopin.

NYQ: *Do you see those returns as related to something seasonal and a closeness to life?*

MR: I mean recurrence in all things. What they call repetition. The phrase in a different position is new, as has been pointed out by many poets. But I think I use this as other poets use rhyme. It's a time-binding thing, a physical binding, a musical binding, like the recurrence of the heartbeat and the breathing and all the involuntary motions as well. But in a poem I care very much about the physical reinforcement, the structure in recurrence. And I love it myself.

NYQ: *That establishes the pulse of the poem in a way.*

MR: Well, the pulse of the poem is established in the first breath. The poem is established in the title. The "Ode to a Nightingale" is established there. The two words are very difficult for us, are almost out of the language for us, but for Keats—Keats did not need to say nightingale once he had it in the title. He could say "bird" from then on.

NYQ: *You use slow rhythm in some cases. "Pouring Milk Away"—you have to read slowly. Again "A Smell of Dying in the Milk-Pale Carton." In your poem "Speed" we say you have established your rhythm in the title—then reinforced it with such lines as "the jet now, the whole sky screaming his name; speed."*

MR: I hope so.

NYQ: *Also in your poem "Cannibal Bratuscha" you not only combine rhythm but you combine opposing styles in the last line of each verse.*

MR: There is a recent poem that might interest you. I was working with some young writers and high school people who were beginning to write, in East Harlem, and to put off going away each day the way we white people rush out of Harlem at the end of the day with our portfolios, I would go across the street to a hot dog stand that had a counter open to the corner. There were two tanks on that corner, there always are.

One says "Orange" and one says "Grape." The man,
whom I had begun to know, was pouring that day,
dark purple into the tank that said "Orange," bright
orange into the one that said "Grape." And I said,
"How are we going to believe what we read and write
and do and say while you go on doing that?" And he
looked at me and smiled and went on pouring, and I
thought it was very much like everything else, and
it worked on me, very much like anything else, and I
thought a poem was beginning and I thought I don't
know what form this could possibly move into. And
I thought I'll be damned if I write a ballad and it's
"The Ballad of Orange and Grape." It's that ballad
with a long line at the end of each verse, like a long
casting out and pulling in. You see and hear it in
songs like Miriam Makeba's songs. Casting out and
pulling in.

NYQ: *This is an example of one of your verses that is in the
        "Cannibil Bratuscha":*

> *Spring evening on Wednesday,*
> *The sky is years ago;*
> *The girl has been missing since Monday*
> *Why don't the birches blow?*
> *And where's their daughter?*

MR: I would like to go back to one thing which I think I
        skipped, evaded and dodged, and that's about advice.
        I care very much about working with young poets. I'm
        lucky in that young poets come to me. I didn't mean
        that advice was not possible, but by advice I think
        more a kind of confirming of what they're doing.
        Somehow setting things out for them, something that
        works against what's always called depression.
        Something that allows them to keep going. I would
        very often say "NO." I would say "No" always when
        a poet says, "Should I go on writing poetry?" I would
        say, "No" and then I would say, "If they can't go on
        writing poems in the face of that No which they will
        get from everybody, they are not going to go on writing
        poems." If they would bring the poems back to me
        then, I would be glad to do whatever I could.

NYQ: *I know you have taught children—two years old up through teens.*

MR: And college, and graduate students, and continuing education and labor school. I like to read poems with people.

NYQ: *How do you feel about punctuation? You use spacing a great deal too.*

MR: I like punctuation very much. It is breathing. I had a rubber stamp made—"Please believe the punctuation." I have needed that very much in dealing with printers. It has saved me a great deal of everything.

NYQ: *Maybe you should have also "Please believe the spacing."*

MR: Yes, that I think has to be added onto another line. But I care very much about the air and the silence let into a poem, and I would like to work with other poets on ways of making this visual. Certainly the placement of a poem on the page can do most of it, but many readers do not take that meaning to be what it is, a metric rest. It's a question of a measured rest in the poem. I've tried to work out a visual form for rest but it clutters the line very badly.

NYQ: *Would you say that your poems come easily or are they somewhat of a struggle?*

MR: Oh, all different ways. Sometimes they come right through as single units, some of the short ones in the group *The Speed of Darkness.* I've been struggling to bring through a poem that I'm now working on which is searching/not searching, a poem out of the long digging for a lost man, a lost set of meeting places in man and history, and all the things I was not searching for during that time I want to get at, and I want the poem out of that. What about all the other things not done at that time?

NYQ: *In your poem "To Enter That Rhythm Where the Self Is Lost" you seem to equate the feeling you get from "Writing a Poem, Lovemaking and Bringing to Birth."*

MR: Yes, and of course the extreme joy in coming into
        those rhythms. The three rhythms. The feeling that
        these are the rhythms most to be alive. There is
        extreme joy. As far as satisfaction with the poem, joy
        is a better word. It is the thing that is present as one
        travels through the making of a poem. That seems to
        me to be alive in a rhythm which I want, which makes
        me feel most alive.

NYQ: *Yet where the self is lost.*

MR: Where the only way to move into self is to know that
        it is lost. I know that it is a way of moving, as a verb.

NYQ: *As for subjects, are there any particular things that
        interest you?*

MR: I don't think I work that way. It's much more the
        meeting place, the coming together of a theme (if it
        is a theme) with something which is extremely
        immediate and present in my own mind. My work—
        poems at the center, and the other things—seems to
        me very much a coherent thing, not a set of
        discrepancies. But I think it is held together by
        something other than theme, other than specific forms,
        and it would be very hard for me to say what is it that
        holds it together. It is what holds me together. And
        there is sometimes great difficulty in that.

NYQ: *You've said, "In poetry, form and content, relation
        and function, reach and merge." You yourself use a
        great variety of subjects and a great variety of forms.
        They seem to come together and to merge.*

MR: They merge in what I suppose is the voice—a
        recognizable voice—a recognizable music if they work
        at all. Again I am unable to get outside of my poems.
        I had great difficulty in making a book of *Selected
        Poems;* I can choose according to kinds of poems in a
        way but my poems don't fall into kinds from where I
        look. Maybe from where you see them.

NYQ: *You spoke of the "Orange and Grape" that did take
        the form of a ballad.*

MR: I want to do another ballad about the Jews and the
        blacks. I see those as ballads.

NYQ: *And you called the one about Timothy Dexter. . . .*

MR: No, it's not a ballad. It's the form of a person's life. I worked at that again and again. That was satisfaction, it seems to me. It is a fan-shaped form, in which choices are made—the form which cannot be seen until the entire life is accomplished and sometimes not until long after that. Again, going back to Blake, one sees very much what the Auguries of Innocence were, what the refusals to accept anyone else's ideas of innocence were, the establishment of his own ideas of innocence. He had to know what his own ideas of experience were, and the great trust in experience. He had to be able to make something of that experience, had to be able to make the great structure of poems. That stamp of a person, that music, that voice unifies.

NYQ: *It has been said that your poems come out of myth and dream. Certainly the word "dream," with various connotations and images, occurs and reoccurs especially and naturally in your collection* Body of Waking. *Would you describe your poem "Clues" as defining your use of dreams?*

MR: I would be willing to go according to that. That's a use taken from the Thompson River Indians who paint their dreams on their bodies, that is, they do not let them go. I saw *Mary Stuart* the other night and I thought of that piercing thing of Queen Elizabeth and dreams and not acting on her dream in respect to Mary Stuart, and the necessity to act on it. And this acting through art, the painting of the dream itself on one's body. I suppose it's related to the machine in the Kafka story in which one cannot read what is engraved into one's back. The first step is to take what one is deeply deeply saying and one does not sometimes hear—take it into the waking life. It's rather what is thought of as the uses of poetry, which is an expression and still remains very good sense and now people are talking again about what effect a poem has. One does not know at all. But it is like a dream. It can be accepted, or not, as with a curse. It takes two; you have to accept it. You must to let it be a curse. With a poem, with a dream, you have to take it back into your life, to see what it becomes.

NYQ: *As for myth, when your poems come out of myth—in "The Poem as Mask" you say, "No more masks! No more mythologies!"*

MR: And then the myth begins again. At that moment "No more masks! No more mythologies!" the god lifts his hand.

NYQ: *Then it is an acceptance actually.*

MR: As soon as the refusal is made. It's a movement that brings together things that are very far apart. That is what I care about very much.

NYQ: *Robert Payne says you have "Launched a new and serious mythology, a mythology in which people of the world assume heroic and even divine stature," that you have "Charted a landscape of hope." Do you remember those words?*

MR: I remember them very gratefully, when I lose hope. But it is in that relation of the least human impulse—there is no scale in any of this. That landscape is without scale.

NYQ: *Each person can have his little personal hope as well as a large landscape of hope.*

MR: And personal despair.

NYQ: *Besides poetry, you have written prose and you said researching for your biography* The Traces of Thomas Hariot *led to the "Outer Banks." Has this happened in other cases?*

MR: It was the Outer Banks that led me to Hariot and then Hariot led me to the poem. But I had gone to the Outer Banks long before I knew there was a Hariot. I went to the Outer Banks years ago interested in flight and the Wright Brothers. And in beaches. As a child I played on sandbars here. Sand means very much to me, because my father's business in the building of the city was sand and gravel. This is a poured city. This is a concrete city by now, and when people speak of concrete poetry it should be of poured poetry and I wish to do my kind of concrete poems.

NYQ: *Do you think that the writing of poetry serves as a discipline for the writing of prose?*

MR: The writing of poetry is a discipline for many things. Prose is really a footnote to the poems. The Hariot book is a footnote to the Outer Banks poem. The Gibbs book was a footnote to the Gibbs poem. And I don't know what in the future. They have also been ways of surviving, during the writing of poems. They were a sustained work. If I hadn't had to do that I might just have done the reading. And not done . . . I don't know. I have no way of knowing. They became obsessive hunts. Each of them was having to look for the material. I haven't been particularly interested in doing anything where the work had already been done.

NYQ: *You did say that in prose the search may be for the* mot juste. *But in poetry you have to go further and find the* sound juste *too.*

MR: The sound structure in prose is certainly part of it.

NYQ: *But don't you think it's more important in poetry?*

MR: I think everything is more important in poetry.

NYQ: *Your interest in* Akiba *and your poem by that name— Did it spring from your possible descendency from him?*

MR: Our mother told us that we were descended from him. Now that isn't anything that anybody can trace or prove. It was a total gift to a child. My mother was a very strange and nonreading woman, except for the Bible and Emerson. Many of the things that she did and said even when most damaging were marvelously suggestive and open.

NYQ: *Do any of the other poems in your* Lives *have a personal connection? What was the common denominator of the people you have written about? There was a composer, an artist, a painter, a physicist, an anthropologist. Was there anything that drew you to these particular people?*

MR: I think it had something to do with what we were talking about before. The structure of a life being an art form. About the ways of getting past impossibilities by changing phase. The reason I think that I came to do Gibbs was that I needed a language of transformation. I needed a language of a changing phase for the poem. And I needed a language that was not static, that did not see life as a series of points, but more as a language of water, and the things are in all these lives that I try to see in poems. Moving past one phase of one's own life—transformation, and moving past impossibilities. Things seen as impossibilities at the moment . . . Or the transformations that come in any great life. It seems to me that the language of poetry is the best way. Music certainly does hold transformation, but without the verbal meanings that I need. Poetry is a clearer metaphor, if you will. More like a transformation than anything that I know. That meaning is a religious meaning. And a very common plain one too.

NYQ: *How do you account for such an early breakthrough of your own voice as in "Effort at Speech Between Two People" written as an undergraduate?*

MR: I think that was in answer to the silences, the things left out that I wanted to hear about, the—I suppose many of my poems are things that I wanted to hear— and certainly something that has gone through all the way from "Effort at Speech" to a poem called "Fragile" in *Waterlily Fire*—about the nature of speech and what action takes place in speaking. And the relation of speaker and listener.

NYQ: *Doesn't your poem "Waterlily Fire" end on that note?*

MR: No, it's contained within the singing at the demonstration outside of City Hall. It feels like that. The poem "Fragile" that I spoke of relates to something I saw on TV. There was an interview with Suzuki, by an American. . . .

NYQ: *Oh, yes, but those—are they not all different parts of the poem?*

MR: Of the poem called "Waterlily Fire"—when Buddha
        says, "I speak to you, you speak to me"—Can I tell a
        story? What is the most important moment in
        Buddha's life? And Suzuki says, "the moment when
        he holds out the lotus." And the young American says,
        "Isn't that fragile?" And Suzuki says, "I speak to you,
        you speak to me. Is that fragile?"

NYQ: *This element of personalism continues to be strong in
        many of your poems. In your recent poem "Yes, We
        Were Looking at Each Other" published in the sixth
        issue of* The New York Quarterly, *this element seems
        to be fused with a commitment regarding the outside
        world ("We fought violence and knew violence," "We
        hated the inner and outer oppression.") plus also
        a feeling of sensuality and love. William Packard has
        suggested that this might be some sort of an ars poetica.*

MR: Well, certainly all you say and all besides. That's the
        center of it, but it's that in relation with. Even in a
        solitary condition it's in relation with. There is no
        way not to. It's the interior space of one's life. The
        poem seems to be a meeting place just as a person's
        life is a meeting place. And a dance of all these things
        is held, by whatever art can be given to it. We allow it
        because it is perceived as having its art. And it seems
        to me that one's perception is clear or human or not
        obstructed, really, that these things exist and that
        they're life entire and that the great devastating
        activity in life as we know it is to shred all the unities
        one knows. It isn't that one brings life together—it's
        that one will not allow it to be torn apart. And not
        only the wars but the thing that wars are images of,
        the tearing apart of life entire in ourselves and in our
        relations with each other. It isn't a question of making
        them come together. They are together. It's a fighting
        that they not be torn apart and killed that way.

NYQ: *Speaking of wars, would you call some of your poems
        protest poems? There is an element of protest that
        runs through many of your poems. The poem
        "Endless" for instance, or some of the Delta poems or
        "What Have You Brought Home from the Wars?"*

And some of the poems certainly from your book
U.S. I are protest poems against the disease of dust.

MR: I can't stand a lot of things, a lot of things have killed
and mutilated people I love. I will protest all my life.
I am willing to. But I'm a person who makes, much
more than a person who protests, and I think we are
that, and I have decided that wherever I protest from
now on, and a number of people are doing this too
now, I will make something—I will make poems,
plant, feed children, build, but not ever protest without
making something. I think the whole thing must be
made again. I think Beethoven said, "Everything I see
is against my religion," and I feel that way.

NYQ: *Then you want to make an active contribution along*
with your poetry?

MR: I will not protest without making something. I hope
other people will do that.

NYQ: *Some years ago you attended a gathering, quite a few*
years ago, of international poets in Spain.

MR: I landed in Spain by a fluke the first day of the war in
Spain. There wasn't any gathering. Oh, I know what
you mean. It wasn't poets. It was athletes.

NYQ: *But Aragon, Ralph Bates, Stephen Spender and Auden*
were there.

MR: Not at that time, later. This was the first day of the
war. There were no anti-Fascist games. The people
I was among were the Catalans. These were anarchists
—a united front in which anarchists and socialists and
communists were within the republic which won its
war. It was that extraordinary sight of something that
then did not take place. I saw the war won in Spain by
the republic. By the time we left it was at peace, and
people had gone out to help the Madrid armies. But
there was this curious vision of a republic that had
expected help from their brothers from the United
States which had already won for what was the
government. Even the gypsies on the docks in
Barcelona were with this. It was a curious vision of a
twentieth-century world which would not take place.

It may still, but it has been beaten down in place after place, from Spain to Vietnam and many many places in between.

NYQ: *How did you arrive at the title for the poem "Waterlily Fire"?*

MR: That was a fire in New York, a fire that burned one of the Monet waterlily paintings. In that building which cannot burn, the Museum of Modern Art. And I was going there that day and the glass was falling and the firemen were rushing in and the painting was burning.

NYQ: *In that poem you have fused various seemingly unrelated elements—autobiographical, political, philosophical, religious.*

MR: I would have to defend that. I think they are related. I use my . . . I see it as a childhood in New York, the Indians of New York, the building of New York, the demonstration in New York, and underneath that bound by much more than place. The idea of the waterlilies burning, in a fireproof building. And the pilot image was making and discovery of burning things is seen as being fireproof. The gathering of poets, by the way, was really there, because people were singing in City Hall Park, several of the poets. That island was Manhattan and was New York and was us at that time. People do think of these things as seemingly unrelated. I hate to explain poems. This kind of showing I'd be glad to do as with the verbs. Because they are there. I don't work without verbs. I don't work with unrelated elements.

NYQ: *Will you explain your comparison of the techniques used in the writing of modern poetry to the techniques used in the movies or on TV?*

MR: Well, I was trained professionally as a film editor, a film cutter. The work with film is a terribly good exercise for poetry although many people have been seduced away to writing for film. But the concept of sequences, the cutting of sequences of varying length, the frame by frame composition, the use of a traveling image, traveling by the way the film is cut, shot,

projected at a set speed, a sound track or a silent
track, in conjunction with the visual track but can be
brought into bad descriptive verbal things and brought
into marvelous juxtapositions.

NYQ: *Which you have used in your poetry?*

MR: Yes. But I was speaking of exercises. These are games
            actually.

NYQ: *You have said that poetry has no acknowledged place
            in American life today?*

MR: I have in "The Speed of Darkness" four lines which I
            think say it for me. It's called "In Our Time."

                    In our period they say there is free speech.

                    They say there is no penalty for poets.
                    There is no penalty for writing poems.
                    They say this. This is the penalty.

NYQ: *You spoke of fear of poetry.*

MR: That was when I was beginning. It still exists but it's
            in a quite different form now. I have an eleven-year-old
            nephew who said to me the other day, "Most of the
            kids in my class are poets." You have a thing now of
            a great many people writing poems. And a great many
            of the elements of everything, but a kind of
            note-taking. But this was always true. People told lies
            about poems, about poets, and about the rareness, the
            weirdness, of any man or woman involved in writing
            poetry. I have always asked the question in any hall I
            speak in no matter how small or how large: "How
            many of you—all critical questions aside—how many
            of you have ever written a poem?" And I get nervous
            when I ask this. There is a moment of hesitation, and
            then very slowly almost all the hands go up. In a big
            university they will look around to see whether the
            basketball team is putting their hands up. But almost
            everybody—and if I stay around afterwards with any
            luck the five or six people who did not put their hands
            up will come up to me and each will say something

like "Well, I was fifteen, it was a love poem, it stank."
This is a human activity, and they tell us lies about it.

NYQ: *But that's writing poetry. What about reading poetry?*

MR: Well, one doesn't know when a person reads a poem,
         how much is read. Suppose every person in the
         country is writing and is writing bad poems, where are
         we? We then have to come to the critical questions.

NYQ: *How to make a bad poem good.*

MR: Well, if you can make a bad poem good . . . I had a
         very funny job when I was in high school. My English
         teacher asked me to write the tests that were later used
         at Teachers' College here, in which you took a lyric
         and you messed it up four different ways. You made it
         into a kind of rocking Kipling, you made bad free
         verse. It was made up as a test. Five examples were
         given to students and they were asked to say which
         was the real poem and defend their choice. Of course a
         lot of students will choose a messed up variant and
         defend it. So you have only opened the question. The
         fact that the poem is needed by people—when
         people will come out in stormy, rainy weather to hear
         poems—or a marvelous summer night. It's partly
         curiosity and it's partly a need—that you feel the
         culture works against. But there is a real and very
         often a buried need in everyone. And the people who
         cut it out of themselves are deprived and do not know
         they are deprived. They can be reached; they will say
         things like "I haven't had any time for poetry since
         I was fourteen" or "Poetry bores me," and when I hear
         those things I know there is something right
         underneath. But that need in everybody is what comes
         through the devastating inert force that is around us
         now.

NYQ: *Do you feel that the present time provides a fitting
         setting for the poet? You have spoken about the
         Elizabethan age considered the much-vaunted age for
         poetry. But what about the present age?*

MR: Well, one of the attacks on me for writing that Hariot
         book spoke of me as a she-poet—that I had no
         business to be doing this and I was broken for a while

and looked out the window for a while. And then I thought, yes, I am a she-poet. Anything I bring to this is because I am a woman. And this is the thing that was left out of the Elizabethan world, the element that did not exist. Maybe, maybe, maybe that is what one can bring to life.

SELECTED BIBLIOGRAPHY

Body of Waking.

The Early Poems of Octavio Paz, 1935–1955, Bloomington, Ind., Indiana University Press.

The Speed of Darkness, New York, Random House, Inc., 1968.

Breaking Open, New York, Random House, Inc., 1973.

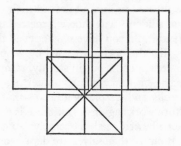

CRAFT INTERVIEW
WITH
RICHARD WILBUR

NYQ: *How long are you likely to work on a poem?*

RICHARD WILBUR: Long enough. Generally pretty long. The last poem I finished concerned a mind reader whom I met in Rome in 1954. Very shortly after I met him, I commenced to think of writing about him. In the intervening years I've now and then jotted down on an envelope, or in a little book, some phrase that might belong to a poem about this man, but it wasn't until three years ago— that is, fourteen years after I met him—that I actually got going on the poem, and now it's taken me three years to finish it. It is, to be sure, a long poem for me, a hundred and some lines. Occasionally I've had the luck to write a poem in a day, but that's not commonly my experience.

NYQ: *When you say, "in a day," do you mean first version or completed?*

RW: Over and done with. I don't actually revise, or it's very seldom that I revise. What I do is write so leisurely that all the revisions occur in thought or in the margins of the page. It can make for a page which is as dense, graphically, as some men's-room walls. Which is not to say that a poem is like going to the men's room.

NYQ: *Is this a recent development, this slow process of writing?*

RW:,   No, I've always been that way. Always extremely slow.
        And I think perhaps it has something to do with my
        respect for the written word—even my own. I don't dare
        set things down, for fear I'll leave them there.

NYQ: *But you do take notes.*

RW:,   I take very, very fragmentary, suggestive or wispy notes.
        I never write out the matter of a whole poem in prose
        or in jottings, and then proceed. I'm aware that some
        august people have done that, but I couldn't do it; I
        think it would take all of the surprise out of the
        experience, so that there wouldn't be any carrot to
        lure me on. Sometimes, to be sure, I've got lost in
        detail toward the end of a long effort, and have made
        a little outline so as to discover its argumentative
        dimension.

NYQ: *What you do write down before, it would be a snatch of*
        an image, a word?

RW:,   A word, yes, or, in a sketchy way, the central idea. Not
        always do these little notes which I put down (and I
        don't keep anything in the way of a continuing
        notebook; I'm not like Ted Roethke), not always do
        these little jottings actually appear in the final poem.
        They're just a way of reminding me that there's a poem I
        might be thinking about.

NYQ: *Do you keep these little notes in any organized fashion?*

RW:,   Pretty disorganized. I have a little blank book in which
        I've been making jottings for perhaps ten years, and I
        may have used fifteen pages of it. And then there are
        scrawled-on scraps and sullied envelopes here and there
        —tucked into that blank book or stuck in the drawers
        of desks.

NYQ:│   *What form does the "carrot" take which lures you on? Is*
        it a vision of a completed, crafted work of art? Or some
        kind of emotion?

RW:,   Both, I should think. I do aim at making a good thing,
        working out a poem which shall be well constructed; at
        the same time I wouldn't be interested in writing a poem
        if it weren't getting a great deal of me and of humanity
        off my chest. I believe I'm not expected to feel this way,

but I agree with Emerson that it's not meter but meter-making argument that's important. To go back to what we were saying earlier, I probably denied too flatly that I do any revisions; but the revisions are likely to be small and local. I showed this poem just finished to Bill Meredith, who's a fine poet and is also the sterling kind of friend who can look at a poem of yours and discuss it neither in a flattering nor in a malicious way. I pretty well trust him. He's pointed out some four words or phrases which he thinks I might profitably tinker with. And I think perhaps I will, in at least two of the cases. But that's the kind of revision I do: finding a better word for the end of some line in a long poem. If there's too much to be done, I tend to throw the poem out altogether.

NYQ: *Do you experience in this process of revision a separate distinct critical faculty?*

RW: I don't know that I can be so analytic about my feelings on such occasions. But I'll try. I do know that, like everybody else, I feel that I have to achieve a certain distance from what I've written before I can mess with it. That must imply, then, that one is allowing the critical faculty a little more prominence and isolation than it had during the process of writing. You become, then, two people, the advocate of your poem as you wrote it and the critic of it. That's dangerous, and should be avoided save when necessary. The poet should be wary of the usurping critic in himself, who is capable of concerning himself with ambition, fashion, publication and book reviewers. The unitary poet, in action, never thinks of such rot.

NYQ: *You wouldn't revise, then, after publication.*

RW: Very seldom. Once or twice I've found that a poem of mine was needlessly confusing, and that a change which was in no way a disreputable concession could increase the precision of the poem, the intelligibility of the poem. I haven't minded making changes of that kind.

NYQ: *You have used notes to explain references and allusions. Do you append those after you have written the poem?*

RW: Yes, it would always occur afterwards. When you offer notes, it's just a matter of being civil. I don't think of it as a patronizing or show-off gesture. There are a great many things which—although I keep my mind fairly busy and self-respecting in intellectual matters—I just don't know and need to be told about. I expect my reader to be tolerant of being told this or that which I happen to have stumbled on. I had a note in my last book in which I unburdened myself of much that I had lately learned about the constellations. I'm sure that many of my readers had not just read the little Simon and Schuster astronomy book which I'd picked up in a drugstore.

NYQ: *Also by using a note you can keep the explanation out of the poem itself?*

RW: Yes, it would be wretched economy to build all one's information into a poem.

NYQ: *Do you have a poet who has served you as a model?*

RW: No, I don't think I've had any *one*. When I was in high school I read all sorts of poets in an extracurricular way —it's so often extracurricularly, I think, that we read the poets who matter to us—and they were as widely separated as Joyce, whose poems are very Elizabethan and conventional, and Eliot, and Hart Crane and Robert Frost. And I read Wordsworth in class with good will though I found much of him damnably earnest, and still do. All of those would add up to a quite varied set of influences and models. And I think that most of my life I've been in luck in this respect. I've seldom been overwhelmed by the influence of any one writer so that what I wrote myself was too imitative. There's a piece of mine that's probably got too much Yeats in it, and which probably resulted from my having taught a seminar on Yeats at Harvard with John Kelleher. There are one or two poems which show how much I've liked Robert Frost or Baudelaire. I expect there are some rhythms out of Gerard Manley Hopkins in my first book, and maybe I stole a word or two from Emily Dickinson somewhere. But I've never enlisted under anyone else.

NYQ: *You don't mention Auden?*

RW: Well, Auden has been a constant delight to me ever since I began to read him. I feel that, at the moment, he's the best presence around—our most civilized, accomplished and heartening poet. I don't know whether at any time I've sounded like him, though Roethke thought my poem "The Undead" showed traces. I can't tell about that. Very often I think we fear that we've been perceptibly influenced by another writer, and yet we're too much ourselves and too safeguarded by our ineptitudes, for it to be perceptible to others.

NYQ: *Or perhaps that influence becomes subconscious.*

RW: Yes, that can happen. Once I was composing a poem called "The Death of a Toad," and at the end of the first stanza of it I had an odd feeling of self-approval, the sort of feeling I don't usually have when I start in to write something. That made me self-mistrustful, and after a few minutes' pondering I became aware that I had reproduced a sequence of adjectives out of Edgar Allan Poe's "Dream-Land," and that's why it felt so proper to me. Needless to say, I revised. I suppose every poet ought to be wary of self-approval, it most likely indicates that there's some kind of hidden thievery operating.

NYQ: *Do you have periods when you're not writing?*

RW: Indeed I do. I suspect that everybody has dry periods. One advantage of getting older is that you have been through it before and before and before: though it doesn't do very *much* good, you can tell yourself that you will come out of it, that you will write again, and therefore you can stay somewhat this side of despair. It's odd, isn't it, that when you have written, and it's mattered to you and to other people, you feel guilty as well as impotent when you're not writing. I don't think this necessarily has anything to do with the parable of the Talents, but you do feel a kind of guilt—or is it shame —as if you were not being quite a man.

NYQ: *How long are such dry periods likely to last?*

RW: They've lasted for many months with me. Happily, I've never had to go through a whole year without getting my hand in again, however briefly. One thing I do when I find that nothing is coming out of me, is to turn to translation—a risky thing to do, of course, because translation is easier to do than your own work, and it can be a way of distracting yourself from poems of your own which you might do if you left yourself exposed to the pain of your impotence.

NYQ: *Do you have a work schedule?*

RW: No, I've never had a schedule. I go simply by impulse, whim. What I do try to do is to keep my life uncluttered when I'm not teaching, and therefore be able to harden to the first whisper of any idea. I very much mistrust, for myself at any rate, the idea of sitting down clerkishly every day at a certain hour and making verses. The Trollope regimen won't do for poets. What would happen in my case, I think, is that I would write more poems, but I would write my poem about the mind reader ten years before it was ripe and spoil it. Oh, I may have spoiled it now, but it would have been worse if I had done it back then in the fifties.

NYQ: *Could this method of working have to do with the fact that you write short poems?*

RW: That's quite true, I think. When you're engaged in a long poem you do have to keep plugging at it, or thinking of plugging at it, because you're waiting not for one inspiration but for a sequence of inspirations. Also because, I think, in any long poem there are going to be non-Crocean stretches, connective tissue. There are going to be architectural problems which you can face and cope with in a state of imperfect frenzy. I remember Robert Frost, one time, talking about the dullness of Wordsworth. He used "dullness" as a term of approval, speaking of Wordsworth's willingness to write prosaically so as to fulfill the structure of his longer poems and make bridges between his more intense passages.

NYQ: *Do you find, just averaging things out, that you're more of a day or night writer, more of a summer than a winter writer?*

RW: I've never figured it out in a seasonal way. I've got to pay some attention to that and see if Cyril Connolly is right. He said something about the month of October, I think. He said if you're going to write a work of genius

you will do it in October. I expect that was a little
personal.

NYQ: *Probably, Keats wrote his great Odes in the spring.*

RW: I used to be a night person, used to be able to work until
three or four in the morning, and now I find that I get
sleepy after midnight, and do a little better at other
hours of the day. Unfortunately, I'm not old enough yet
to be an early morning person. I sleep extremely well in
the morning, and can't get up at five as some of my
slightly older friends do. I'm stuck with the middle of
the day, alas—the period in which the phone rings and
people drop in on you.

NYQ: *On to less practical subjects. What is the importance,
in your mind, of traditional forms of poetry? Are they
essential?*

RW: If by traditional forms we mean meters, stanzas, rhymes,
that kind of thing, I don't think any of those has any
meaning in itself or is absolutely essential to poetry.
There are some poets who are no good at these things.
William Carlos Williams fully proved in his early work
that he was no good at writing with the help of such
means. He found himself, and began to delight us, when
he moved into the use of a kind of controlled free verse.
And I have no case whatever against controlled free
verse. Yet I think it is absurd to feel that free verse—
which has only been with us in America for a little over
a hundred years—has definitely "replaced" measure and
rhyme and other traditional instruments. Precisely
because trimeter, for example, doesn't mean anything,
there's no reason why it shouldn't be put to good use
now and tomorrow. It's not inherently dated, and, in
ways one really needn't go into, meter, rhyme and the
like are, or can be, serviceable for people who know how
to handle them well.

NYQ: *Perhaps their demands put your imagination into places
it wouldn't go otherwise?*

RW: Yes, that's something which is not always recognized,
the freeing effect of a lot of traditional techniques. They
are not simply a strait jacket, they can also liberate
you from whatever narrow track your own mind is

running on, and prompt it to be loose and inventive, to
entertain possibilities it hadn't foreseen.

NYQ: *Do you ever write a poem just for whimsy, a toy poem of*
just pure craft and little else?

RW: I have a desire to go for broke, I think, whenever I start
writing. I find it hard to do anything which is
foredoomed to triviality or to the character of an exercise,
although I don't mind at all writing children's poems—
I've been doing some of that. That's a conscious step,
however, into another genre of poetry in which your
expectations change.

NYQ: *How about traditional forms, like the elegy?*

RW: Well, you're working in such a case with certain
expectations of the convention; and, of course, you're
working against them. If you can't make it new you
won't allow it out of the shop. It is a help to have a
form that you're working with and against. I teach
Milton here very often, and I suppose the greatest
example of working with and against a convention is
"Lycidas."

NYQ: *Is bad art bad, then, in a contemporary way? That is, it*
seems that in order to be a trumpet player you at least
have to know how to move your fingers to call yourself
one, or know how to draw in order to call yourself a
painter. What do you have to know in order to call
yourself a poet?

RW: There are no widely acknowledged qualifications at
present. I'm on the Board of the Wesleyan University
Press. Actually, I've been on a year's leave from the
Board, because I got sick of reading poetry, and I've
just gone back. Rather grudgingly, too, because I don't
feel very much attuned to a fair part of the work now
being done. I don't feel able to distinguish between the
better and the worse of it, because the fashionable
aesthetics seem to me so distressing. I don't like, I can't
adjust to, simplistic political poetry, the crowd-pleasing
sort of anti-Vietnam poem. I can't adjust to the kind of
black poetry that simply cusses and hollers artlessly. And
most of all I can't adjust to the sort of poem, which is
mechanically, prosaically "irrational," which is often

self-pitying, which starts all its sentences with "I," and
which writes constantly out of a limply weird subjective
world. There is an awful lot of that being produced. If
you are given a box containing twenty manuscripts of
verse, and eighteen of them are in that style, it's in the
first place depressing, and in the second place you are
unable for weariness to say that this is better than that.
It's bad to be bored out of exerting one's critical faculty.
I imagine that a lot of poetry which is deranged in a
mild way, and more silly than funny, is trying to suggest
drug experience, trying to borrow something from the
excitement that was recently felt about the drug
experience. There are even some good poets, writing in
other styles, whom I suspect of having been subtly
influenced by the drug cult's notion that vision and
self-transcendence are easily come by. It's not so, of
course; it's hard and rare as hell to get beyond yourself.
Beside yourself is another matter. I like Robert Frost's
saying that before you can be interpersonal you have to
be personal. It seems to me that's what Timothy Leary
forgot.

NYQ: *Would you, then, agree with the statement by Valery
that "a man is a poet if his imagination is stimulated by
disciplines"? Some kind of discipline.*

RW: Yes, I would agree. The idea of letting go is very
attractive to people nowadays; for some, finger painting
and happenings are the norms of the art experience. But
I don't think the kind of art you and I like to consume
was ever produced in a spirit of simply letting go. One
only arrives at a useful precision in spontaneous art if
there's been a lot of discipline in one's life earlier. Dr.
Johnson said, "What is written without effort is in
general read without pleasure." I have trouble with some
of my students and some of my friends at the moment
about this matter of precision. I always say that art
ought to be a trap for the reader to fall into, and that
he ought to know when he is caught, and what has
caught him. There are some people like Jim Dickey who
express a blithe willingness to have the reader's
subjectivity collaborate with the poet's in producing a
hybrid which will be the reader's experience of the poet's
words. I think I'm less generous than he in this matter,

and that, given a good reader, a good poet should make him think and feel precisely what he wants to and nothing else. But perhaps I've overstated my case. It is obvious that we all take possession of art as we can, in the light of our own feelings and experience—every statue is going to be different for every beholder, depending on where he stands, but having admitted that I'm all for demanding of the artist a maximum control of his audience. One of the few ways of judging a poem or a painting is to say that it does or does not make you experience it within a certain range of meanings.

NYQ: *In a recent interview Jorge Luis Borges suggested he thought the way poetry worked on people's imagination to "trap" them, as you say, was through metaphor. That the poem as a whole was a metaphor which brought the reader from the concrete to the abstract. How do you respond to that?*

RW: I think it would be true of some poems I've written, like "The Beacon," which is all one metaphor. The poem is thinking about how much we can know of the world, what the kingdom or province of human thought is, and the poem does its thinking in terms of a lighthouse, and the sea and night. There are a lot of lesser but connected figures in the poem, mostly having to do with ideas of empire, province, kingdom, domain. I'm sure that I could think of a good many other poems which could be reduced in this manner to a field of thought and a scene or situation in which the thought is embodied. I know that's true, for example, of my more recent poem, "On the Marginal Way." There are certain —I shan't say what all the thoughts of that poem are about—but there are certain thoughts on tap, and they're all connected with the stones of a particular cove off the shore of Maine, and the geological history of those stones, and their changing aspect as the light changes, as the sea rises and falls back. I don't think all poems can be described in this way. It seems to me that there are some quite fine and legitimate poems in which the one really pervasive element is the argument, and the metaphors and other figures appear as illustrations of it, are treated in a subordinated fashion. I think a dramatic poem might well do that.

NYQ: *Then the argument would be what would, in a sense, hold the poem together?*

RW: Yes. Metaphor, in the small sense and the large, is the main property of poetry. But there are other elements in poetry, and I see no reason why any of these shouldn't be lead dog once in a while. You wouldn't want to blackball certain epigrams for being nonfigurative. Much modern French poetry, and some English poetry written under French inspiration, suffer from being wholly metaphorical, wholly lacking in statement and thus too difficult to get ahold of. It's interesting to turn back to the Metaphysicals and discover how, in spite of what we were once told about them, the figures are often not sustained and a dramatic argument is the thing most prominent.

NYQ: *On the question of personal style, do you feel your poetry has been evolving or is evolving into new modes and styles?*

RW: I've never tried to initiate blue periods or green periods in my work, and I've always distrusted self-manipulation. All I can say about that matter is that, yes, I do feel changes of direction beginning, but that I can't offer any prognosis. It would seem wrong for me to know or to guess. I'm getting older, and, as Bill Williams said, age gives as it takes away, and I'm just going to wait and see what age gives. Undoubtedly it will give new perspectives.

NYQ: *Do you feel that your later work, as in "Walking to Sleep" might tend to be less ornate than the earlier poetry? The language more simplified and direct.*

RW: I think that's probably so. Another way of saying it might be to say that there is less gaiety in the later poems. I do think that, very often, what may have seemed ornate or decorative in earlier poems was, for me at any rate, an expression of exuberance. I expect that progression may continue, but I do hope not to end in a dull sincerity. I hope to preserve some feeling of exuberance. To lack it is to lack one access to the truth of the world.

NYQ: *You teach classes in literature and in writing? How do you go about teaching literature class?*

RW: I don't think there's anything peculiar about the way I do it. The course I was teaching this year started with Anne Bradstreet and ended in the middle of Williams. It was inevitably somewhat cursory, but perhaps a little less silly than most survey courses in that almost our whole business consisted of the study of individual poems —putting them on the slide, as Ezra Pound said—and understanding, for example, as well as we could, four poems of Anne Bradstreet before going on to Taylor, and doing four of Taylor before we went on to Philip Freneau—in some cases, of course, slowing down and being very careful that we understood what Whitman was up to in the whole of "Song of Myself." I suppose that I do about ten or fifteen minutes worth of generalizing in a class meeting of about an hour and a half, and for the rest I simply talk over with my students —who this year were simply marvelous in their preparation, intelligence and enthusiasm—what's going on in a poem line by line, and, where we can, how this poem might be illuminated by comparison to its neighbor, or why William Carlos Williams' poem "The Catholic Bells" reminds us of Walt Whitman. That kind of thing.

NYQ: *When you go line by line are you trying to determine what the poem "means" or how it was made?*

RW: I think we do both. We talk about how it got its effects, how it made its points, but also what the general position of the poet seems to be—not so much position as concern; that's what we aim at finding out, what's eating the poet. Of course, every now and then there's a dissenter from the method who would prefer to have a somewhat more swooning and less argumentative relation to the poem. My answer to that is that what we do is what can be done in the classroom, and that while extracurricular swooning is admirable, we simply cannot swoon profitably in class. I'm probably making it sound too dry. It isn't dry at all, and we always read the poems aloud. And we allow ourselves parenthetical wows.

NYQ: *Many teachers try to impose symbols and meanings on a poem. How do you feel about that?*

RW: I try to be uncertain even where I feel pretty strongly, not to impose any one way of reading, and to entertain seriously every decent suggestion which comes from the floor. The only time I've stamped my foot this year was when somebody took too seriously the girl-drying-her-hair simile in "Birches" and suggested that the whole poem had to do with climbing girls. I wouldn't have that.

NYQ: *How would you scotch that kind of thing?*

RW: In this case I simply said no, no, and I wouldn't talk about it because it seemed to me so intolerably untrue. But that was, I think, the only time that I ever played authoritarian this year. It won't do to do that; and I'm not in the least disposed to impose archetypal, Freudian or other patterns on the poems we read. In general my attitude about criticism and about teaching is that you look at the thing and see what it wants you to say about it.

NYQ: *You've lived in Europe; could you compare the state of poetry teaching here to that in Europe?*

RW: I think we probably do it much better than they do it in Europe. That's my guess. I'm judging mainly from the attitude of foreign students who come here and are astonished by the openness of our discussions. The French student is likely to be extremely docile and to have been taught to treat the great poetry and drama of his tradition in a very prescribed manner. There are certain things he *is* to find, so that he can answer questions about them on important examinations. I don't think that we feel there are obligatory findings to be made; and indeed I'm glad when people go off on tangents, if they're not perfectly mad. I'm glad to see people take poetry personally—I guess that's what it amounts to.

NYQ: *From your experience with your poetry writing class, are there any poets whom you detect to be large influences on the present generation of young people?*

RW: Oh, I suppose I couldn't produce any names which would surprise you. Any poets in Untermeyer's *Anthology* are likely to be having a continuing effect. It seems to me that most of my students are interested in

Stevens, in Pound, in Williams, in others of that great
generation. But the ones who are very strong about
poetry, and very concerned with writing their own, also
attach themselves to writers of the moment, like
Creeley, Snodgrass, Ginsberg—it's a very long list. Most
current styles seem to have their adherents, in one year
or another. If you'd asked me the question last year, I
think I would have said that people who write a kind of
trickly confessional poetry were the strongest influences
on our students. But this year I noticed in our
verse-writing seminar (in which I don't try to coerce
people at all into writing this way or that) an astonishing
number of voluntary villanelles, sonnets, quatrains and
so on.

NYQ: *Any foreign poets influencing your students? Baudelaire,
         for instance.*

RW: The individual student poet, who is also a French major
         may well catch fire from Baudelaire, as a student of
         German may learn from Rilke. But there seems to be no
         foreign poet in fashion, not even Neruda.

NYQ: *What do you do in your verse-writing seminar?*

RW: I ask them to write an original poem every other week.
         These poems are printed up, anonymously, and
         distributed to the class. We criticize them collectively. I
         also criticize them myself in writing. For the odd weeks,
         I suggest various well-tried exercises—I'll have them
         write a riddle, for example. Once in every semester I'll
         ask that they look through a dictionary of poetic forms,
         find some form which interests them and write in it. But
         that's as far as I go in that way. Then I'll suggest things
         of this sort: I'll say, "It's generally thought enhancing to
         compare aeroplanes to birds; make a comparison of the
         reverse nature, comparing something that is presumably
         exalted to something that is presumably on a lower
         imaginative plane." Some students will find that such an
         exercise jars their imaginations in a good way; for
         others it'll make no difference at all.

NYQ: *"The worlds revolve like ancient women gathering fuel
         in vacant lots?"*

RW: That's right, that's exactly the kind of thing I hope to
         get by that exercise. I have a number of others, all of

which are meant simply to shake up the mind a little,
to disturb its habits.

NYQ: *Wesleyan just recently admitted women. How is it having
co'eds in the class?*

RW: It's very civilizing. There are qualities of feeling missing
from any poetry class if you don't have girls there. And
the effect of it is to mature the male students very
rapidly. I think they don't linger in their prep-school
or high-school attitudes very long if there are girls with
them, raising the tone and legitimizing delicacy.

NYQ: *Do you think there are different difficulties with which
male and female poets have to contend?*

RW: There used to be special difficulties for men, way back
when I was first thinking of writing poetry. When I was
an undergraduate at Amherst, poetry was associated by
some with effeminacy, and I knew one man at Amherst, a
poet and teacher, who rather overstressed his abilities as
a boxer in order to reassure the world about his
masculinity. There's none of that any more. I'm very
sure that it's possible to distinguish between male and
female sensibilities—but I should think that there's now
no subject matter that you would expect to find in a
man's book but not in a woman's. Everyone seems to
have access to everything, and the girls seem to have
found out how to write about the whole range of
masculine topics.

NYQ: *You don't think a man might not have the problem of
saying things just for their own sake whereas a woman
might have more of a problem detaching herself?*

RW: I think women have less capacity for nonsense than men
do. And so, if I understand you, I agree with what
you've said. A man can be a complete abstract-minded
ass in a way in which most women can't be.

NYQ: *Now, we'd like to talk a little about translation. Hayden
Carruth in his recent anthology* The Voice That Is
Great Within Us *describes you in terms of the neo-classic
French dramatists you have spent so much time
translating and refers to your "courtly tone of respect for
order to mask fundamental metaphysical uncertainty."*

*To what extent do you think a poet is attracted to poets
in the languages he has translated?*

RW: Well, it seems to me that Carruth offers a very good
        description of something which happens in Racine. In
        Racine you have the finished and sonorous surface, and
        underneath that an awareness of violence, irrationality,
        disorder. However, if I try to apply Carruth's words to
        myself, as you quote them, it looks as if he's implying
        some kind of faking or bad faith. Is he? That word
        "mask" troubles me. Actually, what he seems to be
        saying was said once before by Theodore Holmes in a
        review in *Poetry*. He said that I had a cheerful, elegant
        surface and a fundamental despair. Where Mr. Holmes
        got his information about my fundamental despair, I
        don't know.

NYQ: *You said you felt you were fortunate in not being
        overwhelmed by any poet enough to imitate him, but
        what about translation as a kind of imitation?*

RW: You write a translation because someone else has written
        a poem which you love and you want to take possession
        of it. I think it also is a matter of imposture, too. You
        want to speak in the voice of that poem, which perhaps
        you could not do in your own poetic person. I think I've
        felt myself drawn to certain jobs of translation in that
        way, feeling that they would be somehow an expansion
        of me, and might perhaps lead to my coping with a
        certain area of subject matter, striking a certain kind
        of attitude, using a certain tone. I detest exercises. I've
        never done any exercises myself, and I've always
        sympathized with my students when they've said, "I
        refuse to do exercises, I'll just write my own stuff, if
        you don't mind." But doing a job of translation can have
        some of the benefits, I suppose, of an exercise. It can be
        an exercise in the use of someone else's palette.

NYQ: *Robert Lowell has said, in reference to translating, that
        poetry is a matter of tone. How do you feel about that?*

RW: I think Lowell was right in saying that. It's not the only
        matter, of course, but it's crucial. The translator must
        catch and convey not only what the poet says but how
        he means it.

NYQ: *Would it be more difficult to translate an ironic tone, do you think?*

RW: Perhaps it's a little harder to translate the special ironic dissonances of a language than to translate the pure vowels of some unqualified emotion. Think how hard it would be to render John Crowe Ransom in Afrikaans. Still, I think anything can be done, with luck.

NYQ: *You have done both translation from poets in languages you are thoroughly familiar with and translating, with help, from languages you don't know. Could you compare the two?*

RW: Translation from languages you don't know works only if poems are well chosen, well assigned, in the first place. And then the linguist must do an extremely good and patient and sustained job of mediation. Working either with Max Hayward or Olga Carlisle, I've asked that the poem be read over and over again in Russian and then, out of my tiny knowledge of Russian, have asked all sorts of detailed questions about the words of the original. I've asked, too, about the meter of the original and its relation to the tone and matter of the poem. I've asked, indeed, almost all of the questions you ask, in a somewhat other way, of yourself while you're composing a poem of your own. Given three days with Max Hayward and a couple of bottles of Scotch, I think you can become quite intimate with two or three Russian poems, and be in a position to take your notes and write something which will be at once faithful and a work of your own.

NYQ: *Has Voznesensky seen your translations of his work?*

RW: Oh, yes. He seems to think well of them, I'm glad to say.

NYQ: *Do you ever have a wish to be doing something else to support yourself aside from translating and teaching?*

RW: Yes, there are other things I've felt an itch to do. I should like to be a farmer. But that, I suppose, would get altogether in the way of writing poetry, it's so hard a life. I've been drawn to a number of other professions, and, of course, one reason I've felt restless at times is that teaching literature and writing poems are far too much the same thing. I find, especially as one grows older and as one outgrows one's initial infatuation with poetry, it's easier to feel after a hard day's preparation and teaching that one has had enough of poetry for the day and doesn't want to go home and write any. At the moment, I think things are working out pretty well. I enjoy teaching and I very much like my students here. I teach only in the fall, and sometime in December I become a free man and write until September. That's good enough. Indeed, I feel pampered.

NYQ: *One final question. Would you recommend poetry as a profession?*

RW: Oh, yes. For someone who doesn't mind a bit of discipline.

NYQ: *What are its advantages and drawbacks?*

RW: There's nothing so wonderful as having constructed something perfectly arbitrary, without any help from anybody else, out of pure delight and self-delight, and then to find that it turns out to be useful to a few others. You have it both ways, if you're lucky: You do exactly as you want to do, you're as lonely and as happy as a child playing with his toy trains, and then it turns out that people are grateful to you for providing them with some sort of emotional machine.

SELECTED BIBLIOGRAPHY

The Poems of Richard Wilbur, New York, Harcourt Brace & World, Inc., 1963.

Opposites, New York, Harcourt Brace Jovanovich, Inc., 1973.

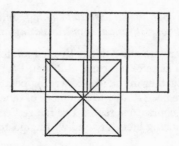

CRAFT INTERVIEW
WITH ROBERT CREELEY

NYQ: *When did you begin writing poetry?*

ROBERT
CREELEY: I didn't write really as a younger man, when I was still in high school, and I think the time I felt it would be a distinct possibility—something I wanted to commit myself to—was when I had just finished school and was contemplating college. At that time in my life I still wanted to be a veterinarian. That was my ambition and I applied for scholarships to the University of Pennsylvania and to Amherst, and also I applied to Harvard. Growing up in Massachusetts that was *Jude the Obscure.* That seemed to be the place. Amherst and the University of Pennsylvania both had good preveterinarian preparation and Harvard, of course, didn't. And I was accepted at all three and given scholarships to Pennsylvania and Amherst. But I chose Harvard. I really did because at that point in my life I decided I wanted to be a writer, not a poet particularly but a writer, and so it was really at Harvard that I began to write in a distinct manner.

NYQ: *What poets have influenced your work?*

RC: Oh, most decisively Charles Olson. Also most decisively, William Carlos Williams. I learned a great deal from Ezra Pound, in the sense that his critical work, his writing about poetry, was to me very decisive. He emphasized the whole condition of writing as a craft, and as a craft separated usefully from academic uses of it or from even, say, senses of literary tradition in an academic context. He really put a very distinct emphasis on the fact that writing is the possibility of doing something, and it has therefore conditions particular to itself and if you intend to be involved with it, you better pay attention to what it is. And really pay attention to what is happening. So, both Pound and Williams at the time I was in college, let's say, were my imagination of what writing could be. I learned a lot from Wallace Stevens. I loved his thinking, I loved the way his mind worked, and I loved the play of his intelligence in his work. It was to me extraordinary and very, very pleasing. But I found that the mode in which he said things wasn't really appropriate to what I had to do.

NYQ: *What about Louis Zukofsky?*

RC: I really didn't come upon Zukofsky's work until I was older. I was introduced to his work by Edward Dahlberg and I was then living in Majorca, and he said that I should get hold of Louis for work to publish in the *Black Mountain Review*. And I was frankly ignorant of him and I dare say a lot of my contemporaries were. Not long after that I met Robert Duncan. He came to live in Majorca for a year. And he had with him Williams' review of Louis' book *Anew*. And he in turn had some texts of Louis', I think. And when I actually held the work in my hands it was instantly something I could use. Its economy, its modality was absolutely attractive to me.

NYQ: *Your work has been described as a bridge from Williams.*

RC: Well, I know what's meant by that. That has to do with literary history, which isn't my interest. Not my ability either.

NYQ: *Under what physical conditions do you work best? At the University of British Columbia, you said if you wanted to change the mood of your poem you changed the color of the paper.*

RG: Not quite. This was the so-called Conference, or gathering of poets, 1963, Vancouver, and the company was extraordinary. Allen Ginsberg and Denise Levertov, Robert Duncan and Charles Olson, Phil Whalen, Margaret Avison, and various other, younger writers and I realized at that point how boxed in my own possibilities had become. Because of the physical habits of my writing. Up to that time I think I wrote primarily on a typewriter; I never wrote anything in longhand or with pencil. Now I have gone almost entirely the other way. I write prose still using a typewriter, but poetry I seem to write entirely in notebooks. Because I realized that I had boxed myself in to a circumstance which only let me write when I was literally in a room with my own typewriter because I never learned to type properly, so I depended on the familiarity with my own typewriter. And also I had to have a particular condition of paper. It all seemed part of a fetishistic circumstance that gave me permission to write. And I really envied Charles and Robert and Allen, all of whom wrote on whatever was at hand. Charles composed on bits of paper, envelopes, anything that was physically to hand, and then he'd work from that collection to the actual draft that he would consider the finished poem. And Allen equally could write anywhere. And that to me was the pleasure that I really coveted. So beginning with *Words,* and altogether in *Pieces* there is a shift from that earlier habit.

NYQ: *That gave you a little more freedom then.*

RG: Far more. It lets you write when you can write instead of when you find yourself in the physically appropriate circumstance—only in a bleakly incidental manner. I tend to write now in a very conventional notebook in a continuity rather than in a series of single instances. I have another book coming out later this year, and it follows the conditions found in *Pieces.* It's a kind of continuity. In fact, I'm hopefully persuading Scribner's not to put in page numbers. I want it to be one continuity instead of a single poem, a single poem, a single poem.

NYQ: *That would make it a little difficult for the person*
        who wants to specify a certain page.

RC: Not any more than in a novel. I don't see why one
        would have that problem. I'm trying to say that the
        poem is not a single instance, not in the kind of text
        I'm interested to get hold of. On the other hand, I
        can't say that it is like the *Cantos* or . . . there is no
        index in the *Cantos,* is there? No. People seem to find
        their way around. Well, *Paterson* doesn't have an index
        either.

NYQ: *In a discussion of yours on free verse, you quote Louis*
        Zukofsky as saying that he wrote "out of deep need."

RC: That made absolute and lovely sense to me. I remember
        Winfield Townley Scott saying to someone younger who
        was interested in writing poems: "If you don't have to
        do it, don't do it." And I think that's reasonable advice
        to give the young. Because they do understandably get
        involved with their sense of the social reality of the poet.
        It's certainly not a thing to do if you don't feel the
        demand upon yourself to do it.

NYQ: *In relation to notebooks, do you keep one nearby at*
        night to note material from dreams?

RC: No I don't, simply because I don't usually recall material
        from dreams. Robert Duncan does a great deal with
        work which has been initiated in dreams. Denise does.
        I don't know if Allen does or doesn't. I think that tends
        to go in and out for him. But myself, I don't tend to get
        material in that way. And frankly, let's say, I wake up in
        the morning and the children are ready to go to school
        and that's where I am in waking up. We live in a
        happily dense kind of family state. The day begins with
        a sort of pleasant abruptness. There really isn't the
        occasion that would permit me the other attention.
        Otherwise I have a shed I work in which is just back of
        the house. I simply go into that shed when I want
        particularly to do something. My wife has another happy
        little shed on the hill. She's a painter and she goes there
        when she wants to do something.

NYQ: *Do your kids have a shed too?*

RC: They have the whole world.

NYQ: *Is there any particular time?*

RC: If usually, I were to recall the times I wrote, I think I
        wrote most, say, starting at eleven in the morning and
        writing until about four in the afternoon. I tend to wake
        up as the day goes on. I can't really do anything in the
        early morning. And by the time the night has come I'm
        almost too excited and I can't sit still long enough. I
        work most easily from midday until late afternoon.

NYQ: *Does the area you live in influence your work?*

RC: We live now in a very pleasant town. It is the most
        extraordinary meld of diverse living styles. There is an
        incredible context of people. Variously the sounds will
        be like some rock group practicing, or some person
        playing a flute walking down the street or kids playing,
        and it is also a small town, not too many cars. One
        thing I deeply respect in this town is that if one is
        working, all you have to do is put a note on the door
        and literally no one will bother you. No one will feel
        offended that you haven't got up to greet them. I have
        friends say that they heard the typewriter and knew I was
        working so didn't come by. We all have that kind of
        respect for each other.

NYQ: *Is it a town of many artistic people?*

RC: Well, we have everything from members of the World
        Bank to members of the Jefferson Airplane, to an
        extraordinary cabinetmaker who has a show presently in
        the Smithsonian, to painters, dairy farmers, to small
        local businessmen, people who commute to the city, a lot
        of hippies, crazily diverse people, two lawyers are our
        neighbors across the way, the lady who wrote the *I Hate
        to Cook* book, Peg Bracken, lives there. One thing it
        does seem to have as a community of circumstance is
        that people who come to live there have really got to the
        other side of this continent. And you can't keep
        thinking of possibilities vaguely over there. Either it is
        going to be made here or it isn't ever going to be found.
        Growing up in New England I understandably had the
        feeling that there were greener fields elsewhere. By the

time you get to the Pacific Ocean you realize that that's as far as the land's going to go.

NYQ: *Is there anything about the climate that affects your writing?*

RC: Well, being born in New England I really love the various climates of the Pacific Coast. There is a kind of lovely shifting weather. The mean temperature is around 65, never very hot, never very cold. A lot of weather comes in from the sea. We have mountains to the back of us so you get a various weather pattern. You have a remarkable diversity of what you call microclimates. You find yourself in a situation where you can move a mile and find yourself in a different environment. It's extraordinary in that way.

NYQ: *What part of California was Robinson Jeffers in?*

RC: Not too far away from us. He was down the coast in Carmel, that area around Big Sur. That's a beautifully dramatic coastline there. When you have mountains literally bordering on the sea, you have a very unstable land form. It's a very dramatic situation in which to live. We live right on the San Andreas fault, it literally goes down the road in front of our house. But that's only one of several, actually. I know that various neighbors are concerned about their houses falling into the sea. We are also right on the edge of the Point Reyes National Seashore.

NYQ: *Do the changes in climate affect your writing?*

RC: I find in a kind of way . . . I tend to a . . . not a cold climate, but coming from New England I like the weather to be decisive, and to be various, and . . . I lived for a time in Guatemala. The heat was . . . I found myself sluggish. I just didn't have the energy I tend to have in a more temperate climate.

NYQ: *Argentina has the same weather as we have, which is reflected in the work of the Argentine poets.*

RC: Sure, I think it's true. I mean the whole so-called sensibilities are based on one's sensual environment, and would seem to be absolutely a modification and/or a condition of what one experiences. I think Jasper Johns,

JAMES DICKEY

MURIEL RUKEYSER

RICHARD WILBUR

ROBERT CREELEY

JACKSON MacLOW

HOWARD MOSS

ERICA JONG

DIANE WAKOSKI

really because of being a Southerner, does do well in a warm climate, and he is thinking about buying land down in St. Martin's in the West Indies, and plans to work down there. It must be hard to get anything done down there, but one can understand that the climate probably is attractive to him.

NYQ: *Do you think there is any connection between the life style of a poet and the so-called life style of his work?*

RC: Well, sometimes it's rather willfully present. For example, the one person I think of instantly would be Charles Bukowski whose life style is very much present in his writing. And not in a strictly parallel sense, but obviously Allen Ginsberg's life style is deeply present in what he has to say. And there are other instances. . . . I remember years ago when I was at college and Wallace Stevens had come to read at Harvard, F. O. Matthiessen had a long conversation with him, and he reported to us that at one point in this conversation, which was very intently involved apropos poetry, Wallace Stevens just suddenly broke off and said, "Wow, what if the boys back at the office could hear me now. . . ." So in that case, the life style had literally no actual connection, and that must have been a very schizophrenic circumstance. I don't think that life style is of necessity reflected in the writing. Or vice versa. I think that's a very interesting fact apropos "creative people," that they just don't conform to a pattern of person. Some of the poets that I have as friends are extraordinarily discreet in their behavior, very formal, very "middle class." Others are quite the contrary.

NYQ: *Well, talking about Allen Ginsberg, as a person is he not quite a gentle . . .*

RC: Extremely gentle and extraordinarily humane. Allen's poetry is, let's say, responsive to kinds of violence he has met in the world, but it has nothing to do with his initiation of that violence. In other words you can be a very gentle man, but if one goes to jail publicly he becomes a jailbird.

NYQ: *What would be your reaction to the statement that unless a poem communicates instantly, the poet rather than the reader has failed?*

RC: I think that's a rather absurd contention. I did once hear an apocryphal but nevertheless lovely story that some people in company with Eliot asked him if he would help them by explaining a particular section of *The Waste Land,* and he simply said, I don't understand it." The assumption that the poet understands all he writes is to me absurd. I don't understand my own children. And I certainly don't understand all of my own poems.

NYQ: *In your opinion, are most contemporary poems ironic? To a greater or lesser degree?*

RC: No. I felt that that was the prevailing mode in the forties. Primarily through Eliot's attitude and his impact on the practice of actual writing then. And also Allen Tate and John Crowe Ransom. Irony gives one a rather quick location of attitudes toward content. It is easily recognized as an attitude and it is a kind of use of what's being said that's pretty simply available. I think irony is one of the simplest attitudes to gain. And make manifest. But I don't think at the moment that irony is one of the . . . it's one of the modes of statement obviously, but I don't think it's the prevailing mode.

NYQ: *But you use some irony?*

RC: As a younger man I used it a great deal. It was simply that that was a way of holding one's own with the dismays and confusions of daily existence. But, at the moment, in my own writing now, it doesn't seem to me to be the most insistent attitude.

NYQ: *You have given your interpretation of the term "free verse" as being related to the literal root of the word "verse." Will you explain that?*

RC: I'm a little confused.

NYQ: *Well, there was a quotation, "If one thinks of the literal root of the word verse, a line, furrow turning—Vertere —he will come to the sense of free verse. . . ."*

RC: I understand . . . well, it's simply to qualify what's meant by free. I don't at all agree with the contention that free verse is like playing tennis without the net.

What I was trying to emphasize was that verse is an activity that doesn't really require attention except as it is happening specifically. Then there are limits and responsibilities that can be recognized. I love that quote of Olson's: "There are limits to what a car will do." If you consider verse as the possibility of a farmer's plowing then that locates what's happening in some specific sense. And the way it turns, as verse does, in contrast to, say, prose, would be an actual place, an actual circumstance, of that turning. If it becomes simply a farmer's meandering all over the field, a farmer who has not as yet mastered either the horses or the plow, it will look simply as such, a man wandering over a surface, whose activity is rather incoherent. Although there will be "lines." And if these do somehow gain a coherence in that wandering, then that will be interesting. I know that Williams, in his later life particularly, began to be very dismayed and depressed and in some ways even confused about what were the actual possibilities of coherence within this context. The very term "free verse" to me indicates a reaction to a previous sense of order, a particular kind of order, that which we had called a poem. One could use set modes of coherence, a sonnet or whatever the mode might be, and could gain a very lovely articulate patterning within that structure. But again, you see, our times, so to speak, have really confronted head on a very altered conception of how the world seems to be. Not only in poetry but in a great variety of contexts. Music, probably, at least in the arts, led the way into that problem and began to make the most articulate solutions. So that free verse is really close to a situation, let's say, that is like the music of Stockhausen or Cage or so many other younger composers. Senses of duration . . . senses of the modality being a diversity instead of one containment. I have felt that to continue forms arbitrarily, no matter how pleasant, the fact that they had been used, was somehow wrong. I didn't want something really new, not necessarily in my own writing, but I did want to know what did the possibilities of coherence have other than what was previously the case. I remember Cage saying he felt it was a little presumptive to tell a hundred and twenty men to sit

quietly and play what you told them to. First of all, it
is extremely expensive to hire a full symphony orchestra.
So therefore he was thinking of this. He also questioned
the kind of music that only used, as he put it, one
quarter of the spectrum of sound that was possible,
while from noise to theoretic silence he pointed out that
so-called classical music only used about a quarter of
that spectrum. He said, being American, he wanted it
all.

NYQ: *Well, do you think it's necessary for a poet to write*
        first in traditional forms?

RC: I think it would be rather regrettable and a little dumb
        not to make use of the full context of what's been done,
        in light of the available material the poet has to draw
        upon. I know in teaching, when I am asked to teach
        classes in writing, I become rather nervous and it almost
        seems to me a little specious for poets or writers
        generally to teach such a "subject." One has all this
        incredible range of example. Just go to your local
        library and see what's been done. I think that if you're
        going to write, reading obviously is part of the process.
        In the lovely sense that Duncan once made clear. He
        said there were times when he couldn't remember if he
        had written something or read it. And therefore any of
        us have to pay attention to the range of the possibilities
        as we have them. On the other hand, I've been reading
        a book on Francis Bacon by John Russell. He is speaking
        in the text of Bacon's respect for and use of previous
        painters. And there would be particular things that
        Bacon had in mind to do. He wanted, for example,
        almost an air of implication or ambiguity, which wasn't
        quite resolved, and he was therefore very interested in
        any painter who could manage that. For example, he
        respects Corbet on the grounds that Corbet really paints
        people naked as actual presences of that nakedness, and
        he said, in contrast, Rubens, for example, and Renoir, I
        think that's the painter he speaks of, gave the whole
        body a kind of lushness that was to him distracting. He
        wanted to see if it was possible to locate that meat in
        a way that wouldn't be descriptive but would be
        presenting, in the sense that Pound says an image
        presents. So when writers look for certain suggestions

or solutions, they find other writers. I think it's very important to emphasize that poets and/or writers are not reading simply to be entertained, or simply to say that they read the right books. They find suggestions and possibilities for their own activity. I read for pleasure obviously, too, but I read also to find out what's possible and who's got some useful answers.

NYQ: *Wallace Stevens said that he never read poetry for fear that he might imitate it.*

RC: Someone might find it out.

NYQ: *Related to your teaching, how do you feel about this in connection with your poetry?*

RC: Well, you see, I began teaching when I was about thirty, and I was both grateful and relieved to find that there was something I could do in the world that had use for others and also gave me an income. Which I then obviously needed as a younger man with a family. Last year, teaching in San Francisco State, and I think coincident with the sad upheaval of education in its daily condition, and also in its attitude toward its own function, I suddenly found myself almost irrevocably bored, really entirely dulled with this insistent confusion. I didn't suddenly get tidy and neat. I was just bored. Bored out of my head and then I unhappily began to be resentful. I was driving, let's say, thirty miles in to teach and then home again, and I wasn't really being asked to go in that frequently, only about twice a week, and we would sit around in this extraordinarily desultory fashion and I couldn't help but feel that I was accepting money under false pretenses, and that off elsewhere all the people I was teaching would be far better . . . and I found myself thinking, why in heaven's name can't you find something specific for your lives, or else get out, go. And I realized that all my students who were stuck in that circumstance were so because they were really rather intimidated by the fact that, at least for the time being, they had an income provided by being in school. Then I questioned their ability to do the kinds of things that majoring in English used to train one to do. Straight-on research, that kind of ability. Reading was extraordinarily desultory if they were

majoring in "creative writing." I thought it was really
sad, I thought it was a fraud to give people a degree in
creative writing. And I felt that gives them no condition
either with respect to writing or the ability to find a
place in the world of some use and self-respect and to
get on with it. It just left them in limbo. To go to the
usual publisher and say, "I got all A's in creative
writing," and to get the answer, "Well, that's nice, you
know, but that isn't going to assure you that your novel
or whatever it is, is going to be published."

Well, it's reflected in a subsequent decision. I had
previously been teaching full time and I was now in my
forties. I was confused, I think, about was I actually
committed to writing, or was I in a sad sense copping
out by leaving teaching? I was living in a town where I
found myself in company with at least a dozen other
younger writers, and I saw them improvising means to
keep themselves together and I thought, well, I really
respect their choices more and more. So I began to
think, do I need to be a full professor at the University
of Buffalo? I mean how much of that do I need? It was
pleasant to take one's family to London for two weeks,
but was that entirely necessary? I mean, if that's the
only way one could find relief from the nine months of
otherwise doing it. So I figured to get out of it as much
as I could. So that when I was teaching I found myself
fresh and responsive to the people I was involved with.
I think the saddest thing in the world is a burnt-out
teacher. You know, plodding on. He or she really resents
the students all the time and has nothing that way to
give them but rancor. So I wanted to cut back to
teaching a semester a year. And I continue happily in an
association with Buffalo because I respect the faculty
and students there. At San Francisco State I sadly didn't.
And it got to be problematic because I certainly liked
the people. But couldn't respect the institution at all.
I think it's a sad, sad place. The sad fact is that I
remember a student once at Buffalo who was a very
active young woman politically. I was very impressed
that she was the possibly usual character of student there,
and that we were getting this thing together. But then
she pointed out to me, very truly and quickly, you know,
frankly, "As far as *all* students in this university are

concerned, I represent 5 per cent at best." That leaves 95 per cent who sadly but truly are the status quo. And who completely refuse to be otherwise. And so it's very hard to avoid the bleak and contemptuous metaphor of the sheep. In a kind of almost goofy or grotesque parallel I went to Juilliard Theatre to hear Virgil Thomson's last opera. Apparently there was the possibility that Kenneth Koch was to do the libretto, and that would have been beautiful. Those two men would have gone together in a beautiful manner. Instead, you have this incredibly tedious and pompous and dull, ridiculous take on Lord Byron. We sat there for three acts. I couldn't believe our own stupidity. I watched the cast come out and take curtain call after curtain call, and this incredible audience—bravo, bravo, and I thought, doesn't anybody in the place have ears? Wasn't anybody there? We really came out looking like we had just seen Dachau for the first time. Just white with shock and outrage. Just incredible— thousands upon thousands of dollars, a Ford Foundation grant, cast of millions, all for this incredible muck. Not that it was just so bad, but it was a travesty—as a thing made of *words*.

NYQ: *Why are some of your poems titled and some of them untitled?*

RC: It seems to me simply that some have no particular relation to a title. A title to me, at least in earlier writing, was most often present to locate a context which was my imagination of the location of the emotional situation being set. So a poem which would be titled "The Kid" had the task of signaling to the reader that this poem would involve some imagination of feeling young, feeling inadequate. Then the poem clarified the particular sense of kidness that I had in mind. It was a way of signaling to the reader or to whoever was listening to the poem that the poem was going to be involved with this particular context. Then I realized that a title might overemphasize something that was going to take place and I really didn't want that to happen in all cases. It didn't seem always to be appropriate.

NYQ: *Gives it away?*

RC: Yes. Gives it away, simply has no use.

NYQ: *You still do title some of your poems?*

RC: Yes, some poems seem to me to need titles. Say, for
        instance, Shakespeare felt his sonnets needed no titles,
        whereas other of his poems he obviously felt did. It
        really speaks better of a poem not to have a title. I
        think of Cummings primarily. He used a title if I
        remember very rarely.

NYQ: *Your poems are characterized by a certain spareness.
        Do they originate in that form? Do you revise?*

RC: No. I certainly deeply respect other poets who work
        through the process of revision. I think the word
        "revision" or "revise" means to see again what has taken
        place, and a poet, say, like Louis Zukofsky has endless
        revisions upon his initial writing. It's like tuning up a
        motor. He really isn't satisfied until all the elements of
        the statement are for him utterly working in congruence.
        I would love to be able to do that at times, but I find
        that I can't go back. I lose the initial energy or impulse.
        And the poems tend to dilute or refute what's been
        said. And that's true both in prose and in poetry. I
        tend not to revise. If something's not working, that is,
        if the motor won't start, I usually give it up and try
        later.

NYQ: *In the original manuscript of "The Finger," which was
        in the* Paris Review, *the first three stanzas only had
        one word change. Then after that it changed
        considerably.*

RC: Yes. What happened there, if you look, you'll see there's
        a false start, and in the full manuscript you would see
        what happens. Those lines are crossed out and then I
        started again at that point and I get past that
        impedence or that difficulty hopefully. When something
        isn't working for me, say, something that's going to go
        on for a while, then I usually stop and then start back
        up and try it again. Like in a car that wasn't getting
        through a ditch. Or else possibly I find a way around it,
        but more usually back up and have another try. And if
        I just can't get through the ditch then I just get out and
        walk home.

NYQ: *Dudley Fitts has called your poems "lyric epigrams."*

RC: Yes. He was reviewing *For Love*. I don't think that the
         basic character in my writing has altered that
         significantly. But I think that the kind of tightness
         that was so insistent in those earlier poems has modified.
         With the kind of emotional crisis one seems to live in
         daily in one's twenties in a difficult situation or
         marriage, there is a need to get it as tightly together as
         it can possibly be done just to survive in the emotional
         nexus, except that emotions seem to be curiously
         diffused and vague. Now I feel much more relaxed and
         therefore don't have that necessity to make everything
         so up tight. I think those early poems, although I
         really liked them when I wrote them, seem to me really
         up tight.

NYQ: *There's a widely influential quotation attributed to you
         —the one about "Form is never more than an extension
         of content." Would you comment on that?*

RC: I still feel that to be true. The thing to be said tends
         to dictate the mode in which it can be said. I really
         believe Charles's contention that there's an appropriate
         way of saying something inherent in the thing to be
         said. Which is really not formally more difficult to
         apprehend than, say, what's the case when you take a
         glass of water and spill it on the ground. It takes
         place on the ground in the nature of itself as water,
         being fluid, etc., and in the context of the ground, that
         nature and circumstance that it's now met with. I found
         that statement actually in a variety of other writers from
         other times. For example, Flaubert says something very
         akin to that in one of his letters. And I remember
         finding it some time after Charles had quoted me, and
         feeling almost dismayed, I was a younger man, that this
         had been said most succinctly—and certainly Emerson
         had it much in mind, in his sense of *spontaneous form*.
         I was thinking of Waggoner's insistence that all
         American verse is from Emerson's, not tutelage but from
         Emerson's perception of its nature. In other words, his
         senses of how poetry takes place were crucial for
         American writers.

NYQ: *What do you think of Peter Jay's descriptive term that
         your works are verbal miniature sculptures?*

RC: I don't really like the word "sculpture" in this context.
I remember there was a lovely thing in Wallace Stevens.
He said something like there are those who speak of
form in poetry as though it were some derivative of
plastic shape. I think the word "sculpture" is a little
assumptive. I can see what he means. But I don't think
poems are sculptured any more. It's like saying someone
is very poetic. I can sympathize with the intention and
the assertion, but if someone took it seriously, then
what would they do? They would have to assume a
three-dimensional condition in the book they were
reading. But the pages didn't fold out or—nothing to
touch. Except old paper.

Some of my best friends are in fact sculptors. But I'm
an absolute failure as a "visual artist." I can't even take
a decent photograph, which is something where one
has every aid. Although I realize being a photographer
is obviously more sophisticated than just having a
camera in your hand. For a long time, as a younger
man, people would qualify my writing as having almost
no experience of visual condition. In fact, all the
writing seemed to take place in a room. Which must
have been very bare indeed, because nothing was ever
reported as being in it. Only two people talking. I
have tried in the last two years writing that simply
says: The road is going this way down the hill and
there are trees here. I mean, I sit down and deliberately
say I want to make a statement of what seems to be
physically actual in this place, and I really don't want
to involve more than that in the statement. I don't feel
I have any particular prowess in the visual aspects of
my work. It really isn't something I can do with much
confidence.

NYQ: *You seem to have many aphorisms in your writing.*

RC: Well, Pound again, in that kind of circumstance he
found really so useful when he spoke of writers, or
poetry, as having several modal possibilities:
phanopoeia, logopoeia and melopoeia, that is. The
writer might be primarily decisive in one or more of
these modes, and probably the phanopoeia situation in
my writing is the weakest. The image-making quality in

my writing is really not what's happening. I think logopoeia—head trips—are what I'd be into.

NYQ: *They say the great poems combine all three.*

RC: All three. Well, one day. Not in my time perhaps.

NYQ: *One poem of yours starts: "How the fact of seeing someone away . . ."*

RC: That's from *Pieces*.

NYQ: *That seems to consist of one aphorism after the other.*

RC: I'm fascinated by the way one states something and this very curious activity, not merely compressing, but this very curious activity follows. For example, I really love people like Wittgenstein who can so state the case that it creates an entire, not merely possibility, but creates an entire *activity* in the statement. As a younger man, for example, when it came time for me to go to college I took college boards and I must report sadly that I was somewhere in the upper two percentile in mathematics whereas in literature and English I was down sluggishly in the middle or lower fifties. At least in that kind of testing I didn't seem to have any particular aptitude, or more than the average aptitude, for what reading and writing seem to involve. In the kind of intellectuality that's involved with mathematics I seem to have a very high ability.

NYQ: *That shows up in your poetry?*

RC: I think that's true. I know people, friends and otherwise, who feel that there are qualifications to understandably make about what I'm doing, really think that I think too much. A generous friend like Allen would say, "We have too much mental garbage in the world and I don't think there should be any more of it." I would not argue that kind of emphasis, but I would not want to get away from the pleasure that thinking can be. I don't think that one can go mindless in order to accomplish experience. It's as much the body as the fingers.

NYQ: *The mind's eye.*

RC: Yes. Well, that is, like Melville's "The eyes are the
        gateway to the soul." Archie Moore charmingly quoted
        that when asked after a particular fight how he
        managed to keep on top of his opponent. "Well," he
        said, "I kept digging his eyes." The eyes are the
        gateway to the soul. He could tell what his opponent
        was into by just watching his eyes. Also the brain
        surfaces in the eyes directly. The physical eye is like the
        brain surfacing. It's where the brain comes to light
        literally. Outward from its own physical place. If you
        put your finger in your eye you put your finger in your
        brain.

NYQ: *You quite often use an unexpected end rhyme. Is this a
        device or does it come to slam the poem shut?*

RC: It comes from impulse and to lock it up, so to speak,
        when it can be locked up.

NYQ: *And you also sometimes end your poems with an
        ingenious turn of thought—with an epigram.*

RC: Yes.

NYQ: *That "Poem for WCW" you end: "In time of trouble a
        wild exultation." Which is almost an oxymoron.*

RC: I know.

NYQ: *Does that derive by any chance as a connotation from
        the words of the Apostle Paul, "Rejoice even in our
        troubles"?*

RC: I wasn't familiar with that. A few weeks ago I found
        myself possessed by the statement, not from this
        particular source, but, "Make a joyful sound unto the
        Lord." And it was always paradoxically true. I found a
        great energy field and paradoxically a great interest in
        voices that had extraordinary and sometimes painful
        difficulty. Other friends regretted that it did prove so
        insistently the case that the ideas came so directly from
        situations of human crisis and pain and agony. "After
        every major war a major literature." It did seem that we
        were energized by situations of extraordinary crisis. And
        that is what I think I meant by the "wild exultation."
        Williams did really seem not merely to thrive on

difficulty but at least in some very actual way to depend upon it.

NYQ: *In his medical career?*

RC: No, in his personal life, I think. The kinds of difficulty he felt as a man were very fruitful. If one goes through his poems, especially his later poems, you find that there are periods of happiness which are not so much meager but they are not the periods in which his most intensive writing took place. Also Charles Olson's emphasis on "the blessing that difficulties are once more." Again, paradoxically and obviously unhappily, human beings tend to find location in difficulty. And find and build happiness.

NYQ: *To speak of images, your images are more of real things.*

RC: Yes. This is what you could call particularism or literalism. I'm by nature and circumstance a very literal man. There was a sign over a diner as one drove from Albuquerque to Santa Fe, and it said: "Ly'n Bragg." For years I drove past that cafe and it never occurred to me that it was a pun. Lie and Brag. I thought that one owner's name was Ly and the other's name was Bragg. As far as being literal, I can be extraordinarily dumb in that way. I begin by believing that you put your name on the cafe and accept it as the name.

NYQ: *Don't you have trouble interpreting cartoons, then?*

RC: You mean such as political cartoons or comic strips? Yes, sometimes I find that I don't get the joke. I find that most truly when I try to tell a joke that has tickled me, and I find that I get so involved with the literal thing that happened that I tend to lose the joke.

NYQ: *Then you would say you do not use surrealistic images?*

RC: With no intention they occur at times, but again they come out of literal states of feeling. They are found in a literal circumstance rather than in fantasy. This book that I've written for Marisol has many surreal situations in it that are literal. They are surreal but they are literal. I was again thinking of Bacon, Francis Bacon, the presences of the images that one finds in his painting are surreal, to put it mildly, but their impact on consciousness come from the fact that they are a literal reality. They're not about something. It has to be actual, otherwise it's simply an echo of something or a description of something that's not present.

NYQ: *In some of your poems you seem to leave it entirely to the reader to create his own images. The poem you have: "Before I Die.|Before I Die.|Before I Die.| Before I Die."*

RC: It's called "Four." There the insistence was not intruding merely but *was* insisting. That insistence was unavoidable. I don't know why, but that's what I was speaking of earlier, that I began to notice about the time I was getting into my forties this sense provoked by biological fact and also other senses provided by experience, that one's life was finite and the condition of what one hoped to do and realize was absolutely contingent on that existence. And so "Before I Die" is a small ritual of that conviction.

NYQ: *You have a period after each line. Is that the finality?*

RC: That's to let it be insistent instead of some accumulating statement. Each time it says it, it is insisting that that be recognized. I wanted it as flat as possible.

NYQ: *To what use do you put punctuation generally?*

RC: Commas are used to make manifest the physical thing being said, for instance. How it should break or how one's feeling of breaking or hesitating or moving takes place. I tend to use question marks when there is otherwise no indication that the thing being said is a question. I really respect Gertrude Stein's notes on punctuation. I can't quickly recall the title of the piece, but it's in a book of her writings that's published by Beacon. She says, why use question marks when the thing being said is obviously a question. Then it's only an addenda. Also like situations: *Why did you come* is a very different statement from: *Why did you come?* "*Why did you come*" with a period seems to me to indicate already a resolution in the speaker's mind that doesn't really want to hear an answer, just wants to experience this person's presence. The period there simply emphasizes that there's already a resolution in the speaker's mind. If you put a question mark, then you do want an answer.

NYQ: *You use punctuation to direct the reading of the poem?*

RC: Sure. I can think of no other use for it. The reading of the poem and the physical way I want it to be said and also at times to clarify simple syntactic circumstances. Like colons or dashes. Semicolons I use very rarely now.

NYQ: *Do you think it's characteristic of contemporary poetry to make the reader as well as the poet work? More in contemporary than in previous poems.*

RC: I wonder. I was thinking of a conversation with Tom Clark a few days ago. We were talking about radio and then we were thinking of various conditions of television reflected in the discussions of the various political candidates for the presidency. One thing that happens to things being said on television is that the sensory demand of all else that's being seen means that the focus upon the thing being said is much diffused and diminished. I was thinking of old-time radio plays in which the door closing and squeaking had incredible effect whereas if you saw a contemporary TV drama with a squeaking door you'd be watching the door and saying, "It looks like it needs oil or something." It wouldn't have nearly the impact. The focus, you see, is diffused because, simply, there is more happening. I therefore wonder what was the experience in a culture where when you heard something and/or read it you didn't have the diversity of other things happening to distract you from that kind of occupation or focus. I think equally that the world changes in its own experience of itself, that humanly we are in a time of great crisis. Not simply political and social but biological. And I think that the apprehension of that, either as a conscious attitude or just intuitively, is going to mean to the reader he is not going to work harder simply to be a good student but simply that the demands upon his consciousness are now very large indeed. Poetry obviously manifests these demands also, and the complexities of "experience" now in our consciousness will occur in poems too. They are going to make great demands on the reader and the writer alike.

NYQ: *Your work is well known for its use of the colloquial.*

RC: It's a language I feel very at home in. One thing that dismayed me when I was still in college was the predominant interest in a poetry which I felt myself excluded from by virtue of diction and social situation. In the same way that, let's say, contemporary black writers feel that the norm of white American writing isn't part of their vocabulary. I felt that to a much lesser degree. Nevertheless, I felt as actually that the writing of Tate or Auden or Eliot was all the habit of diction and therefore of an experience which was not mine. I mean I literally grew up in the Depression years when my mother was a public health nurse in a small New England town. And I sure couldn't come on like T. S. Eliot. It would be absurd. You know. So the colloquial was part of my daily material. John Chamberlain said in a lovely fashion—someone asked him why he used old cars as materials for his sculptures, and he said, Well, Michelangelo seemed to have a lot of marble in his backyard, and what he had was a lot of rusty cars.

NYQ: *Do you ever visualize the work of a poem on the page?*

RC: No, I don't. I'm only interested in the typography and/or the visual appearance insofar as it will inform the reader as something he can hear. I use notation in the same way a composer uses a written score.

NYQ: *Would you say that the subconscious played any part in your poem "The Finger"?*

RC: Yeah. Sure. From the situation that gave it its primary material, the whole experience with LSD. Then, as it came to be written, there was the dictation of that subconscious.

NYQ: *A little different from most of your poems?*

RC: Well—but that woman, whether it be the woman of that particular poem or the poem called "The Woman" in *Words,* or the woman in "The Door," for example. That woman was very insistent, and she comes apparently from my subconscious. In fact, somewhat sadly about two years ago now I really was feeling in some crisis and couldn't locate it, and was in Boston and went to see a psychiatrist at the Massachusetts Medical Center and we got talking very briefly, but then later I went to a psychiatrist in San Francisco for three or four visits and both of them told me that the nexus or the circumstance of this woman for me was not located in a literal person. It wasn't my wife. It wasn't specifically my mother, it wasn't specifically my sister. It wasn't specifically a person who had created this experience, it was a rather dense and complex thing. And so the woman of "The Finger," the guise of that presence, is to me most relieving, really. That woman can also be the woman in a poem called "The Cracks," and she is really pretty scary to me. It's a poem that is toward the end of *For Love*. That woman is really kind of threatening.

NYQ: *You have made the statement: "I write what I don't know."*

RC: That leans heavily on Franz Kline. Mitchel Goodman and Denise were at that time living in the city on Fifteenth Street, and I was having a sort of messed-up time in my own life and was teaching at Black Mountain, and when I was in the city I'd usually stay with them. And I'd go every night to the Cedar and spend time there until four in the morning. Then I'd come home halfway discreet. I didn't make a lot of noise or anything, but I'd babble about what an incredible man Franz Kline was. And Mitch after hearing this morning after morning simply said, "Aren't you really masking the fact that you're spending an awful lot of time in the local bar? I really question Kline, not so much his painting, but I question his whole condition as a painter. Simply that I don't think he pays any attention to other painters." Anyhow I persuaded Mitch to come with me one night and happily Kline was there, and Mitch very politely questioned Kline's interest in painting that might have little to do with his own activities as painter, and he spoke of a particular show of a friend of his that was then on. And Kline said,

"No, I haven't been to see it, but let me tell you what it
looks like." And he described every fact of those
paintings. And Mitch kept saying, "Yes, that's true,
but—" and then Kline would continue to tell him even
the kind of framing. He told him all the dimensions. He
told him every color, he told him the techniques. He
told him, you know, he told him all the physical
qualifications of these paintings. And after he had
finished this recital he then said, "Now, if I paint what
I know, that bores me, if I paint what you know, that
bores you, so I paint what I don't know and I paint
very little of what I do know because that's a repetition
of what's already in hand." That made great sense to me.
Hopefully I write what I don't know. I know in teaching
simply telling people again and again what you know or
what they know, the whole thing sags entirely. So it's a
delight to teach in a circumstance where something's to
be learned. The teacher has equal possibility with the
students. In fact, also one time when I was teaching in
Black Mountain, Olson asked me if I would teach
biology. And I said, "That literally is the one thing I
know nothing about. Somehow I never had it in high
school and didn't have any involvement with it in
college. How can you propose that I teach these college
students?" and he said, "Ideal circumstance, man.
You'll be learning along with them. Which is the best
possible state."

NYQ: *And in this connection, what about poetry readings?*
           What are your feelings about poetry readings?

RC: They're lovely feedback. Sadly, having seen Virgil
           Thomson's opera last night and seeing the audience's
           response to it which was ostensibly one of approval—
           they should have thrown stones at it or some awful
           thing—but anyhow to me public readings are most
           interesting feedback and it doesn't have to be something
           like "Gee, that was a great poem you wrote" and
           discussion of it analytically. One can tell pretty quickly
           what the intuitive response of the audience is, not to
           the performance sense of reading but to the actual
           place that they are given to be as they are hearing
           something. I have lived a great deal of my life in
           isolation humanly speaking, that is, in a very close

intimate nexus of persons . . . I was so extremely shy
that the sense of reading poems in public when I was,
say, twenty-five, that would be impossible . . . I just
literally couldn't see how it could be accomplished.
Then as I got older and got confidence and literally
took the risk, as I think everyone has to, in the world
rather than in some sheltered small place, public
readings began to be a lovely information as to what
was getting through and what wasn't. And I realize too
that there are various kinds of poems that can't be
heard in public and have no reason to be heard in
public, in the sense not that they're private in their
information but they just can't be heard. And going
down in the middle of Times Square and starting to
read one of Shakespeare's sonnets—I don't think many
people would get much out of it. On the other hand,
you could read certain kinds of poems there. I was
teaching the plays of Sophocles to a class of about
twelve people in New Mexico, and they asked, "Does
he have to keep saying, 'I think I see them coming now.'
We saw that a page ago, and here's the lookout saying,
'Here they come even now' and they said that at least
five times. There must be some reason for this." So I
went to look up what was the condition of Greek
theatre and found out that it had a usual audience of
about forty thousand people. So you had to say it five
times to allow for the possibility that someone was
eating popcorn or something else. Readings really give
you a lot of information about what's getting through.
In a kind of intuitive way. For example, Saturday night
I'm going to read up at a friend's loft. In a literal sense
it's a public reading. Probably the audience will be
primarily friends here in the city. That's a good group
to read to because I'm going to get some very useful
information as to what the condition of what I've been
involved with seems to be. It will be really useful to me.

The only times when I don't like public reading is
when it becomes just like show biz. I mean you don't
have to do it fifty thousand times—like Yeats being
asked to read "The Lake Isle of Innisfree" once more.
He apparently loathed being asked to read that poem.
Because that was the poem that everyone wanted him
to read. And he had read it ad nauseam. I think as

Olson put it, one is always interested to read what one has just finished writing.

I've always been suspicious of drama for myself. I think of a friend like Kenneth Koch who has made drama a lovely playful kind of writing. Some of my friends can work very ably in that mode. Duncan is another very different instance. But for me it turns phony. It's false and I can't locate the emotional field and I can't get ahold of it. It tends to blow up the condition of the thing being said in a way I can't keep track of. So dramatic poetry for me is really bad news. I would go again to prose and write a prose narrative, a story. That's the only *drama* that I really have any ability with.

NYQ: *You read your poems in a contained manner.*

RC: Well, I've had a lovely meeting with a lovely old-timer in Los Angeles who wrote a book *The Holy Barbarians,* Lawrence Lipton. Allen Ginsberg took me over to his house to meet him and he had no sooner said hello to me when he said, "You have literally the worst reading style of anyone I have ever heard. I'm going to read you a poem and you take note, young man, and see if you can't improve." A lot of people have come up after I've had a reading and said, "We really felt for you. You seemed so nervous—so distraught—you kept stumbling over the lines." I don't like to argue about it but I say, "Actually I wasn't as nervous as you perhaps thought I was, this is really the way I want those poems to be heard. They are written in an intensity of that order and it is hesitant in what it feels it can say and to read it as though it weren't the case would be to mistake its actual condition."

NYQ: *Different poems require different readings.*

RC: Well, I would hope so. Much as I admire him in roles involved with Sherlock Holmes, I sure don't want Basil Rathbone to be the great reader of our time.

NYQ: *Have you read in connection with the American writers against—*

RC: Yeah, I've read with resistance groups.

NYQ: *What poems of yours would you designate as being protest?*

RC: Very few. A poem called "America" is one such instance. A poem called "The Signboard." But basically I haven't been able to write a poem of direct political protest. I excused myself, but I did not want to let the war, let's say, eat that up too. It's as though you're sitting in the house with your wife and family and it doesn't mean that you're safe but you're aware that you have that as a possibility and you don't want to yield to that other demand entirely. I know that Denise, that dilemma has eaten at her very harshly. It entirely occupies her attention as a writer. And I deeply respect that. But it would be false for me to say it has done that to me. Politically and humanly and socially I protest the war, but I haven't been able to speak of it in the way that she has or that Allen has or that Duncan has or that Robert Bly has. Actually "The Finger" got the largest response I ever got from an audience so involved. I keep thinking if we could simply state or gain a situation of experience that would make the war seem as bleakly and painfully and brutally unnecessary as it obviously is, then possibly people's minds might change concerning it. People might walk away and just refuse it as a commitment. Just not accept its quasi- or phony-serious demand. If the distortion and ridiculousness of that conduct was simply revealed as such and admitted as such, then possibly we could stop. In painfully small instances like refusing to pay taxes insofar as they are used to support the war, but really in ridiculing all those people, I felt that Ed Sanders had possibly come closest than any of us to protesting the war when he got that lovely permission to exorcise the Pentagon—which wasn't really as "funny" as it might seem. I think that kind of address to the war might be very useful. I think that in like sense Abbie Hoffman was an extraordinarily alert political intelligence in his way of demonstrating at the Democratic Convention. I heard a lovely tape of him talking about the whole situation. There were literally four or five yippies present and all the news media were reporting like a takeover of the Democratic Convention. *One is coming tonight. We'll have five thousand federal troops facing*

him, etc. Either walk away or laugh or ridicule them out
of existence. Out of their appropriation of existence.
Once you engage it in terms of argument, it's like tar
baby. You're stuck with it.

NYQ: *Your little poem:*

                    Change

                Turning,
                one wants it all—
                no
                defenses.

         Does that poem have any special significance?

RC: It was written for a friend's birthday—Ted Berrigan—
         and when it was printed it had a dedication to him, and
         it simply is that when there's a demand in one's life that
         one change, it's like Williams': "Men heretofore have
         been unable to realize their wishes. Now that they can
         realize them, they must either change them or
         perish. . . ." And I believe that entirely and when
         there are demands upon one's life that one change,
         there can be no defenses. You know, you can't take
         anything with you. Someone says: Get out of the house
         quickly. It is on fire and momentarily going to collapse,
         you can't start worrying about whether you can save
         the radio or even the baby, bleakly. You have to move.
         You have no defenses against that demand.

NYQ: *Did it have any significance as far as your work is*
         concerned?

RC: Only in the sense that when there was a demand that
         I change, some habit or some circumstance that had
         become a habit and had become reassuring, there was
         no defense that could provide for the possible risk of
         the change involved.

NYQ: *Would you like to comment on what you have termed*
         your present writing and situation generally?

RC: At the moment I'm involved with prose, as it happens.
         I have in mind a short novel using much the same
         approach that I've used with this book for Marisol, and

poetry is interesting to me but I simply haven't been writing it. . . . I've been writing "occasionally" . . . we have something that delights me in Bolinas—birthdays are celebrated endlessly, so people write odes to each other. Those are really the kind of poems I've written mostly in the last six months. They're lovely. You can't throw them away in contempt but then you don't have to worry about them. Now I'm much more able to explore what's on my mind with prose than I am with poetry. This book, *A Day Book*, will be—again coming to that change in my life which moving to the West Coast really meant—not just the change of a physical place but the change I had to get into my own physical consciousness of life, take it in hand and really accept its reality. The poems of the book go through that consciousness.

SELECTED BIBLIOGRAPHY

For Love 1950–1960, New York, Charles Scribner's Sons, 1962.

The Island, New York, Charles Scribner's Sons, 1963.

Pieces, New York, Charles Scribner's Sons, 1969.

Gold Diggers, New York, Charles Scribner's Sons, 1972.

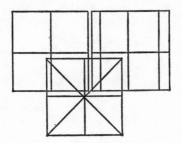

CRAFT INTERVIEW
WITH
JACKSON MACLOW

NYQ: *When did you start writing poetry?*

JACKSON   Sometime in 1937, when I was fifteen. I remember I
MACLOW: wrote a little bit before that, but no poetry. This was
               in my third year of high school.

NYQ: *What kind of poetry?*

JML: The first poetry I really liked was Whitman's and
               Sandburg's—Whitman's was the first poetry that really
               turned me on, and then Sandburg's. The first few
               poems I wrote were very much influenced by Sandburg.
               Then very rapidly I began coming across other poets—
               I ran into Pound's work when I went out to the
               University of Chicago one day to—I wanted to talk to
               Bertrand Russell, who was then teaching there, he was
               a great hero of mine. He was too busy to see me, but I
               went into the bookstore there, and they had a new book
               of Pound's, which was *Culture* (U.S. title, New
               Directions, 1938). And this was so exciting that on the
               way home—I lived in a northern suburb of Chicago
               and the university's on the south side—I stopped in
               the public library downtown and picked up several
               volumes of his poems. Also, I got into contact with the
               editors of *Poetry* around then and used to go up to the
               office to try to get things published, and they used to

tell me, "Why don't you try reading Williams or Eliot?"
And so within that year or so from late '37 to summer
'39 I guess I came in contact with most of the
well-known modern poets up through Auden and
Spender.

NYQ: *Do you think any of them specifically influenced your*
        work then?

JML: Then, or my work in general?

NYQ: *Then, and in general.*

JML: Well, in general, Pound was probably the most
        important of the early influences, and also Whitman.
        There were a lot of people, like Sandburg then and
        Eliot to some extent I guess, off and on. Around the
        same time (mainly through the people at the
        University of Chicago Poetry Club) I began to hear
        about and began reading Donne and the other
        metaphysical poets such as Herbert, and I also found
        Herrick and Shakespeare's sonnets. I remember the
        poetry books I took to the university in September
        1939 were Donne's, and Blake's. Donne was always
        quite an influence.

NYQ: *It's interesting that you came across them in high*
        school.

JML: I used to go to this club of poets that met at the
        University of Chicago. I guess the editor of *Poetry,*
        George Dillon then, suggested I go there. I met several
        people who were friends of mine most of the time after
        that: Paul Goodman, David Sachs and some other
        people. Goodman's poetry was always a very important
        influence. He taught me to say things very straight,
        which wasn't popular in those days. Saying things
        straight, but doing it in a formal way. Then what
        people usually thought of as "straight talk" were poems
        written with a sort of "proletarian" (i.e., Stalinist)
        flourish. Paul's were quite different!

NYQ: *Was Goodman at the university then?*

JML: He was just at the end of his stay. I got there just
        before he got kicked out because of his openness about
        his sex life and related "misdeeds."

NYQ: *Are there any poets who influence your work now?*

JML: I think everything I've ever read influenced me. You mean the modern poets writing now? During the long period from '55 on I was more influenced by composers than poets: first, John Cage, Earle Brown, Christian Wolff and Morton Feldman—later, La Monte Young.

NYQ: *You also compose music, don't you?*

JML: Yes, but many of the poems after 1954 were composed by systematic-chance operations (the way I constructed the *Stanzas* for Iris Lezak, for instance, is a development of the chance operations idea that Cage introduced in music). So during that period (after '54), I guess Cage was the most important influence. Before that, Pound was a very important influence, Pound and Yeats and Donne and Hopkins and Mallarmé, and a lot of others, including Wordsworth, who pointed me in the same direction as Goodman's— toward saying things straight, but in a formal way.

NYQ: *How did you get into composing?*

JML: I studied music from a very early age, from the time I was four on. I went to musical colleges where I studied harmony, theory and piano. I went to the Chicago Musical College and the Northwestern University Musical School when I was in grammar school and high school, so I was doing harmony-class composition then, and I knew how to read music before I could read letters. But I think I started composing seriously at exactly the same time I started writing, when I was fifteen, in 1937.

NYQ: *What were the influences on your composition?*

JML: Ah, gosh, a lot of things. At different times, medieval and Renaissance music, Schoenberg's twelve-tone method for a while, and later Cage. See, at the point where I started using chance operations, the music and the poetry came together, so the same works are very often music and poetry.

NYQ: *When was that?*

JML: At the end of 1954. I had known John for a year or so before that, although I'd first met him at a concert he gave in 1948. He lived in a co-operative community out in Rockland County where other friends of mine lived too. At first, I sniped at him about the idea of chance operations! I talked to him a lot about it. I used to ask, "Why compose by chance? Why not just listen to the crickets?" And he would say, "I do." And toward the end of '54, I was living over here on Avenue C near Tenth Street in New York City. I remember I was invited to a party out there in Rockland County, and I didn't feel like going anywhere. It was just before New Year's 1955. I was thirty-two then. I started writing these "biblical poems"—they were the first ones I wrote using systematic-chance operations, and I was fascinated by them. I thought, "Well, I'll just see what happens." The materials I used were one small die and a copy of the Hebrew Scriptures. Each time I had a decision to make, I threw the die first for the number of times to throw it. Then the first thing I did in writing each "biblical poem" was to throw the die to get a certain structure of numbers of events. That's when I invented a kind of event structure, a kind of event metric, where the number of "events" (words or silences) in each line and the number of lines in each stanza constitute a repeating structure. These numbers were determined by throws of the die. Then I filled out the structure with words taken from the Hebrew Scriptures and silences.

The silences are equal in time to any word that you can think of, so they're indeterminate in length. For each "place" in the event structure, die throws first determined whether the event was to be a word or a silence. If it was to be a word, several die throws would determine (1) whether to count lines from the bottom or the top of a column, (2) which lines so counted should yield the word, and (3) which word in that line was to be put in that place in the poem. I took one word from each column from the beginning of Genesis to Zechariah 9:9. And then eventually the fifth of those was my first "simultaneity," for three voices. The three-line stanza of 21, 21, and 29 events is repeated three times (each biblical poem has as many stanzas as lines in one stanza—the event structure is the first part of each title—e.g., "21, 21, 29, the 5th biblical poem [for 3 simultaneous voices] the 1st "biblical play"), and the words for each "voice" were taken from the same series of columns in the Scriptures (Ezekiel 48:25–Zechariah 9:9). That way there are duplications. The first 4 biblical poems were written between 30 December 1954 and 6 January 1955; the 5th, on 27 January 1955. In the interim I experimented with other types of systematic-chance operations, notably, "translating" the notation of musical works into words via lists culled from various sources. "Machault," written then, "translates" a modern notation of a multiple-text motet by the fourteenth-century French composer Guillaume de Machault, who wrote the mass for the coronation of Jeanne d'Arc's Dauphin, into a gamut of words from a nineteenth-century children's book on natural history. Later I presented the other biblical poems as simultaneities, too. In fact, in my first concert I presented one of the others as a simultaneity.

NYQ: *Have you done any happenings with poetry integrated into them?*

JML: Well, that's what these are—yes. I haven't called them "happenings," I've called them "simultaneities." But they've been on programs of happenings from the beginning of the happenings movement. One of the earliest happenings programs was at the Pratt Institute in May 1960, arranged by Al Hanson. Allan Kaprow was on that, as well as Hanson, George Brecht and others, and I did one of the "simultaneities" with the help of the other composers and students. Gradually, I began to use more and more different elements in "simultaneities." For instance, you'll notice in the *Stanzas* record (in *Alcheringa* No. 4) musical-instrument sounds and noises as well as spoken words read by several poets and artists. Later on, in the middle '60s, I began to use more and more visual elements. For instance, in April 1969 I did a piece for the Whitman festival here at NYU. It was called "Waltspacer," and used prose and verse excerpts and whole short poems by Whitman, which were read by about eight different poets all around the Eisner-Lubin

Auditorium at NYU. One of the other people in the
festival had photographed a lot of portraits of
Whitman for his presentation, so I got copies of those
portraits on slides and I also had a lot of full-color
planetarium slides of nebulae and planets and other
celestial objects, and also Geoff Hendricks' sky slides.
(He photographs the sky all the time.) My wife, Iris
Lezak, the painter, arranged a way of projecting these,
and four or five people ran carousel projectors and
moved the images all around the room (we had
screens in front and paper all around the other three
sides), while the eight poets were at all different
places, moving around the hall, reciting these Whitman
things. And the late Paul Blackburn was there live and
also on a repeating tape, saying, "I contradict myself.
Very well, then, I contradict myself. I am large. I
contain multitudes." This kept repeating throughout.
Jud Yalkut had an eclipse movie going continuously as a
loop in one corner.

I've done several pieces with projections. I did a
"Velikovsky Dice-Song" in which six people read
sentences from Immanuel Velikovsky arranged as
found poems—skinny found poems read over and over
by different people at different times and places all
over the room (we first presented it in the New School
auditorium on Halloween in 1968). That's when I
first used the colored planetarium slides of planets,
nebulae and galaxies—projected alongside
black-and-white pictures of the moon's pitted surface,
and one of a huge meteorite crater in Arizona. (In
later performances we have also used NASA slides of
the moon from the moon, and of the earth from the
moon and outer space.) It is Velikovsky's theory that
anyone who really sees the surface of the moon must
realize that catastrophic events are happening all the
time, that Lyell's hypothesis (the so-called "theory
of uniformity"), which posits only gradual geological
change, can't be true. (The sentence where Velikovsky
says this is one of the six found poems.) The two sets
of slides were projected next to each other in front,
while six readers roamed around the auditorium in the
dark, each carrying a tiny flashlight, a die and copies
of the six short found poems. Whenever each reader

wanted to, he or she would throw the die and then read the poem designated by the number thrown. (That's why it's a "Velikovsky Dice-Song.")

I have also participated in a collectively composed event, "Jacajurismetics," presented in May 1967 at Utica College of Syracuse University. The other composers were the poets Carol Berge and Emmett Williams, the painter Iris Lezak, and the filmmaker Jud Yalkut. At various times in the evening we read solo poems, simultaneities and a sequential permutation poem for five voices by Emmett, as well as showing movies, ringing bells, giving out oranges, letting loose balloons—and other things happened; Iris painted big signs with single words on each, which the audience was encouraged to modify (they also stole them) ; we used a strobe light to make a bluebird on a big black banner Iris made seem to fly; and the students nearly rioted halfway through.

NYQ: *How do you write now? Do you write with a specific presentation of the poem in mind? For example, do you write differently for a simultaneity than you would for the printed page?*

JML: I hardly ever think of writing for the printed page primarily. Not even in writing poems like the odes. I always think of poetry as being primarily speech or song. It's the sound of words even when it looks like it's just for the page.

NYQ: *Do you ever use words primarily or exclusively for the sound, independent of the meaning?*

JML: No.

NYQ: *Even in some of the simultaneity readings?*

JML: No. In all of them the meaning of the words is at least equally important with the sound. Even though I sometimes have things in "sound-poetry" programs, the meaning of the words in my things is always essential. This is true not only of pieces like the simultaneous version of the *Stanzas* (record, in *Alcheringa* 4) and in the "word events," where the performer permutes and combines the phonemes of a single word or phrase in free improvisation. He can make new words and phrases, even sentences, speak or sing syllables or single speech sounds, and so on. Even in these, though, the meaning of the words is very important, whatever words you choose to start with or to make during performances. Occasionally, you may just have an "aaaah" or another vowel sound, and even that's emotionally meaningful the way this is done in performance, in free improvisation.

NYQ: *For one of the simultaneity readings, free structured, you write that the audience could recite words or sounds as they choose.*

JML: They can choose anything from a sound to a whole sentence or paragraph even. Yes, that's the most generalized one, "Thanks," written late in 1960. Anyone present can choose to produce any vocal sound and repeat it or fall silent, then bring in something else (speech sound, word, etc.) and repeat it or not, and keep on going as long as they feel like keeping it going. But I never think of it as only sound—as long as you've got words, you've got meaning, inescapable. Whether it's the lexical meaning of single words or whole sentences. I never think of it in terms of pure sound.

NYQ: *Do you think poetry readings and listening to poetry as it's performed is more important than reading a poem? Should a reader try to read aloud rather than just read?*

JML: I think he always does read aloud. Even if you read silently—if you're reading the poetry you're hearing the sounds.

NYQ: *Yes, unless you're speed reading—for a course in school.*

JML: Well, then, you're not reading poetry. It's impossible to speed read poetry. It's just not poetry that way. If you're not hearing the sounds in your head, you're not reading poetry. The sound of poetry is one important and inescapable dimension of it. All merely "terminological" analysis of poetry is incorrect. For instance, there is a method of practical, structural

analysis of poetry that was first used at the University
of Chicago, a method derived from Aristotle's *Poetics,*
primarily by Paul Goodman and Richard Peter
McKeon, the philosopher. Goodman paid a great deal
of attention to sound when he used this method—see
his *Structure of Literature* (University of Chicago
Press, 1954). But by the time I got there, Paul
Goodman had gotten kicked out, and they were still
using a lot of his same examples, but without Paul's
close attention to the sound. It's all analysis of the
structure of the "terms." Well, that's very important,
but that's only one dimension of it. When I actually
read Paul's thesis, which later became *The Structure of
Literature,* I saw how much attention he paid to the
sound as part of the inner structure of poetry.

NYQ: *Tell us about critics. Do you write criticism yourself?*

JML: Very little. I've written a few reviews over the years,
and some practical and theoretical essays about my
chance-composed work.

NYQ: *Do you think it affects your work? Does it make you
think about things that you hadn't thought of before?*

JML: I don't think so.

NYQ: *Does it make you break your own rules?*

JML: I don't have any general rules, except for those used in
composing or performing specific works. No, I just
don't write very much criticism. If I got more
opportunity to I probably would, but I'm not asked to
review very much, and I don't really go after such
things enough. That's one of my worst troubles, most of
my work is unpublished. I have piles of notebooks of
works unpublished and most untyped.

NYQ: *Do you read much criticism? Are there any critics you
consider important?*

JML: Aristotle, Longinus, Coleridge . . . maybe some of
Eliot's criticism. Of course, I like Goodman's *Structure
of Literature* very much. I used to read more criticism
when I was in Chicago in the early '40s. I used to read
the New Critics, and so on. Pound as a critic was very
influential. And the whole Chicago-Aristotelian

approach: it was part of my main training at Chicago.
That sort of turned me off—that kind of precise
structural analysis turned me off of the impressionistic
kind of criticism, as well as most of the "New Critics."
More recently, well, in the period from the middle
'50s to the middle '60s, John Cage. Not so much his
written criticism as his ideas. Also, in the early '60s,
La Monte Young's ideas influenced me a lot.

NYQ: *The New York Quarterly doesn't publish criticism. Our
emphasis is mainly on the prosody and craft of writing
poetry. What do you think of that approach?*

JML: That interests me much more than the "This is bad
poetry/this is good poetry" type of criticism. I always
feel that there is a cutoff point below which, somehow,
"it isn't poetry," but I think above that, as long as
someone is working seriously—if you don't see it, you're
just not hearing the poem. You can certainly make
choices among them, but they're mainly personal, and
if you can't react positively to some elements of a poem
you have no right to say anything about it. Because
you're not reacting to the poem; you're just being cut
off from it. I tend to be very anticritical in general,
though I read the *New York Review of Books,* more
for the ideas than for the criticism as such.

NYQ: *Getting back to your own work, is there an element
which is paramount—for example, sound, visual
image—?*

JML: That depends on the particular work. I think it
changes a great deal from work to work, because there's
a difference between works written primarily for
performance and those that are more like poems in the
ordinary sense. Sometimes it's the idea; sometimes it's
the idea of how it goes, the experiment itself. A lot of
my experimental works are literally experimental: I'll
think of the idea of how to do something, but I won't
know until it's performed how it will actually come out.
Even the simultaneities range all the way from purely
instrumental musical ones to completely verbal ones,
some of which deal with one particular group of ideas.
For instance, there is a record in the eighth issue of
Aspen of a simultaneity called "The 5 Young Turtle

Asymmetries," and the score is also there. That's all from one little caption in *Natural History Magazine* about how nobody knows where young turtles go to develop into big turtles. They set off on a journey—to somewhere. (Some zoologists think they go to the Sargasso Sea.) I just took that and used chance-selected fragments of the same thing in all five parts, so things just keep repeating. The first set I wrote was for the Utica College piece ("Jacajurismetics"). These are "The 10 Bluebird Asymmetries," where I used the asymmetry method to choose phrases and sentences from two encyclopedia articles on bluebirds. And there's the set in *Alcheringa* 4, the ones for Dr. Howard Levy. All six of those asymmetries are drawn from one little news item, so the poems bring out ideas by reiteration. I do that often with news items. The anthology *Inside Outer Space* (edited by Robert Vas Dias, Doubleday-Anchor Books, New York, 1970) has two long ones about neutron stars.

I did several political poems from news items during the war, such as the one about marines burning villages (*Some/Thing #3,* 1966). In these, reiteration of parts of the news item selected and repeated by use of a systematic-chance method, brings across the idea. My methods after 1954 range from "pure" chance systems, as in most things written from '54 to '60, to those where the material itself is more chosen. Then more and more choices of the performers get into them—choices made during performances (an idea I learned first from the composer Earle Brown).

NYQ: *You have been active as a pacifist and anarchist for about thirty years now. Do you think that poets should be very much involved in political or social or philosophical issues?*

JML: It depends on the poet. If someone isn't interested in such involvement, I don't know who's going to make him do it! I don't think you can say a poet should do anything. It's according to the person. If a person is moved to political action, then he should do political action. If he's disgusted by political action, he should stay away from it. I have always been politically active

in one way or another, so I've written a lot of straight
political poetry. It's not all composed by chance; even
in the chance period, I wrote a lot of direct antiwar
poems. And then there are the political "word events."
The first version of "Word Event" was for George
Brecht, one of the guys who was in our Cage class in
New School. (Cage used to gather people in; he'd say,
"Come sit in on my class," and a lot of us did.) George
does things like exhibiting a white ladder. He also does
events like having two persons coming across a stage
and shaking hands or moving a vase of flowers onto a
piano; that's a *Flowerpiece for the Piano*—you know,
very simple things. So I got this idea of a word event,
because he was doing some one-word poems, like
exhibiting the word "Exit" (on a sign) as a one-word
poem. The idea of a word event, taking one word and
producing all sorts of permutations and combinations
of its sounds by improvisation, began as a
nonemotional sort of working in an uninvolved way.
But I waited a long time, and George never performed
it in Europe, where he was living, so finally in '67 we
had the Angry Arts Week—maybe you remember that
—and they had a "Napalm Poetry Reading" over at
Loeb. I was coming across the park on the way there,
and I couldn't decide what to read. I'd brought a few
things, but I thought, "Oh, I should perform a word
event on 'napalm.' I should do the piece for George
Brecht. He never will." And many other word-event
performances were specifically political and
expressionistic. It started out as a "deadpan" kind of
piece. But that first performance ended up by my
yelling, "NAH! NAH! NAH! NAH! NAH! NAH!"
about a hundred times: "NAH! NAH! NAH! NAH!
NAH! NAH!" Then I did one at the Village Theatre
(later the Fillmore East) on a program with the
Russian poet Voznesensky when he was in town and
agreed to read with us in an antiwar program. The
last piece on that program was my doing a word event
on the phrase "antipersonnel bombs." I just started
with the phrase "antipersonnel bombs," and did
improvisations on it, like,

anti-person, anti-person
I bomb persons, I bomb persons
Aaaaaaaaaannnnnnnn, anti-person bombs, ahhh!

and so on. That was recorded and filmed by Shirley
Clarke. We ran into each other in jail once—after the
Whitehall Street draft board demonstration—and she
said, "You know, I have a recording and movie of
that." She was going to make a movie with that
material, but she never used it, so she gave me my
section of it, along with the tape, so I later blanked
out the other poems on the tape, and in place of those,
I scrambled the improvised word event, changed it
electronically, and so on. So the first part of the tape is
the word event scrambled, and is played with the
movie of my reading direct antiwar poems. Then it
ends up parallel with the movie when I'm doing the
improvisation, and shows the curtain coming down
while I'm still reciting. Somebody's yelling, "You
bastard!" Sounds like someone's after me, but what
actually happened was a poet named Piero Heliczer got
mad because whoever was organizing the program
wouldn't let him read. So he threw a bucket of piss at
the audience. There wasn't a bathroom back of the
stage there, so the poets were using this bucket
backstage. He suddenly tossed it out into the audience
and it just ended the whole thing. They were supposed
to have a big rock festival afterwards with Ed Sanders'
bunch, The Fugs, and all sorts of things—but that was
the end. They just ran down the curtain and shouted,
"All right, everyone out!" and you can hear that on the
tape, too. And so I play that tape with the movie, and
do a live improvisation against the taped one. Now I
have several layers of performances where I have
improvised live against the original tape; I play tapes
along with the original tape, and the movie, and a live
improvisation.

NYQ: *Do you use videotape?*

JML: Yes. But the only thing I've done with it is several
versions of "Tree Movie," a piece I wrote in '61, the

instructions for which are just to focus your camera
onto a tree and leave it there, and keep substituting full
cameras as long as possible. I've never been able to do
it as a movie: I've never had the money. The critics
tell me that Warhol started making all his static
movies from that after reading my instructions for
"Tree Movie." It was published in the Fluxus
newspaper *V TRE* in '64. Warhol's friend Gerry
Malanga got a copy of this paper from me. A few
months later Warhol did *Sleep*, his first static movie.

NYQ: *Have you ever taught poetry?*

JML: I'd like to, but I don't quite know what I would do
about it. I did a course at the Free University of New
York for a short while, where I simply talked about
methods of making simultaneities and other kinds of
pieces that involved all the time arts. I've never really
taught a poetry course, no.

NYQ: *Have you ever been in workshops?*

JML: Yes, very often. I do readings at universities quite a bit,
and very often they'll ask me to do a seminar or
workshop. Robert Vas Dias organized a poetry festival
in July 1971 at Grand Valley State College, near
Grand Rapids, Michigan, a place recently made famous
by Jill Johnston; she wrote a column about going there
to lecture. In that workshop they had me produce with
students a multimedia work. I've performed pieces with
students and read in many courses, like Diane
Wakoski's at the New School, but I haven't run such
courses myself.

NYQ: *Have you participated in workshops with other poets?*

JML: In what sense?

NYQ: *Like Bread Loaf, writing with other people—*

JML: Very little. I was up at Cummington in 1953 for a few
weeks. But, no. In the earlier '60s, serious readings in
coffeehouses began. I met Diane Wakoski around then
through the composer La Monte Young, and she finally
persuaded me to come down to one of them to read.
We used to have open readings at a place over here on
—you remember that?—the Ninth Street Coffeehouse?
It was run by the guy who now runs Max's Kansas City.

A lot of these early sessions were open readings with a
good deal of mutual criticism. It was that kind of
informal workshop we had at readings in the early
'6os. We also had one at the Blue Yak Bookstore—a
place on Tenth Street run by Jerry Rothenberg, Bob
Kelly, George Economou and others—we used to have
workshop sessions there, too.

NYQ: *How do you work physically? Do you have a routine?
How do you write?*

JML: No, I have no routine. When I work on a job, a good
deal of the writing is done on the subway.

NYQ: *Can you write on the subway?*

JML: Most of *Stanzas for Iris Lezak* was done on the subway.
And practically all the *Pronouns* dances were written
on the subway. And I am quite a kitchen writer; the
first biblical poems were all written in my kitchen on
Avenue C. I think I got into the habit when I lived on
Avenue C in an unheated apartment with a little coal
stove. So the only warm room a good deal of the time
was the kitchen. Now that I have a big apartment,
with a big living room, I have a desk I hardly ever use
except to type on. I do most of my writing in the
kitchen.

NYQ: *Do you keep a journal?*

JML: No, but I have. When I was younger I kept a journal
for many years. I haven't done it regularly for many
years. I think somewhere in the '50s I started keeping a
journal for a short time again. The nearest to a journal
I wrote recently were the *Odes for Iris*. That is a series
of formal syllabic odes. The whole series has the same
syllabic pattern, 7,7,7,3—five stanzas of that constitute
the *Odes for Iris* pattern. That series is a journal.

NYQ: *Random technique is the starting point for most of
your poems?*

JML: Sometimes it is, and sometimes it isn't. Sometimes it's
more or less controlled by a chance-operation method.
Lately I've just written freely from one kind of light to
another. The recent "41st Light Poem: for Sharon
Mattlin" started out as one light poem but turned out

to be thirty-one short poems where every so often a kind of light comes in until I've spelled out her whole name.

NYQ: *When you think of a line, do you write it down—do you carry a notebook?*

JML: I usually carry a writing notebook with me, almost always. Whatever is the current book, I carry wherever I go. Now I do much more of my writing at home. It's just a habit—carrying a notebook.

NYQ: *What about single lines that are great, but you can't use them at the moment?*

JML: Yes, I do often jot them down—sure. But the chance-operations things always depend so much on the ongoing process that I don't do that much when I'm writing them. More of them come now in the course of a poem. A line that just comes to me like that will usually generate a whole poem, if I'm writing nonprogrammatically (not using systematic chance alone or the like).

NYQ: *Do you use automatic writing, or stream-of-consciousness writing?*

JML: Sometimes. Not very much. And not when writing purely systematic-chance poetry. When I was younger, I did—in the '30s and '40s. Then I sometimes wrote "from the top of my head."

NYQ: *Did you stop doing it for some special reason?*

JML: No. But now, when I'm not composing poems by chance systems or the like, I'm writing about a particular thing—the way it is. I try to tell it as it is. I think it is very important to tell the news. That's one reason why I like Diane Wakoski's work so much. She's always telling the news.

NYQ: *How long have you lived in New York?*

JML: Since 1943. I got here from Chicago on my twenty-first birthday—12 September 1943.

NYQ: *Do you find New York City affects you specifically as a poet?*

JML: Probably. But just how would be hard to pin down.

NYQ: *Would you write differently if you were still in Chicago?*

JML: Oh, sure. For one thing, I wouldn't write on the subway—the Chicago subway isn't long enough. I don't really know. I have no idea. I think one reason I want to stick around New York is that it's a place where I can arrange performances and get people to perform in my things. Also, here if you make a work that's, say, as much a sculpture as a poem, people will just say, "Oh yes—it's as much a sculpture as a poem." No sweat.

NYQ: *Do you play word games?*

JML: All the time.

NYQ: *Do you ever sit down to write a villanelle or a sonnet— just to work in a certain form?*

JML: I've written a couple hundred sonnets and quite a few villanelles (I got turned onto the villanelle by those of William Empson). Besides, all the chance-operation poems and pieces are partly "word games." And writing the odes was a word game in that those very personal thoughts and feelings had to be fitted into a specific syllabic verse form.

NYQ: *But do you ever sit down to write a sonnet just to write in the sonnet form—like a game?*

JML: I don't think so. When I've written sonnets or villanelles, I think I've done so because I thought I could best say what I wanted to in those verse forms. But, you know, chance-operation work is much more like a game. I invent certain rules and follow them to see what'll happen. But I usually want to say something when I use traditional verse forms.

NYQ: *Do you play games like doing crossword puzzles or making them up?*

JML: Well, sure. I have poems that look like crossword puzzles—a whole series of poems, called "Gathas," that are lettered on graph paper. There's one of them in *Alcheringa* 4, which uses the Great Prajnaparamita

mantram, "Gate Gate Paragate Parasamgate Bodhi
Svaha" ("Gone, Gone, Gone Far Away, Gone over to
the Other Shore, Enlightenment! Hurray!").

NYQ: *What is the most important thing for someone to do
         in performing one of your pieces?*

JML: The main thing in performing a Gatha or any other
         simultaneity of mine is for the performers to listen very
         hard to everything—to other performers, other sounds
         in the room, street noises outside, etc. One must be
         intensely aware, intensely conscious, of the whole
         situation, of the sounds one is producing and of the
         ways one's own sounds affect—change—the total
         situation. One must only produce sounds that one
         really wants to add to that situation. And one must
         often choose to speak softly or fall silent entirely. In
         performing a Gatha, for instance, one can choose to
         circle around in the empty squares until one decides to
         add something new to the situation.

         Thus performing a simultaneity is (or ought to be)
         an intensely communal experience. It demands a great
         deal of tact, consideration and taste. One must care
         about one's fellow performers and the total aural,
         emotional and semantic experience the whole group is
         creating for themselves and the audience (if any).

NYQ: *Do people sometimes perform your simultaneities
         without an audience—except at rehearsals?*

JML: Not only that. I've often passed out parts to everyone
         that has shown up at a public performance. I did this
         at the Kitchen (in the Mercer Arts Center) last May.
         I mingle experienced performers (and sometimes tapes
         of earlier performances) with audience members.
         Everyone participates. The distinction between
         performer and audience vanishes. Everyone in the room
         becomes both.

NYQ: *Do you write concrete poetry?*

JML: Well, before "concrete" began so generally to be used
         as a synonym for "visual," I used to say that all my
         chance-generated work was concrete because it brings
         the words themselves, their sound and their meaning as
         well as their appearance into the foreground. I often

insisted on calling my chance-generated poems
"concrete" because so many people referred to them as
"abstract"—by analogy with abstract painting. One's
attention is directed to the words themselves rather
than to situations, thoughts or feelings which words
may be used to "convey." But later I dropped the
term because it had come—internationally—to be used
to denote poetry of which the visual element was the
most important.

However, many people who consider themselves
concrete poets in the now-accepted visual sense of the
term still consider much of my work concrete in that
sense. Emmett Williams, for instance, included nine
pages of my work in his *Anthology of Concrete Poetry*
(Something Else Press, 1967). But most of my things
that, visually speaking, are concrete poems can also be
used as scores to produce audible performances. They
can be exhibited, like drawings, but also read from—
realized audibly—like musical notation. In fact, John
Cage included one of my Gathas ("Hare Krsna Gatha
4: In Memoriam A. J. Muste") in his anthology
Notations (Something Else Press, 1969).

NYQ: *Do you play with acrostics and anagrams?*

JML: Oh, yes. Acrostic-producing chance is the whole basis
of the many poems in *Stanzas for Iris Lezak*
(Something Else Press, West Glover, Vermont, 1972)
and of the several hundred nonstanzaic poems I call
"Asymmetries." And I've often used gamuts of words
made by recombining some or all of the letters of a
single word, for instance, in *Port-au-Prince,* the first of
*The Twin Plays: Port-Au-Prince and Adams County
Illinois* (Great Bear Pamphlet ⚡10, Something Else
Press, 1966). Also, the word events are really
superanagrams—or more properly speaking
"anaphones"—for you improvise freely, using only the
component sounds of a single word or short phrase.

NYQ: *What do you mean by a "word event"?*

JML: You choose a word or phrase to work with. Then you
analyze it to see how many different speech sounds—
"phonemes"—it contains. In improvising, you may
produce the sounds separately or variously combined

(into words, phrases or sentences), repeat them, sing some of them, prolong the sounds of vowels and nasals, and so on—as in the example I gave earlier, the word event on the phrase "antipersonnel bombs." The earlier (1961) version of the instructions for performing a word event—entitled "A Word Event for George Brecht"—calls for speech only. Also, it allows the performer to produce any sounds the letters of the chosen word can represent, not only just the actual phonemes of the word. However, in the course of performing word events, I came to include more and more singing, but came to restrict myself to the actual phonemes. So eventually (in August 1971) I wrote a new set of instructions (entitled "Word Events(s) for Bici Forbes") that tells the performer to "sing a lot" and eliminates the possibility of including other sounds the component letters may stand for—ones other than the actual phonemes of the word or phrase.

NYQ: *Do you revise much?*

JML: It depends on what kind of poem or piece it is. In these indeterminate pieces, each of whose realizations may be quite different from every other one, the piece itself consists in the description of what to do. The act of performance depends on what you choose as material and on what the performers choose to do with that material. So it's very important to state as exactly as possible what you want. Therefore, I revise that kind of thing a lot. But a chance-generated poem of the determinate kind is unrevisable. The generative method determines the poem. The only things I can revise are mistakes I've made in following out the method.

NYQ: *In what sense are the poems in* Stanzas for Iris Lezak *acrostics?*

JML: They're completely acrostic—stanzaic acrostic. Every one of the *Stanzas* poems is in some way an acrostic of either the title or some other word string. (I call such a series of words an "index string.") Each word of the index string determines a line, and each whole "spelling out" of the index string constitutes one complete stanza. Often I use units (each beginning with an "index letter") longer than single words, such

as phrases or large fragments of sentences or whole
sentences. In some stanzas the units are repeated every
time the letters with which they begin are repeated in
the index string. In other stanzas they aren't repeated.
In the course of writing the *Stanzas,* I eventually
developed forty different "species" of stanzas, which
differ according to the kinds of units they contain and
whether units are repeated. In some species, there is a
mixture of several kinds of units.

After August 1960, when I typed all the stanzas
written up to that time on 5-by-8 filing cards, to use
them as texts for a simultaneity in a program of "New
Music" a group of us presented at the Living Theatre,
I used these filing cards as sources of
"second-generation" stanzaic-acrostic,
systematic-chance poems. The poems so made "mix" all
the different kinds of units in all the *Stanzas* poems
written previously.

NYQ: *Why did you start using acrostic chance methods?*

JML: The reason, I think, that I started using acrostic so
much is that it is much more convenient than number
methods or other ones employing auxiliary means. If
you're riding on a subway, it's hard to work with a
random-digit table or a pair of dice!

NYQ: *Do you still use acrostic chance systems?*

JML: Sometimes. But in January 1963 I began using
something similar to acrostic, which by analogy might
be called "diastic." You see, the Greek root "acro"
refers to the "extremes." In acrostic verse the initial
letters (or sometimes the final letters) of words spell
out the "index words." In diastic, the words of the
verse (or the first words of word strings) have the
letters of the index words in corresponding places—
they "spell" the index words right through ("dia"
means "right through"). For instance, if my index
word was "run," the first word "spelling it out" might
be "rage." But the "u" wouldn't appear at the
beginning of the second word; it would be in the
second "place" of that word, as in "gut." Then "n"
would be in the third place of the third word, as in

"ponderous." Here's an early example of diastic chance verse:

> Orang-Outang (written 8 January 1963)
> *O*ne *f*rom th*a*t Lin*n*aeus,
> Oran*g*-outang.
>
> "Extra*o*rdinary orang-o*u*tang,
> creduli*t*y orang-out*a*ngs,
> Orang-Outa*n*g enunciating *o*rganization—
> *a*rt,
> th*a*t eve*n* change aband*o*n,
> particu*l*ar diligen*t*ly interrel*a*ted Orang-Outa*n*g
>   neighborin*g* *o*riginal *o*rigin le*a*rning."
> Oran*g*-outan*g*.

NYQ: *How does it happen that your title—your "index word" is repeated so often?*

JML: Well, the source was an article about orang-outangs, so as I read through it, taking out the words containing the index letters in the right places, the word "orang-outang," which of course fitted the bill exactly, came up quite often. I often get such repetitions in using diastic methods. I like that. Not only the recurrence itself, but the "feeling of subject matter" it provides.

NYQ: *What other advantages do you find in using acrostic and diastic methods, besides convenience?*

JML: Well, they're both means of composing by chance, since I never know which word or word string will come up next in my reading, and a way of insuring structure in chance-composed poetry, as well as such features of traditional verse as word repetition, alliteration, assonance, consonance and the like. The latter features are even more frequent in diastic than in acrostic verse because of the similarity of placement of the index letters.

NYQ: *Did you start to use acrostic methods because you had to ride the subway a lot?*

JML: No. I thought of the method at home, soon after Iris Lezak had moved in with me, and I wanted to write

something that was both a chance poem and a love
poem. I therefore selected as a source Rabindranath
Tagore's *Gitanjali* (Love-Offerings). I thought of an
index sentence that I'll let you discover for yourself—
two sentences, really. Then I spelled out those
sentences with words as they came up in reading the
Gitanjali. The result was "6 Gitanjali for Iris"
(*Stanzas for Iris Lezak,* pp. 203–8). Here's the first of
them:

6 Gitanjali for Iris (I) (May 1960)

My you
Gain is rainy life
See
The Here end
Gain rainy end again the end see the
Feet. Utter. Cry Know
Is Now,
The outside when Now,
                   (18 seconds of silence)
Is
Life outside void end
The outside
Feet. Utter. Cry Know
My you
Gain is rainy life

NYQ: *Where did you get the number of silence?*

JML: From my random-digit book, *A Million Random Digits
with 100,000 Normal Deviates,* by the Rand
Corporation (The Free Press, Glencoe, Ill., 1955).
Earle Brown told me about tables of scientifically
randomized digits in the middle '50s, but I couldn't
afford to buy one until 1958; I've used it in composing
many poems and pieces since then.

NYQ: *How did you happen to continue using acrostic
methods?*

JML: Well, I was working at the Living Theatre as an actor
that spring—in Pirandello's *Tonight We Improvise*—
and at the end of June they began doing my own play,

The Marrying Maiden, "a play of changes," my first
big chance-generated play. (I wrote it in 1958, using
chance-operational procedures based on those used to
get answers from the *I Ching* [the Chinese classic,
The Book of Changes], along with random digits, and
drawing its words from the *I Ching,* too. John Cage
made magnetic-tape music for it, Judith Malina
directed it, and Julian Beck did the decor.) So I was
always going back and forth from the South Bronx to
the Village on the subway. It was too hard to lug
along my big random-digit book, and people looked at
me strangely if I sat there rolling dice! And other
chance means were equally inconvenient. But reading
a book or magazine and writing something in a
notebook every so often attracted no attention, so I
used variations on the acrostic method begun with the
"6 Gitanjali" over and over. For instance, I was
rereading *Moby Dick* then, so one of the earliest
Stanzas poems is entitled "Call me Ishmael," the
novel's first words, which I used to draw the following
poem from the novel's first few pages:

        Call me Ishmael (May or June 1960)

    Circulation. And long long
    Mind every
    Interest Some how mind and every long

    Coffin about little little
    Money especially
    I shore, having money about especially little

    Cato a little little
    Me extreme
    I sail have me an extreme little

    Cherish and left, left
    Myself extremest
    It see hypos myself and extremest left,

    City a land. Land.
    Mouth; east,
    Is spleen, hand mouth; and east, land.

NYQ: *Where did you get the punctuation and capital letters?*

JML: I arbitrarily capitalized the initial letters of lines in these early ones, as in traditional verse, but the other capitals and the punctuation came from the source—from *Moby Dick,* whenever a word was capitalized or followed by punctuation, it appeared like that in the poem. I even carried over typeface species: Whenever a word appeared in the source in italics, boldface, or boldface italics, it is printed like that in the book.

NYQ: *These stanzas seem to have something in common with the biblical poems—I mean, besides being composed by chance operations.*

JML: Yes. They're both what I call "eventual" verse, because the metrical unit is an "event"—which in the *Stanzas* may be a single word, a phrase, a sentence fragment, a whole sentence or some other word string —or (in the 5 *biblical poems*) a silence. Lines then consist in numbers of events rather than in series of feet, accented syllables or syllables, as in most other kinds of verse. I have used this kind of eventual prosody since 1954 in many different ways: sometimes the numbers of events have been determined by random means (digits, dice, cards, etc.), sometimes by the repetition of acrostic, as in the *Stanzas,* and the Asymmetries (which, though they have broken lines, which give "empty places" on the page that are "read" as silences, still have a basically stanzaic-acrostic structure). However, the Asymmetries often look as if they have no repeating pattern, and many of my earlier chance poems have a different number of events in each line; and when I began using diastic, I began using a nonrepeating prosody, which I have since used often, both with acrostic and diastic determinants, so that much of my chance-generated verse since 1963 has been more akin to "free" than to metrical verse.

NYQ: *The form seems very much determined in these poems.*

JML: Not only the form, but the content as well is determined by chance operations. The only choices I've made have been those of the source (which was often or even usually what I happened to be reading) and the systematic-chance method of selecting words or word strings from the source.

NYQ: *This all seems very impersonal—quite different from what we've learned to expect from poetry: the intensely personal. Is there any particular reason for this?*

JML: Yes. It is a result of a certain interpretation of the Buddhist doctrine that the ego is an illusion. Both John Cage and I were very much influenced by Zen, especially by D. T. Suzuki's seminars in Zen and Kegon Buddhism at Columbia in the middle and late '50s. Cage and, through his influence, I began composing by means of chance operations in the '50s in an attempt to escape the dominance of the ego— especially the personal passions—in art. We wanted to be able to allow the "world"—the Dharmakaya, as the Buddhists term it—the great underlying "Buddha nature" of the world, to express itself in our works, rather than merely our personal egos.

NYQ: *Do you think you succeeded in doing this?*

JML: I don't really know. We did something or other, and the results are quite different from most previous music and poetry. And I feel that they have artistic validity—they are genuine art, and in the case of John's music, great art. Whether we escaped our egos is another question.

NYQ: *Much of your recent work seems intensely personal— the Odes, for instance. Does this mean that you've repudiated Zen Buddhism?*

JML: Not at all. It is just that in the course of using chance operations over many years, I came to realize that the ego is inescapably there, whether one is expressing one's feelings and thoughts or making works by chance operations or other "impersonal" methods. If you invent a method, you invent it and choose to use it— the ego makes that choice just as much as it makes the choice to express feelings about a lover or a war. The "dharmas"—sensations, thoughts, feelings, etc.—came to seem to be more nearly equivalent in status. Letting a sound come to be without interference—or with a minimum of interference—from composers' or performers' egos (which John has done magnificently in his chance-operation work) doesn't seem so different, after all, than letting a feeling or a thought come to be. As one learns in meditation, feelings and thoughts arise just as "impersonally," just as uncontrollably, as sounds or other sensations. I feel that we've extended the possibilities of music and poetry through use of systematic chance, but not that we've invalidated intuitive methods of making art works.

NYQ: *Was your change back to using intuitive methods gradual or sudden?*

JML: Gradual, if anything, but I've never completely avoided composing music and poetry by intuitive methods. Even when I composed most of my work by systematic chance or similar "objective" methods, I was always also writing "subjective" works—mostly love poems and political poems. And now that I'm writing a great deal of poetry directly about my life as I live it, I still also compose by chance methods or the like. Just in January I did a series of poems drawing words from Tennyson's "Princess" poems. Here's one:

Tennyson 1 (1/28/73)

crimson petal,
droops the milk-
white peacock
glimmers on
stars,

huddling slant
purpose waste
hearth
    Arise
but every sound
breadth
    Of
      Autumn,
Shall move

NYQ: *Can you trace the reincorporation of the personal, of the subjective or intuitive, into your poetry?*

JML: Well, I started using very "pure" chance in 1954, and continued to do so until the *Stanzas,* I guess,

which are less "pure" in that I used everything I was
reading as sources: What I happened to be reading
was, after all, a very personal matter. Then more and
more personal elements began to get in as I came to
realize that the ego was involved inescapably, if only in
choices of methods and sources. In writing the first 20
Light Poems, especially (see *22 Light Poems,*
Black Sparrow Press, Los Angeles, 1968) in 1962–63,
I began to mingle choice and chance in different
proportions—for instance, by having directly written
passages "kicked off" by drawing names of kinds of
light from the chart by chance means. Each of the
22 Light Poems (and the equal number I've written
since them) does this differently—as the notes in the
back of the book show in detail.

So from 1962 to the present, I've "played the field":
I've composed by objective chance and other
programmed methods and by the more usual intuitive
or subjective methods, and I've used all sorts of
mixtures of the two principles: the 117 *Odes to Iris*
(1970–71) are intensely personal and often a daily
journal, but they all have the same pattern: 5 four-line
stanzas of which the lines contain respectively 7,7,7
and 3 syllables.

Also the Word Events, though they are indeterminate
pieces in the sense that every performance, even every
one based on the same word or phrase, is completely
different from every other one, are completely personal
and spontaneously intuitive in their process of
realization. Not only was the composition of the sets of
instructions personal, but the performers are
continuously making personal choices. (From 1967 to
1971 I only did the Word Events as solos, but in 1971
began performing them with others—as simultaneities.)
These choices are made during the performances—
spontaneously—a method I first learned from Earle
Brown.

You see, some of the people who played John Cage's
music used to make a realization of a chance piece
ahead of time—before a concert and then play that
—but in Earle's pieces, the idea was for the performer
to play the piece, making the choices right then and
there. That's what happens in the Word Events. You

decide to improvise on a particular word or phrase,
e.g., "environmentally" or "antipersonnel bombs" or
"Central Park," but then you're on your own. You
never know what the actual performance is going to be.
These performances come from within the performers.

Thus it's fair to say that while my poems before 30
December 1954 came from within me, the ones
composed by the earlier, more nearly completely
objective systematic-chance methods came more from
without. Then, as I allowed more and more personal
elements to enter into the chance-generated poems, my
work began again to come more from within. However,
as I said, I've always continued to write personal poems
alongside the systematic-chance work and
"instructional" performance pieces like the general
plans for Word Events. But lately, I've been writing
many more completely personal poems, and almost all
of my recent performance pieces call for spontaneous
personal choices rather than the use of in-performance
chance operations to determine sounds, actions, words,
etc. Nevertheless, there are plenty of more nearly
objectively composed recent poems and pieces, like the
Tennyson series.

NYQ: *Do you worry about not writing?*

JML: Sometimes. Sometimes. For instance, this notebook
contains everything I've written since 19 June 1972.
In other years I would have filled up several notebooks
this size. I've written nothing in February and March.
The last thing I did was a piece for the Swiss composer
George Gruntz, who's writing a jazz opera. He asked
many American poets to write texts for arias in it. He
contacted me last spring when he was in New York,
and at first I felt enthusiastic—recommended poets for
him to contact, etc. But after I'd read over the libretto,
an adaptation of *The Magic Flute*, I couldn't figure
out what the hell to write. Finally, way after his
deadline—just at the end of January—I thought of
adapting the Word-Event method for opera singers.
The general instructions, entitled "An Aria for George
Gruntz," which can be realized outside his opera as
well as within it—I intend to try to do it here soon—
ask the singers themselves to choose a word relevant to

the action at whatever point in the opera he wants
them to do it. Having chosen the word (probably
before the performance), they are asked to improvise a
completely sung Word Event: They sing the different
sounds (phonemes) of the chosen word, combine the
sounds into new words, phrases, sentences, etc., and
sing those, and so on. It's a logical development of my
more recent realizations of Word Events, which contain
a great deal of singing.

Anyway, I haven't written anything, I think, since
then (1/31/73).

NYQ: *Have you been writing any more love poems?*

JML: Yes. Last June and July I wrote a sequence of 31
one-page poems that began being a single Light Poem,
the "41st Light Poem: for Sharon Mattlin—19 June–14
July 1972." As I wrote it, I continually brought into it
kinds of light whose names spelled out Sharon's name,
but after I wrote the first few pages, it seemed obvious
that they are separate poems, even though they're a
connected sequence (I still call them the "41st Light
Poem"). Here are the 3rd and the 29th poems. As you
can see, they do not follow a regular pattern of any
kind. They're quite "free" in all respects:

3rd Poem from the "41st Light Poem"

my fantasies are very literal
I fantasize scenes that may well be
but I'm still filled with wonder when they happen
when we make love together
I live my fantasies

must I burn olive oil
in Aladdin's lamp
to shine a light
magical enough
into these lines
for others to share
this ordinary wonder

I have to write my poems
in natural light

or at least in artificial
full illumination

you & our being together
are not beautiful like anything else
or painted by some kind of beautiful light
but are being itself being light

29th Poem from the "41st Light Poem"

But why can't we always see
everyone's infinite worth
Why must we fall in love
fully to experience another person's value
another person's being
falling in love's pulling back a curtain
or at least a corner of a curtain
The truly enlightened person feels this way
about everyone & everything
Satori's falling in love with all the world

Sharon reality shines thru you & is you
Truth shines from your eyes even when you're
    anxious
Your inward light shines   I speak to it
I *can* speak to your most inward light
with words with caresses with my eyes
The sky's getting light   I sit here writing
I keep trying to say I love you & what it's like
to love you & be loved by you
A natural azure light fills the kitchen window top
I turn off the bulb to see it better   To see

I write quickly as the sky grows lighter
I want to go back & lie beside you as you sleep
I want to see your face when you wake
I want to smile at you & see you smile
I want to stroke you & be stroked by you
I want to kiss you & be kissed by you

NYQ: *That's what you mean by "poetry from within."*

JML: I guess so.

NYQ: *Do you always write longhand?*

JML: Yes, almost always. That's one of my worst troubles, because it's very hard for me to type. I'm a terrible typist, and it takes me a long time to type anything, so I have stacks of notebooks from a long time back—at least a decade! Every so often, I'll type something up, but most of the stuff's untyped. You know, I flunked typing in a high school summer course just before my first year high. Now I halfway look and halfway don't, and I'm never fast. If I go fast I make many mistakes. I think it must take me at least an hour a page to type something and get it neat. It's really hard for me to type.

NYQ: *For writing, do you feel there are certain elements necessary? For instance, do you feel a need to be alone or isolated a certain amount before you can write?*

JML: No. Obviously not, or I couldn't write in the subway— or in my apartment with two lively children doing what children do. (You know, I take care of the children most of the time when they're not in school, although Sharon helps in many ways and stays with them—as a regularly paid sitter—when I'm at work.) I write more when I'm alone, I guess—which is why I write so many things late at night—but I can write with people in the room, and often do.

NYQ: *You don't need a period of isolation every day before you can write?*

JML: No, no. You see, I don't have any regularity—that's my main trouble. . . .

NYQ: *Do you do anything else besides writing poetry? Do you translate poetry?*

JML: Well, obviously, I do many other things besides writing poetry—eat, sleep, make love, teach, take care of my kids. . . . And I not only write other things besides poems—performance pieces, plays, music, but also often draw and paint—used to make assemblages, etc. As for translations, I've done a number of them from Greek, Latin, French and German—but not very many. And hardly any recently.

NYQ: *Do you show unpublished work to friends?*

JML: Yes. Even to people I hardly know—I just showed some to you!

NYQ: *Do you seek advice of friends and other poets, like Ezra Pound?*

JML: I used to send poems to Pound—in the late '40s and early '50s, but he never gave me much useful advice. However, Paul Goodman used to give me useful advice from time to time, and more recently, both John Cage and La Monte Young have provided useful comments. For instance, when I had finished composing the words —the speeches themselves—of *The Marrying Maiden* in summer 1958, I was vacationing out at the Gate Hill Co-op, in Stony Point, New York, where John used to live, and I showed him the completed script. He read it and said, "It's very nice, but if you don't regulate the delivery, they'll just recite it as if it were Shakespeare!" So I worked on it for a year more, trying out different kinds of delivery regulations, and ended up with three types: 5 degrees each of loudness and of speed, and 500 adverbial expressions (ranging from "quickly" to "like a stage Frenchman") regulating the "manner" of delivery. These continually changed the way an actor had to say the lines—sometimes requiring changing speed, loudness and manner several times within one speech. But except for those and a very few other people, I hardly ever ask friends for advice about my work, though I'll often show it to them.

NYQ: *Would you describe your recent computer poems?*

JML: They were very nice. There's some printout from some of them in *Alcheringa 4*, in *Stony Brook 3/4* (1969, pp. 99–102) and in *A Report on the Art and Technology Program of the Los Angeles County Museum of Art* (1967–71, by Maurice Tuchman, which includes seventeen pages of printout, besides several pages of description of my project, photographs, etc., pp. 201–33, published by Los Angeles County Museum of Art, Los Angeles, 1971). Recently, the *Partisan Review* accepted a run of printout from one of the *PFR-3 Poems*, entitled "Space." It should be published soon.

As to what they are like: well, the printout is a sort of by-product of the real piece—a series of appearances of words on the screen of a cathode-ray tube (CRT), along with sounds produced simultaneously with the appearances of words on the CRT. You see, the *PFR-3* propagates images on a CRT by making series of dots, instead of scanning lines, as with a TV CRT. They programmed the *PFR-3* to produce letters for my project. I had shown the programmers some of my earlier work, so they made me a permuting program. I could put into the computer—as "data" for one poem—a certain number of "messages," each consisting of only forty-eight characters (letters or spaces) at the beginning of the project. The programmers who worked with me, one, the director of programming for the corporation, John Hanson, the other his main assistant, Dean Anschultz, planned originally to work closely with me all summer. But I had a rival—a corporation called Computer Micrographics, which bought one of the other film-reader setups (the *FR-80*). That one cost over a half a million dollars; mine was slightly more expensive—I think it cost $800,000! So my demon programmers were pulled away from me (after all, this was just a public-service art project—the corporation lost money on it, they didn't stand to gain hundreds of thousands of dollars!). And the programmers were then just able to get back to me every so often and put a few new features into my program. Eventually, I had a program that allowed me to compose messages consisting of units of several words each—word strings—rather than single words, as at first. And after a while, I had a workable "carriage return"—i.e., I was able to get two or more lines to appear on the CRT at once. Each message consisted of several separable units (once the program allowed me to make phrases or sentences "stick together," I worked with them as units, as well as single words). Units (words or strings) drawn at random from the whole series of messages would appear sequentially on the CRT. Eventually, I was working with little sentences as units, My last *PFR-3 Poem*—"THE"—is a very universal one, with sentences

denoting things that happen all the time all over the
world, as units, e.g., "The sun rises. The earth turns.
The mammals drink. The birds breathe. The ferns turn
toward the light." And so on. Here's some printout
from that last poem:

THE MOSSES ARISE
THE BUSHES ARISE.
THE FERNS ARISE.
THE PEOPLE EAT. THE REPTILES EAT.
THE REPTILES FIGHT.
THE BIRDS FIGHT.
THE INSECTS CRAWL.
THE PEOPLE CRAWL. THE MAMMALS CRAWL.
THE REPTILES CRAWL.
THE FISHES EAT.
THE REPTILES WALK & RUN.
THE PEOPLE HUNT. THE INSECTS HUNT.
THE BIRDS HUNT.
THE FISHES HUNT.
THE MAMMALS HUNT.
THE PEOPLE BUILD TOWNS.
THE PEOPLE BUILD METROPOLISES.
THE PEOPLE BUILD VILLAGES.
THE PEOPLE BUILD MEGALOPOLISES.
THE PEOPLE BUILD CITIES.
THE FERNS TURN TOWARD THE LIGHT.
THE PEOPLE MAKE VEHICLES.
THE PEOPLE FLY IN AIRPLANES.
THE REPTILES WRIGGLE & LEAP.
THE PEOPLE HOP & LEAP.
THE PEOPLE RIDE ON OXEN.
THE PEOPLE RIDE ON ELEPHANTS.
THE PEOPLE RIDE ON HORSES.
THE PEOPLE RIDE ON DONKEYS.

THE PEOPLE RIDE ON CAMELS.
THE FUNGUSES DRINK.
THE TREES DRINK. THE MOSSES DRINK.
THE PEOPLE SAIL ON RAFTS.
THE PEOPLE SAIL IN STEAMSHIPS.
THE PEOPLE SAIL IN BOATS.
THE PEOPLE SAIL IN SAILING SHIPS.

As you see, I began to have sentences about people
in the poem, and I'd planned to have many more, but
it turned out that the absolute capacity of the memory
of my little computer was smaller than I thought
(they'd forgotten to tell me this when they added a
"carriage return" to my program which allowed me to
enter messages consisting of several lines, as in "THE"),
so whenever I entered more than about forty-three
multiline messages, the computer had a sudden
"nervous breakdown"—it literally lost its memory like
a person, and you could see it happening on the CRT!
It would start to print out on the CRT just one more
group of letters, and the letters would suddenly all
collapse into one lower corner! Then I'd have to
retype all the messages hitherto composed back into
the machine! I had to teach it to talk all over again,
so to speak.

NYQ: *What did the computer do with your "messages"?*
Are those groups of lines on the printout complete
messages?

JML: No. Those are randomly drawn and rearranged groups
of units from longer messages. Each line is a unit, but
the whole messages consisted of longer series of lines in
different orders (the margin of each original message
slanted evenly down from the left page margin—the
random rearrangements give the "ragged" left margins
in the printout).

You see, each message I typed in consisted of a
certain number of units. A randomizing routine in the
program "roved over" the whole series of messages
which constituted one whole *PFR-3 Poem* and
selected one or more units, in any order, from any
message. It would do this over and over, and each

time the unit or group of units would appear on the
CRT (every tenth appearance on the CRT was printed
out by the teletype). The piece really consisted in the
sequence of appearances on the CRT "screen" along
with the sounds we produced by splitting the electrical
line from the computer to the electron gun that
produced the images on the CRT, and running one
branch of that line through an audio system.

NYQ: *What kind of sounds?*

JML: Much to our surprise, we got oboe-family sounds!
These were the sounds produced by the electrical
impulses coming from the computer to make the shapes
of the letters on the CRT. Just running a branch of
the line from the computer through an audio system
produced different sounds according to the kinds of
shapes the computer was programmed to produce. For
instance, if the computer was programmed to make the
film reader draw circles on the CRT, the sounds
produced would be very pure sine-wave-type tones.
However, always before, they'd just gotten white noise
from drawing letters on the screen. No one really knew
why the series of letters constituting my poems produced
oboe-family tones; a short series would produce high
"sopranino-oboe" tones; a long series (like the multiline
strophes of "THE") produced superdeep
"contra-contra-bassoon" organ-pipe tones.

NYQ: *Where did they exhibit the piece—I mean, with the
CRT screen and the audio system?*

JML: They never exhibited it anywhere! They were
supposed first to exhibit it at the Osaka World's Fair,
and the company was even going to get the poems
translated into Japanese and exhibit them
simultaneously in English and Japanese, but they
didn't. Then they were supposed to exhibit them later
at the L. A. County Museum of Art, when the Museum
had its own show of the Art and Technology program,
but they didn't exhibit it there either. Only a half-dozen
people have seen the real piece. However, luckily, John
Hanson, the head programmer, once asked me one day,
"Hey, would you like some printout from this?" And
I said "Yeah, sure!" So he fixed it so it'd print out

every tenth unit that appeared on the screen when I
pulled down a certain lever. And that's what I've got
left from the summer's work. They just didn't want to
bother sending their machines to Osaka or even
trundling them over to the L. A. Museum from West
Los Angeles.

NYQ: *So you at least have printout?*

JML: Yes, I have a trunkful of printout. As I said, some of it
has already been published; more of it soon will be.
Also I often use separated pages of printout as text
material for simultaneities. I give each reader a few
pages of printout from one of the poems, and ask them
to regulate their entrances and silences and delivery
themselves—by listening hard and exercising great tact,
and so on. Sometimes, it works beautifully.

NYQ: *Our time seems particularly permissive in the latitude
it allows authors in form and technique and discipline.
What effect does this have on the arts in general and
on poetry in particular?*

JML: A lot on some of the arts. On poetry, not enough.

NYQ: *Well, are you for it, or—*

JML: Obviously! I feel that in art, anything you want to do
is O.K. Everything, that is, except hurting people or
animals or senselessly destroying things that some
people want to preserve. (Of course, it's O.K. to destroy
things of your own, as when Paik used to collect old
beat-up pianos in Germany and destroy them in his
"action-music" concerts.) But practically any kind of
poetry is valid. (I say "practically" because if I thought
hard enough, I'd probably think of some kinds that I
didn't think were valid!) I do think there is better and
worse poetry, somehow, but it isn't something you can
decide ahead of time. You can't legislate for poets.
Critics can't legislate for poets; that's what I learned
from Aristotle (and from the Chicago Aristotelians
and Paul Goodman).

And I think the fact that poets can combine media
now—much more extensively and variously than in the
past—is a fine thing! I float from multimedia works
and chance poems to "confessional" poems like the

Odes and the 41st Light Poem. (I think the term "confessional" is a stupid one, but it's the one that's being used now for poems in which the poet talks directly about her or his own intimate life, so I use it under protest.) And, you know, I go from concrete poetry (in the present accepted usage, meaning visual poetry), that I also use as notation for audible performances to things that some people call "sound poetry" (often the concrete poems performed audibly). So obviously, sure, I'm all for permissiveness—both in poetry and in all the arts! Why not?

NYQ: *Is there anything you'd like to add in conclusion?*

JML: I think people should stay away from hard dope and should drink very little alcohol, if any, and in general, should try to live healthily and eat good whole foods. And don't hurt people (unless doing so is absolutely inescapable) and don't kill people—and do all you can for liberty and peace!

SELECTED BIBLIOGRAPHY

Twin Plays, West Glover, Vt., Something Else Press, Inc., 1966.

Stanzas for Iris Lezak, West Glover, Vt., Something Else Press, Inc., 1972.

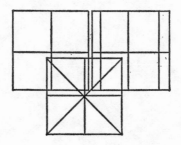

CRAFT INTERVIEW WITH HOWARD MOSS

NYQ: *When did you begin writing?*

HOWARD MOSS: When I was a kid. I used to write when I was in grammar school. I wrote in high school. Poetry. I wrote theatre reviews for the high school paper. But always poetry.

NYQ: *From what writers do you feel you received your most important apprenticeship in the craft of poetry?*

HM: Stevens. Auden. I don't really know. When I was young, I used to stay in after school at three and read a lot of Edna St. Vincent Millay. That was when I was about thirteen or fourteen. I don't know what sort of influence she had. After her, the poet I began to read seriously was Stevens. I remember reading Auden on the beach, finding *Look Stranger* and being absolutely bowled over by that book. Finding it strange and new and marvelous.

NYQ: *Do you feel those particular writers have influenced your work in terms of craft? You have usually used form— rhyme and meter—over the years.*

HM: Well, that's changed a lot. People talk about craft as though you learned it. But actually you don't learn it that way. I mean, you can go to a class and learn terms and facts but you really learn craft by absorbing it. It becomes second nature. It's a way of perceiving as well as writing. I never sat down and said, "This is iambic pentameter and this is a four-foot line, a three-foot line." It simply happens if you read a lot of poetry, and you are a poet. You absorb it in some kind of unconscious way. When you talk about craft in any other way it doesn't mean anything to me.

NYQ: *One of the other questions deals with whether you set a meter for yourself and fit the poem to the meter, so that would be obviously no. The impulse comes, and that works itself out.*

HM: Well, usually a line comes. The line determines what happens. The line is a clue. It's more like a dream, the way a dream is a clue to something. The line that simply arrives is already established in its meter and its subject and whatever it is, it determines the process and the nature of the discovery—if the line interests you. It may be the first line of a poem. It may *seem* to be the first line and turn out to be the last line. Or somewhere in the middle. But it suggests the subject. It suggests the theme. It suggests what kind of form or lack of form the poem is going to have. By lack of form I mean something which is not strictly formal.

NYQ: *Many of the poems we are going to refer to are from your* Selected Poems *which won the National Book Award in 1972. One thing about images—darkness is used as an image in the poem "Clichés for Piano and Orchestra," and darkness is used as one of your images in "Radical Departures," and there are many years between those two poems. Has that been a recurring image with you?*

HM: Yes, I think that darkness and light are fundamental— of course, I'm being photographed right now— fundamental to anyone who is visually aware, and anyone involved in imagery is visually aware. Sight depends almost entirely on darkness and light, the only other things being color and form, or shape, so of course light's a very pervasive notion. It's a pervasive reality, but it's also a pervasive notion. It has connotations and denotations. I think you can go too far with the use of the words light and dark. In fact, I consciously worked to curb their use. The use of the word "dark" can become automatic. I think it's a very essential notion in my work, and in a lot of people's work. It would be very hard to imagine a poet who did not use the words dark and light.

NYQ: *Does the meaning to you of that concept change? Has it changed much in meaning over the years?*

HM: Well, light darkens. You know, there's that marvelous quote that William Maxwell used in his novel, *Time Will Darken It*. It's a fifteenth-century quote. Where a man is instructing painters and says, "Always make the colors lighter, make the canvas a little lighter because time will darken it." And of course time does. I don't mean that in a lugubrious sense, but time does.

NYQ: *Is there one image that you would feel is your most important image, a recurring theme?*

HM: No, I don't, but I do think there are certain central ones. Stillness and moving. Certain key words like silence, distance, which are also versions of moving. I think stillness, moving, light, dark—very key basic things. Root words. I think one of the key poems is "The Silences." And another important poem for me is "Movies for the Home" which is about a trip from New York to California in which every stanza ends with the word "are." Ends with the present. And it's a poem about time and distance, where, as you travel, the place you just left was always the place where you were about to arrive. Watching the trip on a movie screen you realize that time can be stopped, that it can be reversed. What seemed to be the future and became the past is suddenly the present again. And that's an idea I have played with very often.

NYQ: *That's a kind of Proustian thing, isn't it, in his anticipation and recollection?*

HM: Yes. In the subject and the form of *Remembrance of Things Past*. That's certainly true of the form. In the overture you're never quite sure where you are. It starts out with the idea of the boy going to sleep but of course it's the adult who is finally talking. And there are many places in *Remembrance of Things Past* where you're suddenly shocked to find that the person you think is an adult is a child, or the person you think a child is really an adult. The time sequences are so elaborately maneuvered.

NYQ: *Adroitly?*

HM: Well, it isn't only adroitly but significantly. You're fooled into thinking somebody is still an adolescent, and suddenly the camera zooms away, and you realize he's seventy-five.

NYQ: *Would you say that any poem, any poet's work, is an acting of experience in the area of recollection? That every poem is "In Search of Lost Times"?*

HM: I would say that every poem is a memory. But some people of course don't think that. A lot of poets think *now,* that you can capture the moment while it's occurring. But even what I said a fifth of a second ago is already past. For me, poems are forms of memories. It's much more likely that I will write a poem about something that happened than about something that is happening. If I'm in Venice, I will not write a poem about Venice in Venice. I'll write it in New York when I get back. It may be that in Venice lines will come. I might even write them down. Flashes. They happen to me all the time. *When* they happen. And those are keys. Those I always try to follow. As if you were in analysis, the way you would use dreams. They are clues to what's happening to you, to what you're going to write.

NYQ: *Do you use dreams very much in your poetry? As your point of departure.*

HM: No. But I use the idea of dreams. I wait for the given line. Those phrases that just come. And I use them. In the way other people might use dreams. Opening up a world, the idea of the poem being the discovery of that world. Backwards, forwards, down, up.

NYQ: *But you don't take any particular dream experience as a point of departure for a poem?*

HM: I'm trying to think if I have. I think I have put certain images and things from dreams in a poem. But it's very rare.

NYQ: *Do you keep a notebook by your bed if you get an image during the night?*

HM: I have a notebook. I keep images, lines, ideas, anything. Sometimes it's on my desk, sometimes next to my bed. I always have a pencil next to my bed. I find very often that I get images and lines like this when I'm moving. On a bus, in a taxi, train, plane, ship. Anything where you let go of the moorings. As soon as you start moving. Which is why moving is important. So often, a taxi ride, which seems expensive, isn't so expensive because that's where the lines come.

NYQ: *Other images which seem to recur through your* Selected Poems *were birds, darkness again, water, colors, particularly green and blue and black. They have certain meanings for you, do they not?*

HM: Yes. I grew up in Rockaway Beach, in a place called Belle Harbor. And our house was the third house from the ocean. So I was brought up in perhaps a strange environment, I was brought up on a beach in New York City, so that I had both a beach life and a city life. And I think most people don't quite understand that. When I was twelve years old I was allowed to go to Manhattan by myself. So I used to go to the theatre every Saturday afternoon. And I had a whole life in New York City, in Manhattan. When I went home, the next morning I'd be on the beach again, you see. But the beach was very much a part of my natural life. If you know Rockaway Beach at all, there is the bay on one side and the ocean on the other. When I was growing up, it used to be much more primitive. There wasn't a road. There were just rocks. An old cinder path along the bay. And no Riis Park. It was just wild. Pretty wild, suburban wild. And so I was brought up in this double thing, the beach and New York City. So when you say blue and green, when you say water, they were very much what I actually saw.

NYQ: *They were essential to you. You had a foot in two worlds, so to speak.*

HM: I did. I mean, I had a foot in one world, and I was allowed to have a toe or two in the other.

NYQ: *Do you feel replenished from the country? Even now?*

HM: Oh, yes. Rockaway is like Fire Island in the sense that there is water on both sides. You really can't go very far before you hit water on all sides. Fire Island is like that. So is East Hampton. So is all of Long Island.

NYQ: *All the images in your poem "Clichés for Piano and Orchestra"—Dickey's "Lifeguard" seems like your "Clichés." The underwater, the hair, the death feeling in it. Do you think he might have unconsciously associated from your poem?*

HM: I don't think so.

NYQ: *You see them as very different?*

HM: Yes. "Clichés for Piano and Orchestra" is somewhat in the nature of seven little songs. Whereas "Lifeguard" is a poem about guilt and death. "Clichés" are songs. My poems were always very musical. Until now, when there's been a change.

NYQ: *Do you ever write to music?*

HM: No, but a lot of the poems have been set to music. Not by me but by composers.

NYQ: *But you don't use music as a stimulus?*

HM: No. At certain times music stimulates me. But I don't write to music.

NYQ: *What about other types of stimuli? For example, silence, isolation—do you need these in particular?*

HM: Well, I write best when I am alone—of course. But when I have the promise that someone is coming at the end of the day. I write in a certain childish-reward way. I can stay home alone all day and work, work very hard, as long as I know that at five or six somebody's coming by for a drink or something. I'm not one of those writers who work fifteen or twenty-four hours without a break. I can sit down and work very hard as long as I know there's going to be a break. That's the way I've always been.

NYQ: *So transition seems to be a part of it.*

HM: If I were anything else, a bricklayer or something, I'd do my best bricklaying if I knew I was going to have a drink with somebody at the end of the day.

NYQ: *You probably did your homework that way.*

HM: Yes, except for the drinks, so I don't think it really has to do with poetry. It's a matter of temperament.

NYQ: *Like setting limits.*

HM: Yes. And it's also because you are so alone when you work. I can work best knowing the isolation is going to break. There are some people who can go away for three months and live in a cabin. That's not for me.

NYQ: *Have you tried it?*

HM: No. I spent a summer in Maine. But I do the same thing in Maine that I do anywhere. I'm alone all day but I have friends in at night and I have a drink with them.

NYQ: *So your isolation is for very short periods.*

HM: Well, you may be isolated when you're with people. But at least there's the comfort of other human beings. And it works in reverse, too. I find if I am with people all the time, in a house or something, that is disturbing. Then I find I want to be alone to work. I think this is true of most writers. I don't know. People don't write with other people. They write alone. But they also have lives. So they must do *something*.

NYQ: *Since 1967, 1968, 1969, your poems have been quite different. Or is it before that?*

HM: Well, in *Finding Them Lost* there was a group of poems called Lifelines, which were attempts to get certain people I knew down on paper. And in that attempt I broke away from the usual methods I had used for many years. And in trying to do that I broke into something new. I didn't know quite how, but a poem like "Lu" in Lifelines in *Finding Them Lost,* which was 1965, was the beginning of some sort of change. Then in 1968 with *Second Nature,* the poem that was crucial to me was "Front Street." There are repeated cadences and echoes, and I go back to them, but "Front Street" broke the pattern. And I wanted to. I had been writing plays. And I wasn't very satisfied with the plays because they didn't have enough poetry in them. And I suddenly realized that the place for drama was in the poetry, that this business of drama on the one hand and music or whatever on the other wasn't working, that I was trying to put them together by separating them. I mean I didn't know how to put them together and then I began to see how. The crucial poem is "Arsenic." Which I don't think anyone has ever really understood from what I've read about it. The point is really: Which is the true poison—life or art? And it goes through a whole process of denigration and overcoming denigration, of using certain words that I have used and then using them again, after someone says you shouldn't use those words. It's an attempt to overcome and yet incorporate the habitual and the automatic. I don't know if you know the poem.

NYQ: *You have the italicized sections to the side.*

HM: Right. Those are letters—life breaking in on the process. And then these words are slowly used as the poem goes on. But that is a crucial poem, both in its form and in what it says, and I think it succeeds in a way that "Front Street" doesn't succeed. In other words I began to get a method—and that's true also of "A Dead Leaf," new ways of putting things. I think it is by developing a persona, which is always me but which pretends to be something else, by making characters—the woman in "Front Street" and the woman in "Arsenic" I forget what her name is— Miss Mandarin—work. Some people are not made up. They're just around. Only they're disguised. But it was a funny combination of the theatre and my inability to quite deal with it that made the big change.

NYQ: *One poem I find very interesting in your more recent poems is "Radical Departures" with the use of the syllabic line, the collage—is this a unique thing, or do you think you're going to do more in this vein?*

HM: I have a feeling it was unique. Strangely enough, that poem didn't lead to anything. I thought it would. When I was writing it, I thought to myself: I'm doing something I've never done before. It just wasn't fruitful. Somehow when I was done with it, I felt I was done with it. What were fruitful were the new ones "Lu"—"Front Street"— "Arsenic"—"A Dead Leaf," and other poems I've done since then.

NYQ: *But you haven't done anything else with collage? What about spatial punctuation?*

HM: I don't know if you know a poem called "Chekhov." It isn't collage, no, but it unites a lot of disparate images. But "Radical Departures," I just haven't done a poem like it again.

NYQ: *It stands in that collection as a very differt poem for the obvious reasons. Visually it's different, and you have all those other things working. Are you going in that direction?*

HM: So far, no. It's like doing one thing, and then you just stop.

NYQ: *You hadn't expected it would be that way at the time?*

HM: Well, I didn't expect *it* in the first place. And I didn't expect it to stop. Neither one.

NYQ: *What about concrete poetry, shape poetry? Have you done anything in that?*

HM: I really have no interest in that.

NYQ: *You don't like it?*

HM: It's not that I don't like it. I just have no interest in doing it. I've seen lots of poems I've liked, including John Donne's and Dylan Thomas's and May Swenson's and John Hollander's.

NYQ: *And you find it successful in other poets?*

HM: Yes. But it doesn't interest me one little bit.

NYQ: *Another thing I'd be interested to know—how do you feel about playing games with craft—anagrams, use of puns, play on words kind of thing? Does that happen or do you do it?*

HM: Well, a lot of people say those are playing games. I don't know about anagrams, but I think the use of verbal tricks of some kind is part of the poet's possibilities. But if you *just* use tricks, you end up just being a tricky poet. But the pun—the fact that a poet uses words and that words have double meanings, various shades and so on is simply a reflection of one's interest in words. It's very hard to . . . When Auden writes a line like "Oh, hurry to the feted spot of your deliberate fall" the word "feted" which is spelled f-e-t-e-d and fated are a deliberate pun. And it's a lovely pun. Even the word "fall" is a pun. And in Shakespeare—oh, there are thousands and thousands of puns in Shakespeare. But I do think you can get too hung up on just verbal things. I think you can begin to dislike them. I think it is something I began to dislike about my own poetry. I began to think it was too verbal. I wanted to write about what I knew, things and feelings that I hadn't managed to use—some change of that kind.

NYQ: *Then you tried to draw away a bit?*

HM: I tried to draw away from what was almost too natural, too easy. It was the way I always talked. But it was too much, too much.

NYQ: *The "Golden Rule" image in the Midas poem of course has its own double meaning.*

HM: Yes, well, there I felt it was permissible because—and there I don't mind—because I did use every kind of gold thing in Midas that I could think of. And it was intentional, of course. Goldenrod, and gold mine, and jaundice, gold leaf. Because that was very much part of the subject and the theme. In that poem there are four characters, and I gave each one a song and each one a speech. Then I had a little chorus and then a little final poem. Actually it was set to music by Ned Rorem and there's a lovely edition with a gold cover . . .

NYQ: *We'd like to ask about travel and the effect of it on your work.*

HM: Well, I'm not a good traveler, although I am going to Italy in two weeks. But it does give you new subjects, new thoughts. There are specific poems which are obvious —like "Bermuda" and "Venice." There are certain place poems. I guess the poem that I like best of all that I ever got from traveling—well two, I guess—"Venice" was one and "Movies for the Home" the other. I think there's a lot of new imagery, a lot of new visual things happening. Of course people are rather much the same everywhere. Maybe this is just a limitation of mine as a traveler but the main stimulation is mostly visual.

NYQ: *Environmental visual, in other words. Scenery . . .*

HM: Yes, scenery, strangeness of places, rooms, facades, sunsets, fields. In Italy, for instance, there was so much pink that I hadn't known anything about before I actually saw it. Pink buildings and gold buildings.

NYQ: *Which part of Italy?*

HM: This was going by train from Venice to Florence. There seemed to be pink, which I was surprised by, strange-colored walls of farmhouses. The same is true of Ireland. A lot of the houses are painted. And some are just gray. But I was told it's not a sign of affluence to have a colored house. Maybe because one is made of a different material. Maybe one is clay, and then painted and then the other is what? Stone perhaps.

NYQ: *In different countries there may be different colors predominating?*

HM: Yes, and of course it might be the clay. But these were painted houses. But in a town like Cobh one of the charming things about it—it's dominated by a huge cathedral—but up on the hill, the little houses, it looks like an Italian fishing village.

NYQ: *To get back to working habits—do you work most intuitively through the images of the eye, or the ear or through thoughts—through the mind—in getting into a poem?*

HM: Most intuitively, I should think, through the ear, then the eye, then the mind. It's very rarely that I sit down and write a poem about a subject. I do see dramatic connections. I may see a man—Take a poem like "At the Algonquin." I saw a man sitting waiting for somebody at the Algonquin, and I made up who he was and so forth. I don't know why that should be so telling, why you pick a certain person or a certain moment. Certain people, in certain situations, they are either memories or they tell you something about yourself. They are really perhaps disguised versions of yourself, of your emotions, of your feelings. Because that's what really counts. I mean when you talk about craft, it's really what a poem does behind that craft that really counts. To me.

NYQ: *Would you explain what you mean by "what a poem does behind"?*

HM: When I see *Hamlet* I don't think: What a master craftsman Shakespeare was! I think Ophelia's mad or Hamlet's going to kill the Queen. When I read a poem, I don't read it to see if somebody's counted out the syllabics. I read it to see what it will do, because of what it does to me as a person, as a reader, and although I believe in craft, it's completely secondary to art.

NYQ: *After you read a poem, do you go back and examine it for craft?*

HM: Of course. I'll sometimes change lines because of craft but all of that is at the service of art. Which is something much different from craft. That is, to create a beautiful house you may have to learn the whole history of architecture, and math, etc., but you don't learn that for itself, you learn it in order to make a beautiful house. So that the poem is a work of art. I hate to use that word over and over again. But I use it as opposed to craft. Craft is simply a tool, simply a technical thing, to learn how to do something, but that isn't why we do it.

NYQ: *But many people try to talk about a woman, say, who is involved in some act of betrayal to a memory, to a present relationship, but it was only* because *Shakespeare was such a master craftsman that we are able to read* those *words, arranged in* that *way and* care *about Gertrude.*

HM: Absolutely. I couldn't agree with you more. I mean they are absolutely both essential. But the major thing is that the craft is at the *service* of these characters, these thoughts, these ideas. What I mean is think of all the craftsmen who are simply empty. Scribe. People like that, all those French soufflé experts—I don't mean to denigrate them—they have their place but they are not Shakespeare. I feel the same way often about light verse. I feel the same way about detective novels. They can be expert. They can be marvelously crafted by they're not literature because they don't have any themes. They're not thematic. The greatest detective story in the world isn't Tolstoi or Henry James, or Dostoievsky or Chekhov because the mind behind it, the depth of perception, the

interest in character and theme—it's just not there. And
that's what prevents most fiction, which is very well
crafted, from being important.

NYQ: *We didn't talk much about revision yet. How far does
your original impulse carry you before you begin your
rewrite work and refine it into a finished poem?*

HM: Oh, I revise a great deal. Incredible. I revise over and
over and over and over.

NYQ: *Do you see that as a creative process—your revision?*

HM: Oh, yes. But I see that as a craft process.

NYQ: *A creative craft process?*

HM: I see the creative process as—well, I see them both at
once. The creative process is to begin to see what you're
trying to do, begin to sense the form, the notions,
whatever it is. But the craft is a kind of dogged pursuit of
the right form, the right lines, the right tone, the right
everything. And it takes—God—I'm working on a poem
now called "Buried City" of which I must have about
fifty versions. And I do what Dylan Thomas did, I'm
afraid. I can't revise very well unless I start all over again.
I try to break myself of the habit. Say, if I'm changing
a word in the third stanza, or a line, I have to start again
in the first stanza. My real feeling is to go ahead and
finish the whole thing. And often you think it's done. Only
to wait a few days and find no.

NYQ: *You let it get cold, and then you go back and see this
little imperfection.*

HM: I think tone is the most significant thing—tone and
relevance. Because a lot of poems I read as an editor—
what strikes me and what is almost impossible to explain
to somebody—is that something is not really relevant.
When somebody is writing a poem, they are starting a
process which for me, has to go from here to somewhere.
Although there are people who don't believe that any
more. They think that's not spontaneous enough. And
anything that gets in the way of the particular structure
being created should be taken out. And I find that, in my
poems, there's an enormous paring away, of cutting,
refining. Anything that can be said in four words shouldn't

be said in six. Anything that can be said in three words
shouldn't be said in four.

NYQ: *James Dickey's comment on your* Selected Poems—*he said
something about the execution being flawless. You
used the word "paring" just now—something almost as a
sculpted thing.*

HM: Yes, I do try for that. And then I try—because one gets
to be afraid of strait jackets and being *too* sculptured—I
try to break out. I try to break out of habits. In fact it's
a strange thing to try to do the opposite of—not to try
to go against yourself—not for its own sake—just for
fun. That sounds frivolous but I mean in order to see
where it leads you. That's why I took up plays. Not that
they're so different. They have their own little strait
jackets. But because I could never deal with character. It
was always me—me, me, me. I really wanted to deal with
all these people and all these things I observe and think
I know. So I guess theatre *is* an opposite. But you know
what I mean. The difference between painting and the
drama. Between scene and action. And I've been trying
to do that. The poems become much more dramatic. At
least that's the intention.

NYQ: *Do you ever count how many phases or levels you have
gone through since you first began writing?*

HM: No.

NYQ: *Do you think you've gone through many?*

HM: No. Just two—the way I was and the way I am.

NYQ: *Is craft conscious or something that just comes after
enough bad stuff has been written and thrown away?*

HM: I don't think either of those things. I don't think that
question can be answered. I think craft is learned, but it's
not something someone can teach you. So you learn it, as
I said before, by absorbing it, by reading. You learn craft
by reading.

NYQ: *What poets do you read now for pleasure?*

HM: For pleasure I read Elizabeth Bishop, James Merrill—
you mean contemporary poets?

NYQ: *Well, if you read now and read older poets—*

HM: I read John Donne. I read—just the other day I was
reading Sir Thomas Wyatt, whom I love. But the two

contemporary poets I read with the greatest pleasure are Elizabeth Bishop and James Merrill. I read Ted Hughes for pleasure and Sylvia Plath for pleasure. Roethke, Merwin, Jean Garrigue, May Swenson. I read a lot of people for pleasure. I've read Elizabeth Bishop's poems a million times.

NYQ: *You were talking about your second, third, fourth draft at the typewriter. Your original impulse, is that done on the typewriter? How is that done?*

HM: If a line comes, I just jot it down, in the taxi, or wherever. But I do everything on the typewriter.

NYQ: *For example, if this were your writing time, and something came to you, you would immediately go to the typewriter?*

HM: Yes.

NYQ: *Do you travel with your typewriter?*

HM: No. I use whatever I find. And when I travel, as I said, I don't really write very much. I may jot down lines, but I just travel. I don't travel that much. It may seem that way because I'm going to Italy in two weeks. But I haven't been to Europe in two years. I'm not a traveler.

NYQ: *Is there an effect on your poetry from the sound of the languages in the countries you go to?*

HM: I am influenced by—in England and in Ireland—in fact in Ireland, it is the most beautiful speech I ever heard. That speech is of a musical quality you don't hear here and you don't hear it even in England. It's another thing. I could stand on a corner in Dublin, just stand there, and listen. I'm fascinated. It happens too in London when you get all those different dialects, like Yorkshire, the variety of sounds in the English language, which we hardly know anything about, is so amazing in England and Ireland, it absolutely floors me. And I love to listen to it. I would do anything anyone asked me if someone would ask me—in that particular way of speaking—give me a pound or buy these shoes or something. I find it extremely seductive. It must be what some people hear in southern accents. There are some— Cockney I guess and Yorkshire—which are completely enthralling to me.

NYQ: *You find it more attractive than the American southern accent?*

HM: I think it's only because it's more strange. And it seems to go through every kind of sound—vowels, diphthongs that I've never heard. Combinations of o-i which are really combinations of o-u-i—just like quarter tones in music. They sound everything. The whole scale is there.

NYQ: *Do you ever work outdoors?*

HM: Only when I'm typing something, like a manuscript, otherwise no. It's too distracting. Wind, insects.

NYQ: *Negative distractions, in other words? It's not that you're enraptured by the beautiful sunset . . .*

HM: No, no. It's just that—I have typed a manuscript in a backyard when I have rented a house—say, a few times— but the sweat runs down onto the paper, a piece of paper blows away, you get a stone to put on it, the stone makes a dirty mark . . .

NYQ: *Have you ever done poems from particular senses? For example, based on taste, based on scent—just for the experiment?*

HM: No, I can't think of any.

NYQ: *We were talking before in the area of obstacles—going to drama to stretch in different ways. What about writing poetry in other languages?*

HM: No, because I don't know them well enough.

NYQ: *What about very specific types—sestina, villanelle, that type of poem?*

HM: I've written a sestina. I've written a villanelle. I don't like the sestina.

NYQ: *Your own or sestinas in general?*

HM: Mine. But of course unless a sestina or a villanelle seems natural it's just an exercise. I don't like haiku either very much. I don't like anything where you're made aware of the effort of the artist and are supposed to applaud that effort rather than the work itself. When I see a dancer, I want to see the dance. I don't want to see someone who wants to tell me that eight thousand hours were spent at the bar. But there's something lovely and exciting about finding out that what seems natural has been contrived. There's a pleasure I guess in both the naturalness of it and the skill of it, the achievement.

NYQ: *Even in reading it. There's that extra . . .*

HM: There are forests. And there are gardens. I don't like gardens to be too formal. So I guess what I just said about dance is true. But there's also a little corollary to that, which is that sometimes it's very exciting to see someone do thirty-two *fouettés*. But what's nice is to have them both at once. It's nice when somebody wears beautiful clothes, but you're not aware that they're beautiful clothes. Until you look a little harder.

NYQ: *Do you have any strong feelings about a poet's engagement in social-political issues or philosophical issues?*

HM: No. I think poets are always engaged in them to some degree. You mean the question of how specifically. I think that some poets engaged in social activities write very bad poems and some write very good poems. I think the trouble with all of it is that when there is a popular issue, and a real one, like the Vietnam war . . . which I am against, was against, I wrote one poem called "The Wars" . . . I wrote a lot of poems about it, but I never wrote one that was very direct. Because I hate the idea of the bandwagon, of a poem being printed not because it's good but because it says what you believe in. Or it says the right thing. And then artists become propagandists. Then you lose even the idea. That's what's happening now to Yevtushenko, I think. He's writing poems now about anything. To me, it often ends up as slightly phony because of the pressure of social issues. I can't write short-order poetry. It's marvelous to have a poet who writes a good poem about something important and immediate. But it's rare. The whole thing usually degenerates into something that is not personal. And as soon as it becomes impersonal, there's nobody talking, as soon as it's a group thing, as soon as it's agreed upon, you lose the writing that makes for individuality, for something really felt. My personal feeling is that if you are a poet, you should write whatever you were going to write in the first place regardless of social issues. And then *act* on the social issues as a citizen.

Of course, there are certain poets who are naturally social poets, where that separation wouldn't exist. Of them that wouldn't be true. For example, I see Neruda as successful as a social poet. Take Picasso. I think "Guernica" is a great painting. And that's a political painting. But I don't think there are many other things by Picasso that are political. I believe there are great possibilities when something has to be said. Look at Goya's war etchings. Those are superb. But to have a million people do etchings on the horrors of war . . . The horrors are real, God knows. That doesn't mean the etchings will be. They might just turn out to be just so much crap. That's what I'm afraid of. Does that answer your question?

NYQ: *Yes, of course.*

HM: There are social things in my poems. There are in "Radical Departures" for instance. About surveillance, about certain political attitudes, about intimidation. The wars again. But I wouldn't think that I would be a political poet.

NYQ: *What about readings and their value to a poet?*

HM: I've always been suspicious of reading because I think most people who come to a reading come for the poet rather than the poem. It's a great thing. Poets make money. I do it. Not very often but I do it. And it's exciting sometimes. Unless you're afraid. Which I have been. It's exciting to have an audience. But I have a feeling that they really come to see who you are, what a poet is rather than the poem. Most modern poems are too complicated to be taken at one hearing. People tend to read either their simplest things, or, in defiance of the need of the audience, they read something very new and rather complicated. I think it's a lie that poetry is an oral tradition. Our poetry is now a written tradition. And I need time to look at a poem, to read and reread a line, to see how something connects. If I read a poem once, there are certain poems I would never understand. And

I don't see how anybody else could. So I have mixed feelings.

NYQ: *What about poets who see it as a meeting place?*

HM: Yes, it's a meeting place, and you do hear new work there, because since a poet's books are so few and far between, when a poet is working, you know that if you go to a reading, you'll probably hear someone's new work. That's the first place—you may have to wait three years to see it.

NYQ: *Or maybe never hear it at all.*

HM: Right. So for that reason . . . But I see it as having mixed advantages.

NYQ: *You don't see it as having any effect on a poet's work to interact with an audience?*

HM: I'm trying to think. Do I see it in mine or in general?

NYQ: *Well, either one or both.*

HM: I'm trying to think. There may be something to be said for a kind of spareness in certain poets possibly having something to do with reading. Not consciously. I don't think they do it as a compromising thing, but because of that direct connection with the audience. They do something which is more immediately dramatic.

NYQ: *What is the importance of criticism in your own work?*

HM: Some. Someone pointed out that I use the word "love" all the time and that gave me pause. There are very few people I really trust. Critics. Because you read so many things about your poems that are so contradictory. But there are certain critics that I do trust. When they say something about a poem, I listen.

NYQ: *Is there any particular critic you would like to mention?*

HM: Robert Mazzocco.

NYQ: *How do you feel about your own criticism, your other writing, and its effect on your own poetry?*

HM: Well, the Proust book, *The Magic Lantern of Marcel Proust,* felt more like writing a poem. It had the same impulses, as it were. The other things I slave over. I sweat blood. The reviews. And there I do things like ninety revisions. So when I do a review in *The New Yorker* I have a little novel by the end. I dread it because there's so much work but I like to do it, too, like the endless refinement of thinking, the way you get to what you really think and then you get to how to say it, and then how to *really* say it, and that's very good I think for poetry. They go together. You compress. You say something, maybe twenty times, until you find the best way of saying it. There is a tie-in. But one hopes there is a different kind of psychology and mentality, because in the poems I try to release myself, I try to free myself from consciousness whereas in criticism it's always thinking, it's always reasoning.

NYQ:　　*The feeling happens, and then the criticism is analyzing that feeling?*

HM:　　Well, that's the best way if you can do that without stopping yourself.

NYQ:　　*How do you feel about a poet's interpreting his poems once they are published?*

HM:　　Who has a better right? I should think that the poem should speak for itself. But, if someone asks, and people sometimes do ask, I'd rather have the poet tell me than somebody else, like his mother or his wife or a stranger. Sometimes poets know a great deal about what they are talking about. Sometimes a critic can illuminate something a poet might not be aware of. But, if asked, the poet is the person who should answer.

NYQ:　　*Do you think he can be as objective, perhaps, as a critic?*

HM:　　Well, the critic is involved with the quality of it, where the poet is involved with the psychological origins of it, or what the poet was trying to say, perhaps. So he's not evaluating it. The critic's function is really different. The critic is not explaining, not always. He is saying: This is good—this is worth reading. This man fits into this or that group. He compares with so-and-so. So they're completely different.

NYQ:　　*Do you keep a notebook on craft?*

HM:　　Never on craft, but I do keep a notebook of lines, fragments. I *have* written down, when I was trying to

write a poem like a sestina, I have written down the
whole verse form.

NYQ: *We talked about fragments before and about lines. How
long have you carried unfinished lines before they have
been included in a poem?*

HM: Some of them still haven't been. Ten years. Twelve years.
Sometimes they never are.

NYQ: *Do you have any books you feel might be helpful to a
poet in a particular area of craft?*

HM: I think to read good prose is enriching. To read a book
like Auden's *The Commonplace Book*. There's a man
named Corbett in that book. I think that's his name.
He's a man who talks about lead mining and the
landscape of mines. I found it marvelous writing. The
language is so brilliant, the syntactical brilliance. I
always find that very exciting somehow. I also find
exciting certain books—I don't know if this answers your
question very well—because I talk of books which are
exciting to me—but you wanted craft books.

NYQ: *Well, no, not necessarily. What books you would
recommend for someone to read?*

HM: Well, a book like *One Hundred Years of Solitude* is
obviously a good book to read. Or *Out of Africa*.
Certain books that are really splendid. Or Rilke's *Journal
of My Other Self*. Somehow the books I consider
superb are prose books like the Rilke and the Marquez or
Nightwood—any book of that nature somehow is very
enriching for poetry. I don't know exactly why. I guess
because you're not stealing from a poet, and if you're
stealing at all you're stealing from a prose writer. I think
because it's close but different. The point of course is not
really to steal but to be enriched, to be stimulated.

NYQ: *Do you feel we live in a particularly permissive age
insofar as education and discipline are concerned, and
do you feel this has any effect on poetry?*

HM: Well, I hate the word "permissive" since it's used by the
Nixon administration . . .

NYQ: *Well, change it, by all means.*

HM: I think the fact that there are no standards of craft in
        poetry makes it very difficult to make judgments for a
        lot of people about what's good and what isn't good.
        Anything goes. There was a time when, if a sonnet wasn't
        a perfect sonnet, you'd say: "Well, that isn't a perfect
        sonnet"—and that was considered a judgment. When
        there is no standard of craft you have a lot of
        undifferentiated work, which is difficult to judge. It's
        very hard to say what the standards are. I think it takes
        a long time of living, a long time of reading, mostly
        reading, to know, but I don't like to read sestinas, and I
        don't like to read laundry lists either. There's an awful
        lot of junk that passes for poetry, people who think they
        can write down anything and it's a poem. If you mean
        that—then yes, the people who think it's all
        self-expression, for them it's a different way of writing
        their names. I think a lot of it is just junk.

NYQ: *How much of the poetry that comes in to* The New
        Yorker *do you see? Do you have a screening committee
        or assistants, or what?*

HM: I have a reader, a full-time reader. Just one, and
        everything else comes to me. If, at the end of the week,
        she sees anything she likes, she brings it to me. I would
        say that we get between 750 and 800 poems a week. And
        I would say that coming to me direct would be 75 to 100
        poems.

NYQ: *Do you feel there is any effect on your work from
        screening all the time? Seeing the not-quite-so-good
        poems all the time.*

HM: Well, I see the best that we get. Of course, I can't control
        what I see, but I can control it to the extent that I don't
        see what the reader sees. I don't know. I've arranged it
        so that I'm only there twice a week. I never go two days
        in a row. So that when I work at the office, I work
        Tuesdays and Fridays, and I never go in Mondays,
        Wednesdays, Thursdays, unless there's a real crisis. And
        I never take work home—never, never take anything
        home. So I have developed a kind of—possibly schizy
        thing of a cutoff. When I leave the office at six I forget
        about it. On the other hand, people still treat me very
        much, on the other days, as the poetry editor of *The New*

Yorker. I mean, people call me, or I get poems here at home, or mail. But for me, I can make some sort of cutoff. However, I think if there *has* been an influence on me, I wouldn't know it.

NYQ: *It would be an unconscious thing.*

HM: Right. I don't think so, but I would be the last person probably who would really know, if there really has.

NYQ: *You've been there about thirty years?*

HM: I went there in 1948. I was fiction editor for two years. And I've been poetry editor since 1950. So I've been there twenty-five years. There was one poetry editor before that. But I did organize it into a department, went after people I liked. I organized it into a thing, because I realized it had to be if it was going to be anything.

NYQ: *We were under the impression that you were responsible for opening up* The New Yorker *for some of the free poetry. Did you have difficulty with any of the editors?*

HM: Well, Mr. Ross didn't relate to poetry the way Mr. Shawn does. So it is much easier with Mr. Shawn. Mr. Shawn likes poetry. And he has given me quite a free hand. Once in a while there's a difference, but on the whole it's been very nice. He has the ultimate authority. That's true about the entire magazine. I don't know how the *NYQ* works, but when there's an editor in chief, there's an editor in chief. His position is final. There's a lot of leeway, you can fight back and forth. But in the end that's the way it works.

NYQ: *But there haven't been big problems in terms of getting newer types of poetry published?*

HM: Oh, no.

NYQ: *Ginsberg's poem "Wales Visitation," that was first published in* The New Yorker. *There was no problem involved with this one?*

HM: No.

NYQ: *What about directions poetry magazines are going in?*

HM: Well, I think there's a lot of variety, which I think is
        very good. I don't like splits and cults and schools. I
        think that happens when people can't get printed. I wish
        there were more communication between them. Like the
        St. Mark's Poetry Project—I like some of the people
        there. And the New York School of Poets. There is much
        more of a fertilization than one would think socially, yet
        they seem to be rather distinct culturally. I think it would
        be good to mix it up. Have the American Academy of
        Poets invite somebody that's not their sort of thing. And
        I think it would be good for someone from the St. Mark's
        group to invite someone from the American Academy.
        You know what I'm talking about?

NYQ: *Yes.*

HM: I think schools and cults are not only dangerous, they're
        bores. Because sooner or later, they get away from poetry.
        In the end I think you have to go your own way.

NYQ: *You had said there's that danger in a workshop, going
        in one direction because of a teacher.*

HM: I think if there's a good teacher, it doesn't matter too
        much if he says, "Go home and use the following six
        words in a poem" or does it by having private
        conferences with you, and says, "Look—your work lacks
        this or that." Anybody or anything that helps you write
        is very important. Anything that restricts you and makes
        you lose confidence or overpraises you when you don't
        deserve it or doesn't help you develop as a writer is bad
        for you.

NYQ: *What about your own work—the reading of Proust, the
        criticism of Proust, the involvement with him? Do you
        feel this has much bearing on your own work?*

HM: To my own work? Not really. Except for that one book.
        I feel he's a supremely great writer. I wrote that book
        because I felt so. But to me he's an epic poet. He's a
        novelist and an epic poet. And I was fascinated by him.
        What I said about character before—his is a completely
        metaphorical book which uses character. It's very
        strange. In fact I don't know any book which is a great
        poem and yet has such extraordinary characters and set
        pieces of social observation in it. It's fascinating,

psychologically. And it's a story. And a philosophical drama. Anyway, I became very involved with it, and I think the reason it hasn't influenced my work is because that book was written. It did influence my work to the whole extent of that book. That book is a critical book but it is also like a book of poems. To me. You might say it's my missing book of poems.

NYQ: *Proust examines something from as many possible directions as he can, so that one incident could go on for pages and pages and pages. In your own work, your lines are so condensed that it opens up perceptions. That would seem to be paradoxical or contradictory.*

HM: I understand what you mean. Yes. He works by expansion and I work by compression. Yet it's very strange that in Proust in those four thousand pages there is not one inaccurate metaphor. I think it's most extraordinary. Every metaphor counts. A lot of people who imitate Proust are just slobs. They don't understand the precision of his mind. It allows for any kind of elaboration. Because everything he says really is true.

NYQ: *There are so many directions from which you can examine any object, thought, incident.*

HM: Particularly if you're dealing as he is with time. And he has that marvelous section at the end where the narrator thinks it's a costume party and then he realizes—and you realize just a second before he does—that it isn't a costume party—that everybody's just old.

NYQ: *Isn't there something about snow?*

HM: Hair. They're not wearing costumes, they're just old. And he describes in great detail every single one of them. I think it's one of the most fascinating pieces of writing that exists.

NYQ: *What about your current work?*

HM: I'm working on a book on Chekhov now. I'm trying to make certain connections between the plays and the stories. Certain characters from the plays appear in the stories and certain characters from the stories appear in the plays. It's funny that my two favorite writers are so different. The one thing is that they're both truthful.

Nothing could be plainer than Chekhov. Nothing could be more elaborate than Proust. I guess that's why I like them because they're both truthtellers. And to have them both so different.

NYQ: *You have the two, the poems and the plays. What is your thinking on verse theatre in general?*

HM: Of course, my plays were in prose. But I feel that most plays are stupid. I think the audience is stupid. The plays are stupid. Film is so far ahead of it. Poetry is so far ahead of it. Every art is so far ahead. If you can watch Balanchine, why go to the theatre? I think it's partly a deadly combination of audience, playwrights and criticism. Every time a good playwright comes along, nothing much happens. I like that play by Edward Bond —*Saved*. But I don't think there's much activity, much vitality. It's like a dead thing.

NYQ: *For how long do you think it's been so bad?*

HM: I don't know. I mean the last big figure is Albee. I have his new play here, which I like. There's plenty of talent: Sam Shepard, Terence McNally, Lanford Wilson, but I think the whole business of going to the theatre has become slightly obsolete. It's simply the money, the artificiality, the intermission. I guess what's become obsolete is that there's just no overwhelming play. If you saw a really terrific play then you'd forget everything I just said. Everything I said would be canceled out. There's no excitement—or the excitement is false. It's a kind of false energy. You read about something and you go to see it and say, My God, is this what people were talking about? The theatre is so unsubtle that if you're used to movies or novels or poetry, where new things are being said and done and people are saying something about life, theatre isn't doing it.

NYQ: *So you can have the stage and the clothes and the intermission, but if art itself isn't present in the drama, it's just as empty as the well-crafted nonpoem.*

HM: That's right. But I must also say that there is the *non*-well-crafted nonpoem.

NYQ: *We know. We screen too. We know about those.*

HM: I have to mention those.

NYQ: *Does it get to you after a while when you see a lot of bad poetry? Or are you lucky enough to see the good poetry most of the time?*

HM: Well, I do see a lot of good poets' work. I now do. So I don't think it's quite as discouraging. If you have two bad days of poems and rotten things come in the mail, and you suddenly have a day with three good poems, then you feel elated again. Or if you discover somebody new. Somebody you really think is good. Like Mark Strand. I saw his very first poem. And we took it. And that's always very exciting. After all, what are you doing it for? If you don't have that excitement, then what's the point of it? You might as well be doing something like working in a sardine factory.

   Of course there are a lot of one shots. Sometimes you find one poem and you hope. But there's never anything as good. Does that ever happen to you?

NYQ: *That's supposed to be true of many, many novelists. They write this one incredible novel, and you find out later that that was autobiographical and they have nothing more to say. They've talked about themselves, and they have no other object.*

HM: But a poet you'd think would be different. If he did one, you would think there would be more.

NYQ: *What about translations?*

HM: I did one translation of Valéry. I don't set much store by it. I don't really enjoy translating. Some poets are excellent. I think Merwin is a beautiful translator. I'm also getting very suspicious of translation. There seems to be a sort of international translators' style, where everybody sounds the same. I've been reading poets, Spanish poets and French poets, who all sound the same. And just as stereotyped as English poems can be: you know, the rose bloomed on the blah-blah tree. There's a funny, creepy thing of people who don't know the language and who are given texts, literal texts, who translate and are all sort of imitating each other. And I think something terrible is happening. I think the poet has to know the language. And he has to be a poet. I

can see the problems with Swedish and Norwegian and
those languages. But, God knows, a lot of poets know
French and Spanish and Italian. Of course, how do you
know? They could just be writing anything. I have no
idea if those translations from Yevtushenko or
Voznesensky or any of those are even accurate. Why, we
could make up a poet right here. Some Baltic hairdresser
we could make up.

NYQ: *You do know French though.*

HM: I do know it. But I wouldn't want to get tangled in a
witty French conversation. It was very hard, translating
that Valéry, because that's a poem where everything
means two or three things. There was one word—*grillage*
—which meant grill, and also meant grillwork. The same
ambiguity as in English. It was about a fence, how the
sun cast shadows through the grill, but it also involved the
idea of being broiled. And I just couldn't find the right
word. I wanted to get the idea of food as well as the sun.
I forget what I did.

NYQ: *At* The New Yorker, *did you know Louise Bogan?*

HM: Yes. She was the critic. I liked her immensely but we kept
our separate ways. If I liked somebody and she didn't, she
could say so, and yet his poems could still be printed.
There was the possibility of two different viewpoints.

NYQ: *Is there anything you wanted to say about screening?*

HM: No. I really try to be instinctive. I think it's the best way.
I go by what I like. You try to open yourself, as if you
were still reading while you were in bed or someplace.
For pure pleasure. Because I think once you lose that, I
think you lose the whole thing as an editor. Even if you
make mistakes, you don't make that awful mistake of
losing your sense of yourself. Making mistakes is one of
the risks. I remember one poem I liked and then came
to hate. Of course if you have five days of bad poems,
then one which is not very good may seem much better.
Then also what happens is that a poem on a particular
subject is superseded by a much better poem. And then
it's too late. If you buy three poems on suicide, and then
two weeks later an absolutely smashing poem on suicide
comes in you really hesitate because you know they're

going to have to be printed six months or two years apart. You can't control what comes in and you can't control when it comes in.

SELECTED BIBLIOGRAPHY

The Toy Fair, New York, Charles Scribner's Sons, 1954.

A Swimmer in the Air, New York, Charles Scribner's Sons, 1957.

A Winter Come, a Summer Gone—Poems 1946–1960, New York, Charles Scribner's Sons, 1960.

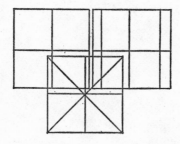

CRAFT INTERVIEW
WITH ERICA JONG

NYQ: *How do you start a poem?*

ERICA
JONG:
That's a very difficult question. My way of writing has
changed considerably in the past few years. At this point,
I usually get a first line. I don't know where that first
lines comes from and I don't know who says it to me. It
may be the Muse. (I really believe in the Muse, by the
way.) But the process seems to be that I get a line and
write it down as quickly as I can and generally from that
I allow things to build. I follow the images one after the
other seemingly automatically. That doesn't mean that
my poems are not revised or edited, but they come in a
very mysterious way. Almost by dictation.

I didn't always write this way, however. When I was
in college I wrote in a much more premeditated manner.
I would struggle from one line to the next, poring over a
rhyming dictionary, counting out the meter on my fingers.
Although I now write very freely, I'm conscious of the oral
qualities of the poetry and of the rhythm. Also, I don't let
everything stand. The second draft is written extremely
critically. Most of the process consists of striking out the
crap—the bad lines.

But I can't tell you where my first line comes from. I
do know that I recognize Osip Mandelstam's description
of the kind of foretrembling which precedes writing a
poem. It's a weird kind of excitement which feels
somewhat like sexual tension and somewhat like anxiety.
It's as if an aura exists around you—and you know you're

going to write a poem that day. The real question of beginning is when you get the hook into the poem, and that hook is the first line. It may not always remain the first line. It may become the last line, or it may drop out of the poem altogether, but it's the line that starts your imagination going.

NYQ: *Do you usually finish the poem in one day or work on it for a while?*

EJ: It depends. Some poems are finished in one day. Others take years. Sometimes the process is merely a question of refining, and sometimes you have to grow into a poem. I have a poem which is just beginning now, and I haven't the faintest idea when I'll finish it. There are two lines that really live. Two images. But they haven't grown into a poem yet.

NYQ: *It's working?*

EJ: It's there working, yes. I'm reminded of the motto Kafka had over his writing desk—"Wait." And it's true. You're not always conscious of working on a poem. And then it happens. It erupts like a volcano. Your imagination is working all the time in a subterranean way. And when it comes time for you to write the poem, the whole thing explodes.

NYQ: *What about ideas for a novel—is it a whole section, a chapter . . . ?*

EJ: *Fear of Flying* was written in such a funny way that it's difficult to describe the process. I had been working for years on sections of it and I had attempted two earlier novels that I didn't finish. I had been collecting autobiographical fragments, fantasies, character sketches, ideas. When the framing device for this book—the trip across Europe—occurred to me, I suddenly found a way to make a coherent story out of materials which had been obsessing me for quite some time.

NYQ: *One of the questions we were going to ask you was about the Muse. Because you do mention her in a very specific person way sometimes.*

EJ: How do you mean?

NYQ: *You talk about her in a very familiar way as if you met her and she's right there beside you. Could you talk about it?*

EJ: Well, I used to think that all this talk about the Muse was a lot of bullshit. But I was wrong. I'm convinced that there are powers we cannot find names for. Maybe the Muse is really the same as the collective unconscious. I don't think it matters. Maybe the Muse is one's own unconscious which connects with the collective unconscious. Or maybe the Muse is a supernatural being. But I think there are forces we have no way of scientifically codifying, and inspiration is one of them. Why is it that at a given moment in your life certain elements come together and fuse in a way that makes a poem or that allows you to write a novel you've been dreaming of for years?

NYQ: *So you call it the Muse?*

EJ: Yes, but that's just one of many possible terms. That quality of inspiration, that sudden chill, the thing that makes your hair stand on end . . . I don't know what else to call it. You see, I think part of being a poet is learning how to tap your inner resources. Probably poets are born, not made. But the training of a poet consists in learning how to tap that secret part of yourself which connects with the communal unconscious. So you spend a lot of time imitating other people's poems. Writing on subjects that, let's say, aren't of interest to you but were of interest to the poets you admire. You're learning your craft. But what you're really learning during those years of apprenticeship is how to explore yourself. And when that happens—I've said this in the poetry seminar about a million times— when craft and the exploration of self come together, that's when you become a poet. All the stuff you produced before that was derivative apprenticeship work. And you usually know it when that point arrives.

NYQ: *One of the quotations you had in your article "The Artist as Housewife" was "Everyone has talent, what is rare is the courage to follow the talent to the dark place where it leads." What has helped you the most to go into those dark places?*

EJ: I had to learn to trust myself. I had to learn to trust that part of my mind which had the potential of being original. I think lots of things helped. Getting older and having more confidence in my own voice. The other thing (unfashionable as it's become) was psychoanalysis. Artists tend to be afraid of it. They think they'll lose their creativity. But what analysis teaches you is how to surrender yourself to your fantasies. How to dive down into those fantasies. If you can do it on the couch—and not all the people can do it on the couch either—then, you may learn to trust the unconscious. To follow its meandering course. Not to look for a goal. As in an analytic session where you begin meandering. "Oh, this doesn't make any sense at all. I'm saying X. I'm saying Y." And then at the end of the session you discover that it does quite make sense. It makes more sense than most "rational" discourse. There are a lot of dreadful analysts around—just as there are a lot of incompetents in any other profession. But about 2 per cent of them are artists and understand artists. I was also lucky to have a couple of teachers who knew where I was going. And who encouraged me when my poetry began to take the inner direction. Mark Strand, for example, said at one point, when I showed him my early poems, "You haven't really been fucked by poetry yet." I don't know if he would remember having used that phrase, but I've never forgotten it. Then, when I showed him the first draft of *Fruits & Vegetables,* he said, "Now you're into something! Keep with it." He recognized that I was dealing with sexuality in a way that was more daring for me and that I had begun to allow my imagination free rein. His encouragement was vital at that time.

NYQ: *You mention voice in that same article. You say that the poet's main problem is to "raise a voice." How did you find your voice and how do you suggest a poet find his voice? Going into himself?*

EJ: Well, I remember my gradual realization that the person I was in life and the person I was in my poems were not the same. When I wrote poetry I assumed a kind of poet role. It probably came out of some old grade school notion of what a poet is. We all have that and it somehow stands in our way. I realized that in life I was a clown, alternately very solemn and serious—and at other

times, kidding around wildly. But I never had allowed
that range in my work. I had always been attracted to
satire, and even in my high school and college poems, I
had tried to write satire. But it was a kind of formal satire.
It wasn't really open and spontaneous. I had to learn how
to let spontaneity into my poems.

NYQ: *You speak frequently of the need for authenticity. Is the
need for authenticity the need for trusting yourself?*

EJ: Yes, because all you have to write out of is your own
kinkiness, the idiosyncrasies of your personality, the special
spectacles through which you view the world. If you censor
those things out in deference to some fear of exposure,
fear of what your family, your husband, your lover or your
friends may think, then you're going to lose authenticity.
When you write, you're not writing for an outer social
world that approves or does not approve. Writing is for
that inner place, that inner place in other people, too.
That's what I mean by authenticity. And it's very hard to
get past this obsession with trying to please. It's especially
hard for women. Men are afraid, too, of course, but in
women the fear of self-exposure is even more cultivated.

NYQ: *Many of your poems refer to specific people who seem to
be in your life. There is a poem called "Chinese Food,"
for example, where there are specific people by name. And
in some of your recent poems you mention your mother.
Do you deal with these poems that are maybe biographical
in one way, maybe nonliteral in other ways—how do
you deal with this issue of speaking from your voice and
also other people?*

EJ: I don't think that any of the people in my poems are real
people in a strict biographical sense. Obviously, they are
people frozen at certain moments in time. My real
biographical mother is not merely like the mother in that
poem. And she would be the first to say so.

I don't think that biographical question is a fair
criterion by which to measure a poem. There's a
wonderful quote from Jerzy Kosinski which I used in my
novel. He says that you can't have such a thing as straight
autobiography or confessional writing because even if you
try to write down literally what you remember, memory
itself fictionalizes and orders and structures. Even if you

make a film or a tape, you have to edit it, and so doing,
you put a controlling intelligence around it. It ceases to be
the same as biography.

What you're talking about in my poems is that they
refer to—yes, I have a mother—everybody has a mother—
I could have written twelve other poems about my mother
in different incarnations, and I probably will as time goes
on. But I don't see the people in those poems as real
people. The Chinese food poem mentions people who were
present at a given dinner. But those people aren't really
depicted. And I don't see my poems as confessional at
all. I see them as "structures made to accommodate
certain feelings." (The phrase Kosinski uses.) Obviously
they come out of my life. But then all poets' poems come
out of their lives.

If the people in the poems were just people in my own
life and hadn't any universal meaning, nobody else could
connect with those poems. They would be so personal that
they would mean nothing to anybody but me. That's why
I think the term "confessional poetry" is an absolute
misnomer. I don't think there is such a thing as
confessional poetry.

NYQ: *One term you do use is "author" in the sense of authority.
          What would you say is the author's particular
          responsibility as an author writing today?*

EJ: When I talk about authority, what I mean is: You are
          the person where the buck stops. You are responsible for
          what you write. You cannot write a book in committee,
          nor with a certain editor, publisher or reviewer in mind.
          Writing is one of the few professions left where you take
          all the responsibility for what you do. It's really dangerous
          and ultimately destroys you as a writer if you start thinking
          about responses to your work or what your audience needs.
          That's what I mean by authority. And that's why I say
          again and again to my poetry seminar: "Don't even listen
          to me. We're offering criticisms of your poems and we're
          saying—'O.K., that line works, that line doesn't work.'
          But if you want to ignore it, go ahead and ignore it
          because learning to be a writer means learning to ignore
          people's advice when it's bad." You have to reach that
          place in yourself where you know your own sound, your
          own rhythm, your own voice. That's what it's all about.

You'll find that with many great authors of the past, their strengths and weaknesses are so intertwined that one can't unravel them. A contemporary author like Doris Lessing is a good example of this. She can be incredibly hard to read, even boring at times. And yet she's a great writer. It's the very heaviness of her writing, the way she works out a detailed portrait of a society that makes her so good. How could an editor sit down with *The Golden Notebook* and excise passages? God knows there are sections of it that are heavy going. Yet the strengths of the book and the faults are so interwoven that editing it would be impossible. You can't make *The Golden Notebook* into an E. M. Forster or Elizabeth Bowen novel. It's a different animal. You try to refine your work as much as you can. But ultimately you have to say: "I am I. I am the author." That's what I want everyone in my seminar to learn eventually.

NYQ: *You mentioned earlier some of the problems of being a woman poet. In your article "The Artist as Housewife" you said, "Being an artist of any sex is such a difficult business that it seems almost ungenerous and naive to speak of the special problems of the woman artist. . . ." What are those special problems?*

EJ: There are many. Despite the fact that we've had Sappho, Emily Dickinson, Jane Austen, the Brontës, Colette, Virginia Woolf, etc., etc., etc., there is still the feeling that women's writing is a lesser class of writing, that to write about what goes on in the nursery or the bedroom is not as important as what goes on in the battlefield, that to write about relationships between men and women is not as important as writing about a moon shot. Somehow there's a feeling that what women know about is a lesser category of knowledge. It's women's fiction, women's poetry or something like that. Women are more than half the human race, and yet since the culture has always been male dominated, the things men are interested in are thought to be of greater importance than the things women are interested in. Also, there is still a tremendous condescension toward women in reviewing. Whenever people tote up the lists of the greatest writers now writing, you get the same male names over and over. Roth, Malamud, Singer, Updike . . . the same old

litany. . . . You don't get Eudora Welty, Doris Lessing,
Mary McCarthy, Adrienne Rich, Anne Sexton. Why?
There is a kind of patriarchal prejudice which infuses our
whole culture. I think it is not always malicious on the
part of men—it's often purely unconscious. The
psychological reasons behind this are many. Probably
womb envy—that most unrecognized phenomenon—plays
a significant part. Since the majority of psychologists and
anthropologists have been male, they've been reluctant to
recognize it. Men have the feeling that women can create
life in their bodies, therefore how dare they create art? A
book I'm very interested in is *The First Sex* by Elizabeth
Gould Davis. It deals with male envy of the female and
its manifestations throughout different cultures.

NYQ: *Do you think women writers have more difficulty getting
published because of this?*

EJ: It's hard to generalize because women are being published
now for faddish reasons. Let's just say women don't have
difficulty being published. But they do have difficulty
being taken seriously as writers. Certain kinds of
commercial writing are almost exclusively done by women
—Gothic romances, children's books. Yet being published
is quite a different thing from being accorded respect as
an artist. Secondhand bookstores are strewn with books
which were published and forgotten.

NYQ: *You mentioned women writers. Do you find it more often
that women are reviewed as women than as writers?*

EJ: I've never seen a review of a woman writer in which her
sex was not mentioned in some way. And frequently
reviewers do things like comment on appearance. Carolyn
Kizer was reviewed (I think in *Time* or *Newsweek*) as
"the Mae West of the poetry world" or some crap like
that. There are many good looking male poets, and people
don't go around saying, "Isn't W. S. Merwin a cutie?" I
mean, he's very handsome. Richard Wilbur is very
handsome. Mark Strand is very handsome. I hope I
haven't left anybody out. But people don't talk about that
in reviews of men. With women they always talk about it.
And if a woman's ugly, they harp on that too. Did you see
that reference to Gertrude Stein's "fat ankles" in the
Times a few weeks ago? It's as if you're a piece of meat.

Besides condescension and not being taken seriously, there's that awful category of "woman poet." Women's conflicts—as if they weren't applicable to all of us.

NYQ: *Now when you go into your workroom and begin to work, and you're a poet and also a woman, what special kind of traps do you have to look out for because of this scene in terms of your craft? In terms of your voice?*

EJ: As I said in the "Artist as Housewife" article, I went for a long time not dealing with my feelings about being a woman, because I had never really seen it done before. In college I read Auden, Yeats and Eliot, and imitated a male voice. I didn't think of it as a male voice, I thought of it as a poet's voice, but it didn't deal with the things that I wanted to deal with. Perhaps the reason Sylvia Plath was so important to my generation of young women was that she wrote about being a woman and she wrote about its negative side. She dealt with birth, menstruation —all the things that male poets don't deal with. So she liberated us. Now I think we can go on beyond that. We don't always have to write about female rage.

NYQ: *Do you have any work habits? In* Fear of Flying, *Isadora writes in the nude. Do you have work habits like this?*

EJ: I don't always write in the nude. Anyway, that's not a work habit.

NYQ: *Do you have any—certain papers—in longhand?*

EJ: I write in longhand and I write very fast. I like to have a pen that flows rapidly because when the words start coming they come so fast that my handwriting is virtually illegible. I can't compose on a typewriter, although my second draft is typed. It gets pasted into my notebook side by side with the scrawled first draft and I refine it from there.

NYQ: *Do you keep a journal?*

EJ: I don't really have time, though I would love to. I've kept journals at many times in my life, starting from when I was about thirteen or fourteen. But it's boring and contrived to keep a journal every day. Better to write as the mood strikes. But I don't even have time to do that except on rare occasions. Writing a novel, writing poems, writing letters to many correspondents, trying to keep notes on poems that come to mind—there just isn't time to keep a journal. Also you use up the energy that might go into poems.

NYQ: *Do you write every day—your poems, your novel. Do you write at a set time?*

EJ: Writing a novel is a very tough discipline. Poems can be written in spurts, irregularly. I sometimes write ten poems at once. But of those ten, perhaps one third will eventually be published. With a novel it's a whole different thing. You sit down every morning and push that pen across the page, and you have to get from one point to another. You know that you have to move your character to a certain city and out again and you must do it that day whether you feel like it or not. You don't always start out inspired, but you work your way into the scene, things start happening. You begin pushing that pen along, and then maybe after two hours you're really going. Things you hadn't expected are happening on the page. There's such a hell of a lot of sheer plugging. Sometimes you write chapters and chapters and wind up discarding them. But you plod along day after day. You have to get up every morning at eight (or whenever) and sit down for at least three or four hours.

        By the way, I think that you can be a writer with four hours a day to write. Although you may need two hours of warm-up time before, and two hours of wind-down time afterward.

NYQ: *We were talking about serving your apprenticeship as a poet and becoming a poet.*

EJ: There was something I wanted to add about that. You have to find that place in yourself where you have great control, yet great freedom. Control over your craft so it's almost automatic. And at the same time great freedom to deal with unconscious material. That's the point at which you become a poet. Both things are not always operating at optimum pitch, however. You may sit down in the morning and feel you're going to write a poem, but the poem you produce may be just a warm-up for some other unwritten poem.

NYQ: *Do you see special exercises like free association exercises or games to get you going?*

EJ: No, I don't, but sometimes I read.

NYQ: *Which poets?*

EJ: Lately I've been reading a lot of Neruda. God help me for saying that. Every time you mention a name in an interview, you get haunted by that name from then on. Critics will clobber me with "influenced by Neruda"—but the reason I read him is that he shows me the possibilities of the imagination. I love the way he associates from one image to the next. It gets my mind going. But when I write, I write poems very different from the ones I've been reading. I may read a poem by Neruda that deals with death. But that doesn't mean I'm going to write a poem about death.

NYQ: *What do you do when you are plunging under water and you hit a block, when you can't write any more, when the poem doesn't mesh and when you sense it's a block rather than just being finished for that day?*

EJ: You leave the poem in your notebook and come back to it eventually. Months or years later you may see it very clearly. I save all my notebooks, and from time to time when I don't know what I'm going to write, I read them over and find the first line of a poem which I started but couldn't finish and sometimes I'm able to finish it. Nothing you write is ever lost to you. At some other level your mind is working on it.

NYQ: *Are there times when you can't write anything? How do you get around them?*

EJ: One of the happy things about writing both prose and poetry is that you always have something to do. We have a funny idea in this country about overspecialization. Lately I've been writing poems, articles and prose fiction, and it's been a good combination for me. Obviously you're not going to be at the peak of inspiration every day. And if you're not writing poems, why should it be dishonorable to write an article?

NYQ: *Then you don't have problems with blocks?*

EJ: Not at the moment. God knows lots of them in the past,
        and may have again in the future. Knock on wood.

NYQ: *In your article "The Artist as Housewife" you wrote about
        the willingness to finish things being a good measure as to
        whether one was adult or not. Could you talk about this
        willingness to finish work as a special problem of the
        artist?*

EJ: I went for years not finishing anything. Because, of course,
        when you finish something you can be judged. My poems
        used to go through 360 drafts. I had poems which were
        rewritten so many times that I suspect it was just a way
        of avoiding sending them out.

NYQ: *You can see it very clearly now.*

EJ: When I look at some of those drafts, I realize that beyond
        a certain point I wasn't improving anything, I was just
        obsessing. I was afraid to take risks.

NYQ: *Is this more of a problem with women, do you think?*

EJ: It's hard to generalize, but since women are encouraged
        not to have responsibility for their own lives, I suppose
        they do have more of a problem in this respect. Of course
        throughout history there have always been women who
        didn't give in to the demand that they remain children.
        Nevertheless, a woman's time tends to be more
        fragmented. (I can just hear all the male poets I know
        who have office jobs screaming and yelling.) But perhaps
        it's not a problem of sheer time; perhaps it has more to do
        with not trusting yourself. Also women want to find men
        they admire and look up to. That's very dangerous.

NYQ: *What started you writing?*

EJ: I don't remember a time when I didn't write. As a kid I
        used to keep journals and notebooks. I wrote stories and
        illustrated them. I never said I wanted to be a writer, but
        I always wrote. Still, it was hard to make the step of
        saying, "I'm a writer" before I had published. I would
        shuffle my feet and look down at the floor. After my first
        book was accepted for publication, I began to think, "Gee,
        I'm a poet." Talk about being other-directed.

NYQ: *You mentioned once that your early poems were in
        traditional verse form and that you came rather late to*

free writing. What would you say about that kind of classical training for a poet?

EJ: I think it's tremendously important. You get letters from people saying: "I love to write poetry and I have twenty-six books of poetry in my desk drawer but I never read poetry." The country is full of "poets" who have never bought a book of poetry. If every person who sends poems to magazines would just buy one slim volume of verse, poets would not be starving. I've spent years reading poetry. I went to graduate school and read ancient and modern poetry, imitated Keats, imitated Pope, imitated Browning. . . . Learning is good for a poet as long as she doesn't become a professional scholar.

NYQ: *Can you write prose and poetry simultaneously?*

EJ: For the first six months when I was writing my novel, I wrote poems simultaneously. But then when I got very deep into *Fear of Flying* (when I got past the 200-page point) it really took over—and from that point on I couldn't write poetry. Many of the poems in *Half-Lives* were written the year before *Fruits & Vegetables* was published, and many of them were written the following year. Some of them were written during the time I was beginning the novel. But fiction takes over your life. The final section in *Fear of Flying* (the chapter where Isadora is alone in Paris, abandoned in the hotel room) nearly did me in. I felt that I was Isadora and was abandoned in that hotel room. It was ghastly. Then I spent months writing chapters which never found their way into the book at all. The ending was finally rewritten about seven times. The last chapter, which is now about six pages long, was rewritten so many times you wouldn't believe it. And I finally wound up with a minimal amount of words but just the right sort of indeterminate feeling I wanted. I had written it every other way imaginable.

NYQ: *Other endings?*

EJ: Yes. And I won't tell you what they are.

NYQ: *Was it coincidence or were you working toward prose poem form that one of the last poems in* Half-Lives *has long prose poem sections in it?*

EJ: I think I'm going to do more of that. Prose and poetry intermingled. It didn't really have to do with my writing the novel, but I'm very interested in mixed forms. Even the novel has a few poems in it.

NYQ: *You mentioned that you raised your own consciousness as an artist while your home was in Germany. (Then you mentioned just now that Paris became a locale for you.) Generally speaking, how do you feel your locale affects the way you work as a poet?*

EJ: The German experience was complicated because it made me suddenly realize I was Jewish. I had been raised as an atheist by cosmopolitan parents who didn't care about religion, and living in Germany gave me a sense of being Jewish and being potentially a victim. That opened up my poetry. I wrote a whole sequence called "The Heidelberg Poems," some of which were published in the *Beloit Poetry Journal* under my maiden name. They dealt with a kind of primal terror and with being a victim of Nazism. After writing those poems, I was able to explore my own feelings and emotions in a way I hadn't before. The experience wasn't pleasant, but it was a deepening one.

NYQ: *How do you find the New York locale as a place for a working poet?*

EJ: I must say that I don't give a lot of importance to locale despite what I just said about Germany. At that point in my life it was important to be in touch with those feelings of terror. But I don't think it matters where the hell you write. You write where you are. You write from your head. You don't write in Paris or London or Heidelberg. But perhaps I'm too harsh about this because I'm not a landscape poet. I write about my own inner geography.

But there are other things in New York that are very distracting. Too many parties. Too many telephone calls. Too many people. Yet when I found myself last summer at Cape Cod sitting alone for hours and listening to the ocean, trees and stuff, I would call long distance to New York because it was too quiet. I couldn't stand it. Still, I do think it's kind of phony when young people say: "I'm going off to Europe with my notebook in hand. I will be inspired by the fountains of Rome or sitting in a café in Paris." What crap. (I did it, too, of course.) You write best in a place where you're familiar and can stack papers on the floor. But beyond that, locale doesn't matter.

NYQ: *When you talk about that room of your own, what do you mean particularly?*

EJ: I mean a place where you can close the door, make a mess if necessary, and nobody bothers you. My mother, who is a very talented painter, never had a room of her own, had to set up her easel in the living room and put away her paints if people were coming over. That's very destructive, especially for a woman. Staking out your territory is the big definition of identity that you win within your family or with the man you live with. That in itself is a very important struggle. When you can say to the person (or people) you live with: "This is the place where I work," then part of the battle of your identity as an artist has been fought. And in a very tangible way.

NYQ: *Could you comment on the question of the selfishness of the artist to demand time and space—the whole question of selfishness as a working condition?*

EJ: We all suffer about this. If you want to have human relationships, it's very hard to say, "Now I am closing the door to work." But the people you live with have to be aware that you are not shutting them out and it's not a rejection of them. It's very hard to be a writer because it means taking seriously your own nightmares and daydreams. If you're a young unpublished writer and you're closing yourself in a room, neglecting other people, it seems very selfish. Almost like masturbation. But you have to believe in yourself. It helps a lot if the people you live with respect what you're doing. My husband respected my work at first more than I respected it. He'd say, "You have to work." And I'd say, "Help, let me out!"

NYQ: *Like Colette.*

EJ: Well, not quite. Willy locked her in a room to turn out these Claudine novels. He was exploiting her financially.

NYQ: *You once suggested writing a poem from a dream and dream images. How do you feel about using dream material?*

EJ: Again, that has to do with total self-surrender. But I've always found that if you try to use literal dreams in your work they're very boring. It's like waking up in the morning and trying to tell your dreams to somebody at the breakfast table. Fascinating to you, but to the other person, incredibly boring. "There was this floating apple and winged eyeball and blood." It doesn't interest anyone else. So when you use dream images in poems you have to universalize them. Like any other poetic images.

NYQ: *How do you feel about the use of drugs to get into a poem?*

EJ: I've never been able to do it. With pot, all I want to do is sit around and eat. I don't have any interest in writing whatsoever. Alcohol also makes me incapable of writing. Hashish is like pot—only more so. And I've never tried LSD. I tend to think that drugs are useless to writers. But that may just be because I have not been able to use them. I think when you write you need a combination of great control and great abandonment. What the drug gives you is great abandonment, but the control goes all to hell.

NYQ: *What special things do you want to happen, do you think can happen in a workshop?*

EJ: The best thing that happened to me when I was in a workshop at the School of the Arts was that I met a lot of other poets. They turned me on to lots of books. Also I got feedback on my work. I met people I could exchange poems with. And from time to time somebody would say something that made me think hard. I don't think a workshop teaches you how to be a writer, but it serves its purpose in indirect ways.

NYQ: *What assignments do you find helpful for beginning writers, thinking over your own workshops?*

EJ: That's hard. Some students come to you with too much freedom. They cannot censor themselves at all. For those you have to stress craft. Other students come to you so hung up on craft that they have absolutely no freedom. For them you stress freedom. What works for one student doesn't work for another. So to say something in an interview like: "Craft is the most important thing" is misleading.

NYQ: *Did the workshops help you in your own writing?*

EJ: Yes. But that was because I went around a lot and worked with different poets. It's dangerous to have only one mentor. What you'll do is pick up all that poet's prejudices and imitate them. It's much better to study with a variety of people.

But the most important education you get is on your own. It's like what Rilke said in *Letters to a Young Poet:* "There's only one way—go in to yourself." You learn in solitude from reading other writers. And from writing and writing and writing. A workshop can accelerate that process, but the basic learning you do is alone.

NYQ: *You've run workshops for high school students and for adults. What do you find happening in the two age groups when you get started?*

EJ: It's really not all that different except that (as you'd expect) a high school student is less sophisticated. I honestly think it's a rare high school student who has her or his own voice. You must have a certain amount of maturity to be a poet. Seldom do sixteen-year-olds know themselves well enough. You can work a lot with students at that level, but it's really preparatory work. I go into shock when I see a South American poet with a first book at the age of nineteen. In North America we tend to have a prolonged adolescence. We're more likely to publish around the age of thirty. I think it was Neruda's *Twenty Poems of Love and a Song of Despair* which was published when he was nineteen or twenty. But in South America they tend to grow up faster than we do. It must be the heat.

NYQ: *It may have to do with the competitiveness of the publishing business.*

EJ: I don't know anything about publishing in South America. But I do know from my experience with other writers that most North Americans don't come into their maturity until they are at least twenty-five. I hate making generalizations like that because I can see people writing it down and saying—Ah, until I'm twenty-five . . . There are always millions of exceptions.

I used to sit around reading books and comforting

myself. Virginia Woolf didn't publish her first book till she
was past thirty. Katherine Anne Porter was thirty-three
when she published her first short story. I would pore over
such facts. If I had known someone in high school or
college and saw something published by him before I was
published, it threw me into an envious rage. Being
unpublished is so painful.

NYQ: *How do you feel about publishing? Do you feel it's
       important for a poet to be published?*

EJ: Obviously if you write, you want to communicate with
       other people. To say that you don't is phony. But I'm not
       sure that publication always reflects quality. Magazines
       buy poems for very strange reasons. And for a young poet
       to determine whether or not his work is successful,
       dependent on whether or not he gets published, is a very
       dangerous business. I think the best poems in my first book
       never got taken by magazines. My name was unknown, so
       nobody cared. Also, many of them were long, and lots of
       magazines use poems as fillers.

NYQ: *What about sending out?*

EJ: Yes, I think it's helpful to send work out depending on
       what kind of reaction you have when it's rejected. If
       you take that as a final judgment, it's dangerous. But if
       you do it in a kind of lighthearted way (who does it in a
       lighthearted way? Nobody!) it's okay. You must
       realize that people who accept or reject your poems are
       not always right.

NYQ: *You can be affected by the recognition after publication.*

EJ: I was helped by the freedom it gave me. You see, I was
       one of these people who was very hung up. I had all kinds
       of blocks and problems and didn't believe I was a poet,
       so when people began saying to me, "Hey, you really can
       write," it gave me a lot more confidence and it made
       writing easier. But this is tremendously individual. I
       think for somebody else, it might be ruination. I am very
       self-critical and don't publish everything I write. I
       sometimes get requests from little magazines which say:
       "Send us anything you have." And my theory is I'm not
       going to publish anything I have. If I publish a poem I
       want it to be something I care about.

NYQ: *What about poetry readings? How do they affect your own writing?*

EJ: They've made me very aware of the rhythms of my poetry.

NYQ: *Would you rather have your poetry read on a page or heard as a poem?*

EJ: Both. I like people to hear me read because I think that they understand the poetry better. When I read, I feel I'm giving life to the poem.

NYQ: *Does this desire to have your poetry read influence some of the forms you use like the list poems or the poems where a certain word or phrase is repeated?*

EJ: No, it isn't premeditated. I do think my poetry has a kind of sound quality. Very often it uses repetition. But I think that poetry by nature is a form brought alive by the human voice.

NYQ: *Could you comment on what you think poetry is?*

EJ: It's voice music. Ancient poetry was all produced for that purpose. And that's still a very strong tradition. I don't think it was produced by the "reading scene" of the late sixties and early seventies. This was the ancient function of poetry. We haven't created a tradition—we've just rediscovered it. There was a period in American poetry in the forties and fifties when verse was very difficult, involuted, and meant to be studied and read on the page. That was partly the influence of the New Criticism. Since tight academic verse was being written by a certain segment of American poets, those of us who went to college at the time thought that to be the nature of poetry. On the contrary, that period was actually rather aberrant. Poetry has more often been a spoken thing than a difficult metaphysical puzzle. When I write, I always hear the voice in my head. I'm baffled that there is even a question about it.

Still, since we're into definitions of poetry, I think I ought to add that condensation is essential. Images are important to me because the image is a kind of emotional shorthand. Poetic language must be rhythmic, fresh, interesting language, but it must also be condensed and pack a lot of meaning into a little space.

NYQ: *Are there any contemporary poets that you feel particularly close to?*

EJ: I could name them but then the people I hadn't named would wonder why I hadn't named them and it would only be because they hadn't popped into my head. There are so many.

NYQ: *Do you think there are many good poets around?*

EJ: I think we're living at a time of great renaissance for poets.

NYQ: *You mentioned once that when you were a beginning poet it helped to get together with small groups of poets and read work in progress. Do you continue to do that?*

EJ: I have a number of friends who are writers and who read my work. There were specific people who were very important to me when I was putting together my first book. I used to get together with Norma Klein and Rosellen Brown and Patricia Goedicke. I think it's very important to find friends whose prejudices you know. And who care about you and your work and will be honest with you. You must share enough values with them so that you can trust each other. Finding such friends might be the most important thing a young poet does. You need a critic, but it can't be just *anybody*. The idea of sending your work to a stranger is perhaps not such a good idea. You need somebody whose prejudices you know.

NYQ: *There must be a need for criticism. So many manuscripts came in to the* Quarterly *with requests for criticism.*

EJ: Yes, and it's so hard to honor such a request because you don't know the person. And often you don't know what kind of psychological problems are going on behind the request. It's not as simple as it looks. If you write a critical letter to somebody, you may absolutely destroy that person. Or make him furious.

NYQ: *Do you get manuscripts from strangers?*

EJ: Yes. Everybody does. It's just impossible to deal with. You don't know how this person is going to react to what you say or what you may be stirring up.

NYQ: *Do you have a favorite poem?*

EJ: How can you have a favorite poem? Your favorite poem is always the one you just wrote. The others are not quite real to you. I read *Half-Lives* now (those poems were finished about a year ago and other people tell me they're enjoying them), but I can't enjoy them. They seem very remote from me now.

NYQ: *What will your next book of poems be like?*

EJ: It's too early to tell. I think I will do some more combinations of prose and poetry like "From the Country of Regrets." Overlapping of forms. I'm also working on a long poem which looks like it might become a self-portrait in verse. I'm writing on very traditional subjects again and poems that rhyme occasionally. I'm writing a poem to Keats and a poem to the moon and a poem to spring. After all the wild stuff in my first two books, here I am writing poems to Keats and to spring.

NYQ: *You've spoken about the frustration of writing from the point of view of a woman. Did you get to the point where you felt trapped by your subject matter?*

EJ: It took me a long time to break through to the freedom of writing out of a woman's voice, and then it seemed to be *all* I was writing about. Now I want to go beyond that. Sexuality is an important part of life, and sometimes it seems to be *all* of life. But there *are* other subjects. One tends to become impatient with oneself and doesn't want to repeat the things one has learned.

NYQ: *That doesn't mean you won't come back to it.*

EJ: I don't know. I don't have any program. I just sit down and write. When I have enough poems, I'll see if they make a book. I didn't realize that *Half-Lives* was a book which dealt with fulfillment and emptiness until I began putting the poems together. Then it became apparent to me that I had subterranean rivers of imagery in those poems. Certain themes repeated themselves and I saw that a lot of the poems dealt with emptiness, wholeness, halfness and so on. And a book began to come together. So I arranged the sections the way they naturally fell. I can't tell you what the third book will be "about" until I see what poems accumulate. But I am quite sure that at certain periods in your life you deal with certain themes; and if you grow, those themes have to change.

NYQ: *We wanted to ask you some questions about translation. Have any of your poems been translated into other languages? And then, do you ever do translations? Do you read poetry in foreign languages?*

EJ: I don't read poetry in foreign languages. Although I know some foreign languages tolerably in a kind of school way, and used to be able to speak some of them when I lived in the countries where they were spoken, I don't really know any language well enough to translate. I suppose I don't try translation because I write prose when I'm not writing poetry.

NYQ: *When you speak of translations as the kind of thing poets can do, what recommendations would you make to a young poet about choosing something in a related field like translations or teaching or something entirely different to be a way of surviving economically while he struggles?*

EJ: I think the best thing for a young poet is to grow up in Latin America. And to be made a diplomat.

NYQ: *Like a Neruda.*

EJ: We don't have ways of rewarding our poets like that. I don't know what a poet can do to survive. Everything you think of has terrible disadvantages. If you're a college teacher you're always up to your neck in bad student writing. If you're an editor you get so weary of books being thrust at you that the printed word almost loses its force. Advertising is not the most joyous profession. (I know poets who do all these things.) Maybe the best "profession" for a poet is to be born very wealthy. When I was in graduate school, I was told to get my Ph.D. in English and to use my summers to write. I found that getting a Ph.D. in English was not conducive to writing at all.

NYQ: *How do you feel about confessional poetry?*

EJ: Who the hell was it who invented that dumb term? There is no such *thing* as confessional poetry. Anne Sexton gets loaded with the term and it's absurd. It has become a putdown term for women, a sexist label for women's poetry. People who use the term are falling into the subject-matter fallacy. Subject matter doesn't make a poem. And so a critic who uses that term is showing his total ignorance of what poetry is about.

There is this tendency to think that if you could only find the magic way, then you could become a poet. "Tell me how to become a poet. Tell me what to do." Is there a given subject that makes you a poet? Well, that's ridiculous. What makes you a poet is a gift for language, an ability to see into the heart of things, and an ability to deal with important unconscious material. When all those things come together, you're a poet. But there isn't one little gimmick that makes you a poet. There isn't any formula for it.

NYQ: *In general, modern poetry requires (underline one): more vegetables, less vegetables, all of the above, none of the above.*

EJ: The answer is: All of the above.

NYQ: *That gets into your whole minimal vs. maximal poetry. You want everything.*

EJ: I do want to get everything into my poetry. I want to get the whole world in. Colette had a term for it. She said that she wanted the "impure." Life was impure and that was what she wanted in her art—all the junk and jumble of things. Wallace Stevens also uses the image of a man on a dump: the poet—the man sitting on the dump. Life is full of all kinds of wonderful crap. Splendid confusion. Poetry should be able to take it all in.

NYQ: *What do you think of interviews?*

EJ: You always read them and say, "Oh, no. That's not me." No matter how candid you are, you *hate* the person you seem to be. But I understand the impulse to get a person down on paper. I'm reading my novel in galleys now and thinking: "Who wrote this book? What kind of shit is this?" And I'm thinking that the only way that I'll ever get it all down is to write another book because I don't like this one any more.

NYQ: *You made a statement a while ago about writing from
your inner landscape. And yet you also talk about writing
as a woman poet. At a point when women poets are
having a renaissance, how do you see this relationship
between writing from this inner landscape and writing as
who you are quite apart from where you live and the
time you live in? And also being alive in a moment when
there are lots of forces—psychoanalysis, the women's
movement, moving down to the end of the century, and
that kind of thing.*

EJ: What should I answer first? One question at a time . . .
Actually, I don't think those things conflict. If you're
writing about your inner landscape you're writing about
that inner landscape as female. It's female first and then
beyond that, it's human. The two things don't cancel each
other out. It's just a question of how you get there. Of
course, you're affected by the movements of your time,
but not in a direct way. Look—I was not living in the
United States between 1966 and 1969—which was the
explosion of the hippie subculture, the flower children,
the student revolutionaries—and yet there were many
people who on reading *Fruits & Vegetables* saw me as a
sort of flower child of that generation. If you're a poet,
you *do* have your navel plugged in to the *zeitgeist* and
you *are* tuned in to the currents of your time. And not in a
literal, obvious way. But your antennae are working.
You don't plan it.

NYQ: *A completely different question that we didn't ask you is if
there are any reference works on the craft of poetry for
students to read or that you particularly love yourself.*

EJ: You know the books I've recommended for my seminar.
And some of the other books I find really indispensable
are: *The Glass House,* Allan Seager's biography of
Theodore Roethke; Rilke's *Letters of a Young Poet:* Keats's
letters; Mandelstam's *Hope Against Hope* (which shows
you what it's like for a poet in a totalitarian country) ;
books on mythology like *The Golden Bough* or *Women's
Mysteries* or *The Great Mother.* I would certainly
recommend *The Book of the It,* a book that really loosens
up the imagination. I would very much recommend
Theodore Roethke's *Straw for the Fire,* Virginia Woolf's

Writer's Notebook, Collette's *Earthly Paradise.* Those are not books strictly speaking on the craft of writing, but I don't think you're going to learn much about poetry from reading about iambic pentameter, spondees, trochees and things like that. If that's what you're thinking of—a handbook. (There are many good handbooks of poetry. There's Untermeyer's *The Pursuit Of Poetry,* which is very complete and good.) But for the most part you learn to be a poet (as Rilke says) by going into yourself and by reading lots of other writers. I think I once told you that when I began writing free verse, I read and reread Denise Levertov's books. I figured that *she* knew where to break a line. Her white spaces on the page *meant* something. So I reread and reread her books trying to figure out where she broke her lines and why. I might have gone to William Carlos Williams too, because that was where she learned. You learn to write by reading the poets you love over and over and trying to figure out what they're doing and why they're doing it. You read Galway Kinnell's *Book of the Nightmares* and you see the way it interweaves certain images throughout the book. Study the poets you love. Read them again and again. That's how you learn to be a poet. Unfortunately though, talent is something you're born with. And that's not very democratic. A gift for language is essential. So is a feeling for the rhythms of prose and poetry. The other gift is stamina—that willingness to *do* it and *do* it and *do* it. I don't know where you get that. I knew many people in college who had plenty of talent but never became writers. They gave up. A good portion of the struggle is just that willingness to keep on doing it. Ultimately, I would say I write because it gives me a great deal of pleasure to write. I would rather write than do almost anything else. Somebody will say to me, "Oh, you've been very productive," and the implication is that I've been disciplined and plodding. But writing is such an incredible joy and pleasure that at times it scarcely feels like work. There are also bad times, though.

NYQ: *Have you ever thought of another career?*

EJ: I thought of being a painter, and for years I did paint. There was a time when I wanted very much to be a doctor. At one time I thought I was going to be a college professor. And, of course, I still teach. But I think writing is the only profession which has enough surprises in store to hold me for the rest of my life. If you keep growing and changing, writing is an endless voyage of discovery. The surprises never stop. All that runs out is time.

SELECTED BIBLIOGRAPHY

Fruits & Vegetables, New York, Holt, Rinehart and Winston, Inc., 1971.

Half-Lives, New York, Holt, Rinehart and Winston, Inc., 1973.

Fear of Flying, New York, Holt, Rinehart and Winston, Inc., 1973.

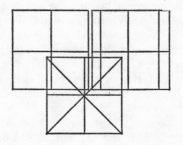

CRAFT INTERVIEW WITH DIANE WAKOSKI

NYQ: *Could you tell us when you began writing?*

DIANE WAKOSKI: I really did start writing when I was a little kid. I wrote my first poem when I was seven years old, about a rose bush, and then I wrote a lot of poetry when I was in high school. I got seriously involved in college, which was when I decided I would spend my life as a poet. Right about the time I was taking Thom Gunn's workshop. That workshop was a wonderful workshop because Thom was very gracious when he said I didn't need a teacher, but what he meant was that there was an unusual situation in that particular workshop. There really were five extremely talented people who would have learned from each other whether he had been there or not. He did what a gentleman and scholar would do. He quarreled with us enough to present his objective, but he also respected the fact that we all were just passionately involved in what we were doing. And would do it. In the true sense, we didn't need him. On the other hand, he really did help us because he understood that. He didn't try to mold us or do anything else. That was a formative period. I was just beginning to find my voice and write the poems that—my publishable poems date from that year.

NYQ: *That was* Coins and Coffins?

DW: Yes. You know, there really are events that happen in
           your life that are significant at the time they are
           happening. No one else may notice that they are
           significant, but they are obviously partly significant
           because you think they are. But you also felt they were
           because there was something significant about them.
           And the event that I will always remember from that
           period—and I date my poetry from that period, though
           I wrote poetry much longer than that—was the result
           of Thom's workshop being very prestigious in a strange
           sort of way. The Poetry Center, which was just
           beginning, invited him to pick five students from
           Berkeley or people who wrote poetry seriously, and
           obviously Berkeley had a reputation, and put us on a
           program in January of 1959 called "Berkeley Poets." For
           me it was a really significant event. The other poets—
           they were all men if that means anything—it didn't
           mean anything to me . . .

NYQ: *So you would say that that was your most important
           apprenticeship—that experience?*

DW: It really was. The first thing Thom Gunn made me
           realize was that there are lots of rules about poetry that
           have nothing to do with poetry in the abstract. Poetry
           is a human art, and we're really talking about our
           lives, and poetry which is most readable is that which
           is most intimate and touching. At the same time, it
           requires a tremendous kind of craft to walk that
           tightrope of talking intimately about feelings or talking
           feelings and not producing a certain amount of gush.
           Thom made me immediately aware of the fact that—
           he didn't say this in so many words—I had a proclivity
           to like beautiful things, that I thought poetry was about
           beautiful things. I still think that, by the way, but I
           have a different idea of what beautiful things are now.
           He made me realize that if I was going to get any
           tension at all in there I would have to stop writing those
           pretty things. I would have to write something more
           powerful. And he did this partly, I think, by being
           British. You know, Americans are very susceptible to a

British accent. It carries a certain authority, especially when you're young.

NYQ: *Do you have your student poets read their own poems?*

DW: I do. I really very much subscribe to the idea that what contemporary poetry is about is partially an oral phenomenon which can only be understood and really appreciated if you hear it. I know for a fact that the experience of hearing the poetry reading is dynamic to many people who would not have had that experience reading the poems on the page. I'm not talking about the poet himself or the good reader of poetry or the scholar who obviously can find many kinds of pleasure in a poem. I really do think that if there is any such thing as a possible wider audience—and even for any of us who think of ourselves as experts having specialized in one poet—the experience of having been to a poetry reading is much more vivid to us than reading the book. Consequently, I think the people should learn to do it. I used to be very, very interested in the prospect of poetry as theatre and having some actors get involved in it. I am against it at the moment. I still believe it's an interesting prospect, but I've come to realize, from talking about this to many people, that isn't really what poetry is about these days. Poetry is about poetry, which means the poet reading his poems. This gives the poems another dimension in the same way that when you try to talk about film as an art as opposed to theatre as an art, you can make all kinds of generalizations. The point is that right now in the times we live most people find the film experience a more vivid one. It's only those of us who have certain kinds of knowledge and certain perceptions that like the theatre just as much. I think that's pretty generally true about poetry. I see no reason why if a person is really serious about poetry, it shouldn't be one dimension of his education. If he reads it, and reading it means presenting his personality as another dimension, and then that's part of the poem. There are poets who have resisted this and their argument is a perfectly good one, a good poem comes alive on the page. But perhaps that isn't really that much to think

about right now. We do and we don't. We have a much
different idea about poems lasting. It makes me think
that if a poem lasts eighty years, it has really lasted a
long time. And I do expect poems to last eighty years.
Although they don't always. I know I tried to reread
Shelley this summer, and found it impossible.

NYQ: *Do you have an imaginary audience in the back of your
mind during a reading, the way you really want an
audience to be, the way you'd like them to respond?*

DW: Yeah, I think so. I think I have several imaginary
audiences. First of all, I always write my poems with the
feeling that I am speaking to someone. Or some group of
people. So I obviously have people in mind. And I
wrote poetry because I had a very narrow and
circumscribed deprived life, and it was a fantasy world.
And the Diane who's in my poems is not a real
person. She's a person I would like to be, that I can
imagine myself being, even though I put all my faults in
my poems, it doesn't mean I'm not a fantasy or
imagined person. I didn't create a fantasy that was
unreal. I'm smart enough not to have done that. But
the Diane in my poems really is fantasy. I don't care
how happy my life ever gets, there's always a part of all
of us that feels deprived in some way or another. We
don't have everything and what the poem speaks to is
that fantasy part of ourselves—and no matter what my
life is and no matter how it's fulfilled, there are many
things that I will not be, and those are the things that
I will fantasize. Part of my imaginary audience are
always those people who have not loved me or are not
in my life because I am not the Diane I fantasize. In
a way I'm always having a kind of duel with my
audience. I don't ever believe they'll ever like me. And
they are the very people who in real life probably
wouldn't like me.

NYQ: *Your early poems have been called "confessional
poetry." What is your definition of confessional poetry?*

DW: I'll give you my parting line first, and then—the term
"confessional" has been a real misnomer. A critical
school, I don't know if it was M. L. Rosenthal who
coined it or not. In general, people think that it is,

when he was writing about Plath and Sexton and Lowell. The one thing that Plath and Sexton and Lowell all had in common, and most twentieth-century poets have this, is they liked physical imagery. They all had been in mental institutions and all had either suicidal impulses or alcoholic behavior. They had in some way had antisocial patterns in their lives. And I use the term advisedly because the term "confessional" is related to poems and poets who are talking about experiences that were not acceptable to normal people —the fact that you've been in a mental institution, the fact that you're an alcoholic, the fact that you tried to commit suicide, the fact that you were a conscientious objector—whatever. They were things that you were supposed to be ashamed of and so to talk about your impulses was to confess them. I think that's a real misnomer because first of all even Plath's poetry, which comes closer to that term than any other, is not confessional in the sense that none of those poets are ashamed of what they did or felt that anything they felt should be condemnatory. They felt they had human experiences. In Sexton's case her poetry was only made possible by her experiences of madness because what her personal experience did was obviously shatter a kind of bourgeois insulation—I don't mean that all bourgeois people are insulated but that life is one that insulates you very easily. And to break through to a kind of feeling perception of the world is something I'm sure she would never have arrived at without her nervous breakdowns. Plath has often been said to glorify suicide in her poems. She's certainly not confessing it as a bad thing. I think in order to read her poems with real sympathy you have to have a tragic vision of the world and it has to be a kind of grand thing accomplished by itself. Sexton's poems really do point to the fact that when you go to bedlam and back and get something good out of it, it isn't a bad thing at all. Lowell's poems, which are the source of that term, are simply autobiographical poems. What he does is speak about being an aristocrat with a certain amount of humility, showing that it wasn't all that it was cracked up to be either. But none of them are confessing. Lowell doesn't feel it was an original sin. He wants you to understand that whatever condition people have, it's a human condition and he glorified it.

NYQ: *Could you tell us about your George Washington poems? Why did you choose him?*

DW: Because I'm basically interested in symbol and allegory. And Washington is the father of our country. And we live in this very paternalistic society, and he stands for the kind of masculine values that have strengths but for many of us have their frustrations. They do stand for the opposite of what poetry is about. For me he's really the symbol of the material world that doesn't appreciate enough how you feel and for me the revelation that that frustration comes out of not any of the things like materialism or the kind of Philistine attitude that penalizes, but really comes out of our inability to communicate, which I equate with our unwillingness to communicate. For instance, nobody ever understands anybody else. The people we think we understand or feel we communicate with are simply the ones who have tried to talk to us and we have therefore been aroused to try to talk back. Washington, as a historic figure, stands for that kind of aloofness that just doesn't give. For me it's the antithesis of what poetry is. It's also basically what I fought in myself all my life. I am extremely shy. It's really hard for me to talk to people. It took many years of writing poetry and then approaching people by talking to them about poetry to get away from this. I sat in Greece for three months this summer and literally did not have a conversation with anyone except one huge quarrel that I had with a man about poetry. And it's not because people bore me. It's because I'm really frightened of them and I am not able to give and they don't want to communicate, and they do seem boring to me. It's always been easier for me to go off and read a book. Poetry is the next thing to reading a book. By putting it down on paper and then by publishing it you're doing the same thing to people as if you had a conversation with them. But for me it's easier because I can do it by myself. I still really fear to communicate with people, unless I have that symbol.

NYQ: *Do you think your surrealism goes closer to the tremendous emotional impact of all that is in conflict?*

DW: Surrealism is a fascinating subject, and it's very easy to have a different idea about it every day. What I would say today about surrealism is that as a technique for writing it's a fascinating way of trying to combine your intellectual perceptions and your emotions about it. All those bizarre placements of things have to do with the fact that every day of our lives we have this bizarre mind living in a body that could be someone else's. Seeing too much and knowing so much more. I've never been an athlete or had any kind of physical prowess of any sort. And I often wonder if athletes, people like those Russian gymnasts, or acrobats you see in circuses, have a different kind of control over the world because I keep feeling how helpless we are. We know—I wonder, for instance, if they have more control over their emotions.

NYQ: *Because they seem to have so much practice.*

DW: To me emotions seem to come so much out of the body. A lot of my imagery is physiological imagery. I really do perceive my emotions as if they come out of different parts of my body. Different parts except my head. And I wonder if people who are wonderful athletes have in some way more of a sense of continuity with their emotions. My emotions are very strong and athletic, but my body just doesn't follow. I really think that part of what surrealism is about and why it's such a twentieth-century technique is that we have all developed our minds so much. They still live in these bodies which are so separate. It's a very good way of presenting that separate but together bizarreness.

NYQ: *What about recurring images in your work—oranges, blood, jewels, flowers, have they evolved?*

DW: Yes. I didn't start out knowing what I was doing, but after a few years of writing poetry I began to realize that there were certain things that were part of my fantasy life. Usually images are what to me seem very beautiful or very terrible things. And I realized that even before I became a poet I was going to be repeating myself. Those were the things I wanted to write about. I think at the point I became aware of that was the time I was taking Thom Gunn's class and even more important I was for the first time reading Wallace Stevens and beginning to understand that beautiful early poetry of his, and I was reading Lorca for the first time, and those are both poets who used very, very sensuous physical imagery, and it was particularly noticeable in the case of Lorca but equally true of Stevens. He used over and over again the same images. And I realized that they used them as symbols—that their landscape became part of their trademark or their voice, and it suddenly was one of those awarenesses that you have known for a long time without realizing it. That was so obvious. There was no reason why I had to keep trying not to write about those things. The thing to do was to be superconscious of writing about them and to make them into a network. So all of those things did stand for my own sense of what is beautiful and durable.

NYQ: *Also, the very short words, the very strong short words. Is that part of this network of symbols?*

DW: I think that has a lot to do with the fact that I always wanted to read my poems aloud and that I come from California and that we have a—I don't know what a good adjective is for the way we speak—but it's very matter of fact, and the poetry in general cannot have a matter-of-fact tone. One of my greatest battles is how to get my matter-of-factness, which I consider part of my vision of the world, into lines and still make it sound like poetry. It's very natural for me. It's my matter-of-fact way of trying to describe things. It's something that I have deliberately allowed myself to use and tried every possible way of using it to see if I could get away with it.

NYQ: *Another one of the things in addition to the short words is the assonance. Is this sought or does this just happen?*

DW: That's a very hard thing to talk about because it's talking about your perception of the use of language. I don't know if anyone, including a linguistic specialist, has really figured a successful way of assessing what that is in a person. I know that my own view of it is

that I studied music for many years, that I started
writing Shakespearean sonnets, that in the back of my
mind I'm always going de-da, de-da, de-da, and that's
the test for me, by the way. If my language gets too
prose-y, too short, it means that at the back of my mind
I've said, "Boy, you haven't been iambic for a while." I
don't mean just iambic, but that's the easiest one to use.
When I feel that there haven't been any regularly
recurring rhythms, even though I don't feel required in
any way to make even-length lines or subscribe to
theories of meter (that strange thing which poetry is all
about), I still keep pulling back to that kind of thing.
Poetic language is everything that's beautiful. In some
way it always comes out singing. And I'm sure that that
has to do with my literal sense of what music is, and the
way poetry is related to that.

NYQ: *What about the parallel line and the parallel structure
that you use? That relates back to music, doesn't it?*

DW: That relates back to music, yes, and it also relates to
the way I like to put things into neat little piles.

NYQ: *Do you find yourself practicing exercises to keep yourself
in shape, writing sonnets and so forth?*

DW: I write short poems as exercises. It's hard for me to
write short lines in short poems. Although in retrospect
I've written an awful lot of them. Whenever I begin to
get very long and discursive, which is when I'm writing
a poem that I really wanted to write, I begin to feel
myself just kind of dissolving out. I have a strong urge
to just kind of pat things back in shape, and I write
short poems. I haven't for a long, long, long time done
any kind of experimentation with what is referred to as
metrical forms. Because I started writing poetry that
way. In high school poetry was a game for me. I don't
mean I didn't take it seriously because I think when
you're young, games are a serious part of your life—
they were challenges—using language in certain
rhythms, you'd get a rhyming dictionary, a thesaurus,
it was really fun to do. The only thing was you couldn't
say too much that way. And that's ideal for young
people because you don't have much to say then except
this is fun, who am I. You can boil it down to two or

three statements, and you don't have to think about experiences to write about unless you want to write for *Seventeen* magazine. So I think game playing is a very good way of starting poetry. If you start writing poetry when you are older, I don't think that's a natural concern. Unless you have the particular sense of language which goes with that, which by the way is not a twentieth-century sense of language. But I periodically go into doing it again. I found a wonderful book of forms this summer. Its name has escaped me. It has I think every peculiar form ever invented. What is that crazy little book of forms and who is he?

NYQ: *But you do write in form. You have a sestina, for example, in* Inside the Blood Factory, *which was five years ago, wasn't it?*

DW: Sestinas are fun. If you break the rule for iambic pentameter, which I insist is an English rule and not a French rule, it's a fun-organizing form, because you keep coming back and back and back like a refrain. If you make yourself very conscious of making very long lines and very short lines then there are really interesting musical sounds to the language. I'm not sure that I could write an iambic pentameter sestina.

NYQ: *That was a free form sestina.*

DW: Yes. The idea of making thirty-six lines all the same length is like being in jail.

NYQ: *Do you keep a journal?*

DW: Oh, I'm a hopeless failure at keeping a journal. The most I can ever do is several weeks at a time.

NYQ: *What excuses do you make up for not keeping a journal? What excuses do you make when you don't write?*

DW: Well, I have a lot of excuses. I'm still enough of an old Puritan to have to have an excuse for myself when I'm not writing. I truly believe in my own self-discipline and that I write when I'm ready to write and if I'm not, nothing valuable will come out. I wrote very little this summer except a few critical articles, and my excuse is that I really am going through a big change in my

personal life and in my poetry. This year is a very
retrospective year. I'm looking back on what I've done.
I don't feel very compulsive about writing anything. As
far as I'm concerned I've written enough so that I don't
have to worry about not writing any more. So I don't
feel obliged to write. On the other hand, I write because
I like to write. I am going to write again when I'm
ready. I wrote three or four poems this summer, which
will be included in my new book, some that I like very
much. They're moving in other directions, much more—
if you can make these distinctions—Apollonian than
Dionysian—and I'm much more interested in prose
as a component of the poem, and for the first time in
my life I'm really interested in writing some amount of
criticism. I'm very interested in theories of poetry, and
ideas of poetry and how poetry has changed in the last
years and what it means, the kind of poetry that works,
and why it works and so forth, and these never
interested me. I mean they interested me in terms of
how you made a poem, but not interested in how you
made articles out of it. I sat down and wrote articles
this summer because I really wanted to.

NYQ: *What writing method do you find most conducive to*
        producing your work, writing in longhand or writing at
        the typewriter?

DW: I'm very unhappy these days working in longhand,
        which is another reason these journals are not kept up.
        I don't write letters in longhand. I really like my
        typewriter. I started—I can remember being appalled
        once when someone told me he composed his poems on
        a typewriter. To me it was appalling, and he said,
        "Have you ever written a short story?" and I said, "Yes,"
        and he said, "Did you write it in longhand?" and I said
        "Yes," and he said, "Well, what's the difference?"
        But I do notice that the more I compose on the
        typewriter, the prosier my poems are. I never compose
        those kind of exquisite little things—lyric poems—on
        the typewriter. I don't see any way of possibly composing
        a lyric poem on the typewriter, because that's the kind
        of thing where every word means something and the
        way you write it down and the shape of it. I have
        notebooks from when I was in college that have an

almost shocking little strange elegant hand—my
hand was very sloppy—that the poems were composed
in. It was like a different state of organization.

NYQ: *The handwriting had to match it.*

DW: Yes, it had to match. There was a kind of elegant
slowness, and just the act of writing down a line and
then another line, I can just feel it. Every once in a
while I get in that mood again. It's not the usual mood.

NYQ: *Do you have to be in a special mood to write a poem?
Or if you feel one coming on, do you know . . .*

DW: I do. I think that's probably fairly typical. I can sit
down at any time and write something. But the good
things, the better things that I write—every once in a
while I just sit down and write—my favorite poem last
year—I was writing a letter to someone and I wanted
to include a poem and I didn't have a thing I had
written, so I just sat down and wrote it out and it's my
favorite poem from that time. Actually I had done a lot
of things that got me in the mood to write that poem,
and I became aware of it in the process of sitting down
and writing the letter.

NYQ: *How about revision? Do you revise a great deal?*

DW: I don't revise a great deal, but I revise after I read a
poem aloud, and if there are what I call dead spots in
it, I bring all my rhetorical skills to bear on it.

NYQ: *When you say read aloud, do you read to yourself or
before an audience?*

DW: Preferably before an audience. But to myself if there is
none. It's very hard for me to type something up, which
is one of the reasons I appreciate hiring a typist. It's
very hard for me to type things up and not want to
change. My kind of revision is not what Dylan
Thomas would call revision. Fifteen drafts or anything
like that.

NYQ: *Then most of it comes through your original impulse.*

DW: The one part of every poem that I subject to rigorous
rewrite is the last three or four lines. I love the last
three or four lines of poems, and I think they are the

easiest part to rewrite. You can rewrite a poem five
days after you've written it and completely change
that poem's meaning by changing the last four lines.
Or you can turn what was a mediocre poem into an
exciting poem. It's impossible for me to put a book
manuscript together without meddling a little bit.

NYQ: *You were talking about craft before in relation to that
workshop in California. Do you think craft is a
conscious thing or something that just happens when
enough bad stuff gets discarded in the process?*

DW: Well, obviously I think craftsmanship is something
that can be acquired in a lot of different ways.
Because I've always resisted authority even though
I'm a very authoritarian person, it's hard for me to
learn neat methodical ways and yet I always want to
see other people learn that way. So the hit-or-miss
method is my method of learning. In terms of the craft
of writing, I think that you learn it by reading. I just
don't see any other way for learning it. I think you
learn more from reading than from hearing people
talk. I don't see how anybody who writes poetry
conscientiously for ten years and reads can help but
get better. I just don't see any way. In a way that's
almost a dilemma with so many people writing today
and so many, many creative writing programs because
it means that any person with a certain amount of
time and effort with a lot of reading and who has a
certain kind of intelligence can write a respectable poem.
That presents a whole other funny vehicle for poetry
these days. No one really trusts reading one poem by
a person. On the other hand, if you read one poem that
you really like, you will remember it and you will go
on and look for something else. Most people don't
even see one poem that they really like in a magazine.
On the other hand, they like the magazine. They say
this is interesting, this is interesting and that could be
and so forth. But it's a very controversial subject of
what the value of publishing poems in magazines is.
I know one value it has and that's purely professional,
and that is you can't get a book published until you get
published in a lot of magazines. They are your
credentials for publishing a book. And they are the

way a lot of people can get to know your name. But I
don't know of a single positive value that I would say
derives for people from reading poems in magazines.
My feelings about this in the past few years have
forced me to forget to submit poems to magazines.
Lots of magazines ask you for poems and I'm always
perfectly glad to submit them, but I never quite
get around to typing them up, and by the time I
sit and think about it, I know that those poems can be
put in a book. The book will definitely have some
readers. It's a very complicated subject, because if you
ask me now if my conclusion is: should there be no
poetry magazines, I wouldn't say that; I'd say it's even
great to have poetry magazines for young writers to
publish in. I can't reconcile that with the fact that I
really don't think people read magazines. Obviously
somewhere I'm working with a prejudice. Maybe my
prejudice is that the magazines aren't good, or maybe
my prejudice is even if they're good, you shouldn't
submit to them.

NYQ: *What books do you recommend that your students
        read for craft principles? You said before that they
        have to read a lot. What do you recommend?*

DW: Well, there's just so many good books. I would like to
        suggest something very different from specific poets
        for people to read to learn craft. I think the way you
        learn craft is the same way you learn criticism. And
        that is by reading everything that you can find. I
        don't think you learn any kind of discrimination if
        you only read masterpieces. When you read a
        masterpiece, you may not like it. It may seem awful,
        and it's not until you read about a hundred more pieces
        that are nothing like masterpieces that you suddenly
        realize how good that was and when you start reading
        things that are badly written, and you suddenly
        recognize how badly written they are, you have already
        learned some craft. You can see students doing this,
        but you can't see them doing it if you say, "Now, read
        Sylvia Plath, and notice how she uses imagery here and
        so forth." There's nothing wrong with doing that in
        retrospect after they've read a lot, but if that's the
        way they learn, they will know that that's how Sylvia

Plath knows how to use imagery and they know that
Auden's lines are all scanned, and they know that and
that, but they don't have any idea of why that is good
poetry. They don't have any of the sensation that that's
really exciting. When you go through a magazine and
there's nothing that you can even stand to read and
then suddenly there's this beautiful poem there. That's
the experience they don't have because they only read
masterpieces. They don't seem as masterful when they
don't have a lot of schlock around them, when we
don't have a whole life of reading to compare them
with. I think at any given time it helps to have models
to write from. I learned to write from models. I think
most people do. Anybody who learns on his own
uses models. I started imitating Shakespeare's sonnets
when I was in high school. It's still the best way to learn
many many things. So I don't see anything wrong in
putting whatever five or six books together at any given
time, and I'm sure they change over the years, and
reading them because it will give pleasure, and pointing
out what you really like about poets, and they'll get
some ideas. I've seen students that I would be willing
to swear will not become poets, even if they have a
certain amount of talent, write some nice pieces
because they found a poem by someone that really
excited them and they imitated it. And it was an
exciting experience for them. But my real feeling is
that if you read five books and that's all you're going to
read, you're almost doing them a disservice. There
should be some way that they could go out and have a
lot available. This is done in the universities because
the libraries are getting better and better and better.
But you still have to go to the rare books room for most
of the poetry books, and most students are shy about
doing that. So they don't really get to sample anything.
Another article that I wrote this summer—and it's a
letter, a response to a man who teaches English at
Kent State—and the whole subject of the letter is
how it is possible to teach poetry today without being
exclusive, because I think that's what the most exciting
thing should be for the student—there's just this huge
gamut of interesting stuff being written. Any time you
make a reading list, it doesn't become a reading list, it

becomes a list of what you leave out. And that's the
biggest problem. And if you're in some place like Kent
State, Ohio, maybe you stick around because you had
a good teacher for a few years, but if you're in an
ordinary college town, you don't have anything to
browse in, to really see what's going on. So if they have
one professor there who teaches Robert Lowell, they
don't even know half the time that someone like
Ginsberg exists. And Ginsberg is a different case
because he's been in *Life* magazine. But they don't
know the possibilities of poetry, they know that there's
one, but they don't know that that one doesn't have to
be in a quarrel with any other one. And they often
don't find out that there are really ten or twelve
things going on instead of two in a quarrel with each
other. Because usually if somebody is teaching Robert
Lowell and then he teaches anybody else, he'll teach
someone and say, "Now this poet doesn't write
anything like that." And they'll spend the time going
over how much less good he is.

NYQ: *And you can't do that in writing. It destroys the
whole idea of creativity.*

DW: The whole idea of making literature competitive—
the great story of your life if you are an artist and you
love nature, is savoring the beautiful things that
you've read and you've heard, the masterpieces, but
the masterpieces aren't beautiful because they're
famous. They're beautiful because they're things that
really hit you and you really like them, and there's no
way that some young person is going to have your
masterpiece experience. I may have loved Beethoven
when I first heard him. But I didn't feel he was a
master the way I now feel. And the real problem is
that you have—I sometimes think that instead of
lectures given by experts, the best teachers would be
people who didn't know anything. I think the problem
of teaching poetry today, I think it has to do with the
way poetry is going to be taught in schools, and I
can't—I'm usually very good at thinking of ideal
systems, I can't think of any ideal system of teaching
poetry. I just cannot think of it. Everything seems to
be lacking. No matter what you do you seem to be

putting something else down, or leaving something out. Maybe that's the way the poetry world is. They're always at each other's throats. You don't seem to be able to praise one poet without putting down another one.

NYQ: *How do you feel about the need for isolation in the life of a writer and how does it affect personal relationships?*

DW: Well, as I told you, I grew up extremely timid and shy and it was very very hard for me to even be interested in making friends with strangers. And consequently I always had a lot of enforced isolation in my life. And I grew up hating being alone, being terrified of being alone. And yet I spent a lot of time alone and it took me many years to learn to be alone and not freak out, to begin to appreciate that I really liked being alone and I didn't have enough privacy for being alone, and I got equally disturbed. And I approached it from the opposite side. I feel like you have to have a certain amount of privacy to sit down and work. But I don't feel that people interrupt that. I don't have that closed-door sanctuary attitude. I really am very seldom annoyed if someone disturbs me when working. And that's a result of compensation from when I was a kid and I would have been delighted if someone had disturbed me. My attitude is that it's natural for me to be alone, and if my life just flows its own way I'll find myself alone anyway, that I'm grateful when there are people there that I can talk to. I'm very much less flexible about it if somebody I don't like interrupts.

NYQ: *Have you ever done any experimenting with concrete poetry?*

DW: Not in the most literal sense. I've done a little series of what I call spells and chants. I did these a few years ago, many of which are just repetitions of words. I think of them as sound poetry. There is very little informational or emotional content. I think of that aspect of poetry as precisely that, an aspect of poetry. I'm not very satisfied with poems that only appeal to your eye on the page or can be listened to by your ear. It seems to me that an exciting poem can be seen on

the page, and can sound good, and can also have all
those other things.

NYQ: *Do you feel that you have a public image because of
your readings?*

DW: I think that it's inevitable that anybody who gives
as many readings as I do and I tend to give fairly
consistent readings—I read many of the same poems
—I present myself in one of two or three ways.

NYQ: *Is it a public image or images?*

DW: Well, that's a good question. I think the people think
that I'm just as willing to talk to them in private as I
am in my poems. Which may be true. I may be willing,
but my old shyness and inhibitions arise and I don't
find it very easy. And there's a real intimacy when I
read my poems because many of them are very intimate
gestures. And there's no way I could have a first
conversation with a stranger that's anything like what
I say in a poem. Now I think that's a hardship because
I think they are disappointed. I keep telling people
that if you love me, you should love me in my poems,
and I could be a mass murderer or something. In fact,
I have always felt that there is too much personality and
silliness in the poetry world, so that if you like someone,
you try to like their poems. I'm a victim of this too.
You dislike someone, you find something wrong with
their poems. I'm a very perverse person, and recently
I've developed a dogma that you should be able to
insult a person, somebody that you don't want to have
anything to do with, you don't like him, you think he's
stupid, and still like his poetry. And if you do, then
he's written good poetry. Because you can transcend
that. Now there are some people who just aren't honest
enough to do that. I always admire people who can
write wonderful poems and be rotten. It seems to me
that they have achieved something. Poetry is a heroic
form. People are idealizing themselves in a poem. I
don't care what you say about confessional poetry and
all of us presenting our weak sides, or our crazy sides,
or whatever, we are presenting them to be loved, and
we are presenting them in our most lovable form.

NYQ: *Do you write best early in the morning?*

DW: Yes, and I find it almost impossible to work at night. I don't find the dark conducive at all. I like real light, the sun, coming in.

NYQ: *Do you have a certain number of hours a day that you set aside for writing poetry?*

DW: Like my journals I'm always trying to do that, but I'm afraid it never did work out.

NYQ: *Do your dreams provide images for you?*

DW: They haven't for many years. I haven't written many poems in the last three years using dream imagery, but I don't really know why that is.

NYQ: *What do you do about fragments and unfinished lines?*

DW: I've always thought that's what journals ought to do. I have one in that journal.

NYQ: *Do you usually use them right away?*

DW: No, sometimes I use them five or six years later. I tend not to look through stuff like that. Because it's not exciting to me to keep a journal. I don't know and yet every once in a while I go through my papers. Sometimes when I'm going to edit a book and I want to put some poems together, I'll find fragments and write a poem from them. It always seems such a waste to have a fragment when you could sit for an hour longer and have a whole poem.

NYQ: *We talked about early workshop experiences, but was there any writer that you felt or you feel now did influence you when you began writing poetry?*

DW: Well, when I was younger I really didn't think anyone influenced me. It was all absolutely out of my head. But in retrospect, you see things slightly different. I really think Jerome Rothenberg had a profound influence on it. He was one of the people I met when I first came to New York and published my first little book of poems, which he liked because they used those surrealist kind of dream images and had a haunting sense of being terrified. It was a way of presenting the world that interested him. He translated a lot of German and Spanish poetry and he himself had this kind of Hassidic tradition. Even though I'm not Jewish, I've often felt like I've had a lot of the same emotional experiences in my life that the Jews associate with their history.

NYQ: *Do you have a sense of where you want your poetry to be, say, in five years?*

DW: No. I don't really know. I guess the best thing I could say is that I want to create the possibility of being as discursive as possible. And discursiveness is not really an attractive quality in poetry. It's like looking for ways to do something that I think basically unattractive.

SELECTED BIBLIOGRAPHY

Inside the Blood Factory, Garden City, N.Y., Doubleday & Company, Inc., 1968.

Greed, Pts. 5–7, Los Angeles, Black Sparrow Press, 1971.

Motorcycle Betrayal Poems, New York, Simon & Schuster, Inc., 1971.

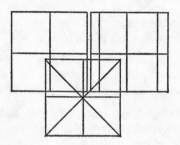